David Nyaluke, Barbara O'Toole, and Ebun Joseph bring together a heterodox group of concerned scholars who are on fire for social and cognitive justice to explore contemporary problematic education discourse and challenge resilient dominant racist discourse. Africa is their legitimate epistemic site because of its misrepresentations, exposure to stereotypes and even epistemicides. The powerful anthology invites us to rethink not only education discourse but also pedagogy as it pushes for decolonial educational transformation.

Sabelo J. Ndlovu-Gatsheni, author of Epistemic Freedom in Africa: Deprovincialization and Decolonization *(Routledge, July 2018)*

Challenging Perceptions of Africa in Schools adds to the growing literature integrating broader concerns of education, development, equity, and social justice. Contributions in this collection cover a complex array of topics, engaging the reader's interest in the challenges and possibilities of counter hegemonic knowledge, subversive pedagogy, decolonial education, and the intersections of knowledge, justice, race, and education. The interrogation of global education brings to the fore salient questions about knowledge, representation, and the politics of authentication of postcolonial realities in Africa and the Global South for that matter. Scholars reading this book, no doubt, will come out with more probing questions about the coloniality of global justice education itself, starting to probe additional questions: What are the redemptive qualities of global education? And, what does global justice education mean for the search for new educational futures? The book is a recommended read for all scholars working on global justice education.

George J. Sefa Dei, Professor of Social Justice Education and Director, Centre for Integrative Anti-Racism Studies Fellow, Royal Society of Canada

Challenging Perceptions of Africa in Schools challenges the racial and cultural hierarchies that dominate Western research and education about Africa and Africans. It is a 'call to arms' for decolonising the epistemologies and pedagogies that pathologise and subalternise people of African, black and brown descent. It takes readers outside the comfort zone of Eurocentrism and whiteness, and the deficit narrative that has pervaded much of so-called 'development education' in particular.

The book is an invaluable resource for educators as it offers a counter-epistemological perspective on the politics of knowledge and pedagogies in white societies about Africa, and people of African descent. It is not only of value to those who do 'Global Justice Education', however, it is a tool box for exploring the privileging of discourses, ways of thinking and ways of living that are contingent on violating peoples and the natural world in the name of modernisation, growth, and progress. It demonstrates how the practice of development-as-charity is contingent on the perpetuation of one's own privileges, reinforcing the colonial matrix of power.

Kathleen Lynch, Professor and Chair of Equality Studies 2003–2018, University College Dublin

Challenging Perceptions of Africa in Schools

This book challenges educational discourse in relation to teaching about Africa at all levels of the education system in the Global North, with a specific case study focusing on the Republic of Ireland. The book provides an interrogation of the proliferation of negative imagery of and messages about African people and African countries and the impact of this on the attitudes and perceptions of children and young people. It explores how predominantly negative stereotyping can be challenged in classrooms through an educational approach grounded in principles of solidarity, interdependence, and social justice.

The book focuses on the premise that existing educational narratives about the African continent and African people are rooted in a preponderance of racialised perceptions: an 'impoverished' continent dependent on the 'benevolence' of the North. The cycle of negativity engendered as a result of such portrayals cannot be broken until educators engage with these matters and bring critical and inquiry-based pedagogies into classrooms. Insights into three key pedagogical areas are provided – active unlearning, translating critical thinking into meaningful action, and developing a race consciousness.

This book will appeal to academics, researchers, and post-graduate students in the fields of education and teacher education. It will be of interest to those involved in youth work, as well as intercultural and global citizenship youth trainers.

Barbara O'Toole is a Senior Lecturer at Marino Institute of Education, Dublin, Ireland.

Ebun Joseph is a Lecturer in Black Studies, Dublin, Ireland.

David Nyaluke is the Proudly Made in Africa Fellow at University College Dublin, Ireland.

Routledge Research in Education

This series aims to present the latest research from right across the field of education. It is not confined to any particular area or school of thought and seeks to provide coverage of a broad range of topics, theories and issues from around the world.

Recent titles in the series include:

The Complex Web of Inequality in North American Schools
Investigating Educational Policies for Social Justice
Edited by Gilberto Q. Conchas, Briana M. Hinga, Miguel N. Abad, and Kris D. Gutiérrez

Fear and Schooling
Understanding the Troubled History of Progressive Education
Ronald W. Evans

Applying Cultural Historical Activity Theory in Educational Settings
May Britt Postholm and Kirsten Foshaug Vennebo

Sonic Studies in Educational Foundations
Echoes, Reverberations, Silences, Noise
Edited by Walter S. Gershon and Peter Appelbaum

Designing for Situated Knowledge Transformation
Edited by Nina Bonderup Dohn, Stig Børsen Hansen and Jens Jørgen Hansen

Challenging Perceptions of Africa in Schools
Critical Approaches to Global Justice Education
Edited by Barbara O'Toole, Ebun Joseph, and David Nyaluke

For a complete list of titles in this series, please visit www.routledge.com/Routledge-Research-in-Education/book-series/SE0393

Challenging Perceptions of Africa in Schools

Critical Approaches to Global Justice Education

Edited by Barbara O'Toole, Ebun Joseph, and David Nyaluke

LONDON AND NEW YORK

First published 2020
by Routledge
2 Park Square, Milton Park, Abingdon, Oxon OX14 4RN

and by Routledge
52 Vanderbilt Avenue, New York, NY 10017

Routledge is an imprint of the Taylor & Francis Group, an informa business

British Library Cataloguing-in-Publication Data
A catalogue record for this book is available from the British Library

Library of Congress Cataloging-in-Publication Data
Names: O'Toole, Barbara, editor. | Joseph, Ebun, editor. | Nyaluke, David, editor.
Title: Challenging perceptions of Africa in schools : critical approaches to global justice education / edited by Barbara O'Toole, Ebun Joseph and David Nyaluke.
Description: London ; New York, NY : Routledge/Taylor & Francis Group, 2020. | Includes bibliographical references and index.
Identifiers: LCCN 2019039351 (print) | LCCN 2019039352 (ebook) | ISBN 9781138607576 (hardback) | ISBN 9780429467127 (ebook)
Subjects: LCSH: Social justice--Study and teaching--Ireland--Case studies. | Africa--Study and teaching--Ireland--Case studies.
Classification: LCC DT19.9.I7 C44 2020 (print) | LCC DT19.9.I7 (ebook) | DDC 960.071/0417--dc23
LC record available at https://lccn.loc.gov/2019039351
LC ebook record available at https://lccn.loc.gov/2019039352

ISBN: 978-1-138-60757-6 (hbk)
ISBN: 978-0-429-46712-7 (ebk)

Typeset in Galliard
by SPi Technologies India Private Limited

Contents

Foreword

'Global Justice' and 'Education' are often two items that do not go together, like mixing oil with water. That is because we conflate 'education' with schooling, and the purpose of the latter is to embed inequalities further into society. Schooling's primary reason for being is to mould young people to be functional within the *status quo*, which unfortunately is currently a racially unjust social order. There are marked disadvantages in access to schooling in the West, let alone in the underdeveloped world where the question is not whether you live in the catchment area of a 'good' school, but whether you will be fortunate enough to be able to attend a school at all. Even the smallest of glances at a map of global poverty will reveal that global poverty is shaped in the image of white supremacy, with the richest nations in the majority white West and the poorest in Africa and with a hierarchy in between. Schooling is central to the preservation of this racist order in a number of ways. For one, the universal access to education in the West justifies the grossly enriched standard of living, whilst legitimising the poverty in the poorer parts of the world. More insidiously, the knowledge that is schooled into societies around the world is based on maintaining racial inequality. Eurocentric ideas and practice can only ever do the opposite of challenging the racist order. A key mechanism of neo-colonialism is schools in the undeveloped world drilling in Eurocentric knowledge to their children. Schooling is part of the problem and not the solution. Those who are successful then gain opportunities to study in the West and become experts in how to maintain their oppression in the global system. Any notion of global justice education in this paradigm can only ever be an oxymoron.

It is therefore not only refreshing but essential that a collection such as this exists. If ever there was a paradigm that needed to be unlearnt, it is the well-intentioned trope of global justice education. By re-examining the discourse and practice of global justice education, we can chart new ways forward. Coming to terms with the colonial roots of 'education' and the continued collusion in reproducing racial inequality opens up the possibility of untangling our efforts from the web of neo-colonialism. No progress towards global justice can be achieved without critical education. Learning about the true nature of society is a transformational process that sparks people into resistance. Education on how to combat the ills of global inequality is essential for developing alternatives to the *status quo*. Schooling may be a dirty word but true education is a fundamental part of liberation.

In terms of what a transformative education looks like, there are some key ingredients that this volume adds into the mix. Critiquing the *status quo* is always a vital starting point. It is necessary to what needs to be undone both at the societal level and also in relation to pedagogical practice. Once we have critiqued, we need to reframe, which means to re-imagine the key concepts that we had taken for granted. Africa is certainly one of these concepts; do not be fooled into thinking it is merely a place. How Africa is understood and, even divided into sub-Saharan (black, backwards) and North (Caucasian, civilised), frames ideas of white supremacy. We need to reconceptualise Africa as the cradle of knowledge rather than a continent allergic to it, as a bedrock of education rather than a passive recipient of Eurocentric schooling. Once we have new conceptual tools, the task then is to apply them, to build the pedagogies and capacities to create new forms of knowledge and learning. This can only be done by respecting the knowledge produced at the grassroots level and by acknowledging the wisdom in indigenous populations and the struggles for justice. A critical global education already exists, just outside the halls of elite Western knowledge. The very communities we are so keen to teach have been developing knowledge through resistance for centuries, we just need to listen to them. It is only by stepping out of the ivory tower that we can appreciate and educate ourselves in the wealth of knowledge that exists in the world.

The world can only be as equal as the knowledge through which it understands itself. A critical global justice education is essential to reshaping the unjust social order and this volume is the perfect start in building the learning we need.

Professor Kehinde Andrews
Professor of Black Studies, School of Social Sciences, Birmingham City University

Preface

This book sets out to challenge educational discourse in relation to teaching about Africa at all levels of the education system in the Global North, and specifically in Ireland. The writers start from the premise that existing educational discourse about the African continent and African people is rooted in a colonial structuring of the world order. This leads to a preponderance of racialised perceptions, comprising views of an 'impoverished' continent dependent on the 'benevolence' of the North, and resulting in the invisiblising of peoples: their knowledge and scholarship, their cultures, the by-products of their labour; indeed every aspect of people's lived realities.

The exploration is framed here as 'global justice education' in that it knits together the dual and usually parallel fields of global learning and intercultural education. One of the consequences of the persistence of the colonial matrix of power (CMP) (Mignolo, 2018) has been the ubiquity of stereotypical depictions of Africa – in educational discourse and in societal representation. This cycle of negativity cannot be broken until educators engage with these matters and bring critical and inquiry-based pedagogies into classrooms; in other words, until educators take a global justice approach to teaching. This necessitates race awareness. Race is thus foregrounded in many of the explorations carried out in the book chapters. Race has been applied as a category imposed by others who use it as a foundation for oppression and discrimination, including the enslavement of people in the USA, colonialism in Africa and other parts of world, and apartheid in South Africa. One of the most contentious uses of the concept of race is that it often assumes the ordering of racial groups, whereby Africans are inserted at the bottom and Europeans at the top (Zuberi & Bashi, 1997). The way Africans are positioned today has its origin in the hierarchal representation of raced people; consequently, when global justice educators do not centre or acknowledge race and colonial mentalities, they only skim the surface without impacting transformative learning.

The impetus for the book was a small-scale research study which took place in Ireland in 2016. Four primary school teachers participated in an action research project whereby they implemented a trade justice module (Just Trade: www.mie.ie/justtrade) with their fifth and sixth classes (83 children, 11–12 years old). The lessons were grounded in principles of social justice: they challenged stereotypes of Africa and African people and they examined trading relationships between Ireland and African countries. The study sought to examine whether the module could change learners' perceptions of African countries and African people: moving students' attitudes from deficit towards equality. The module introduced the concept of 'value added', whereby the monetary gain from production of commodities (e.g. coffee, tea, chocolate) can be retained in African communities rather than stripped away to wealthy Northern countries as is the predominant practice. Holding on to the 'value-added' dimension through commodity production rather than the export of raw materials, has a major impact on local economies.

Trade justice is used therefore as both a lens and a springboard in the book. It is examined in depth in its own right and readers are shown how complex ideas in relation to global economic justice can be mediated for learners at all levels of education: from primary school to university. Chapter authors also demonstrate how such patterns of wealth extraction from African countries are symptomatic of and a reflection of the colonial world order with race at its core. These patterns emerge in areas such as 'sending' programmes which have become increasingly popular in Northern countries in recent years, whereby Africa is seen as both a classroom and a pedagogical playground for wealthy Northern students and student teachers. These patterns are also evident in Eurocentric epistemicide through which the scholarship and knowledge traditions of African people have either been eradicated completely or relegated to 'undeveloped' or 'underdeveloped' status. Colonialism has thus not only been a process of European territorial expansion, but also a "mode of knowing and representation" (Andreotti 2011, p. 323) which continues to this day.

These are just two examples of the areas under scrutiny in these chapters. Other foci include representations of Africa, Africans, and African Irish characters in primary school textbooks, racial stratification, and its impact on the African diaspora, and pedagogies to support inquiry-based learning in classrooms. The chapters also unravel some of the complexities of unlearning, a process which requires deep self-questioning and self-reflexivity, followed by learning which is grounded in critical perspectives. The book provides insights in three key pedagogical areas: active unlearning, translating critical thinking into meaningful action, and developing a race consciousness. We hope the chapters provoke thinking, stimulate debate, and offer an alternative discourse grounded in social justice perspectives. We hope they provide insights to educators who are concerned with these matters and who are, like ourselves, committed to challenging the single story of Africa and of African people.

Lastly, this book was made possible because of the community of enquiry involved in its creation. Authors from the North and South worked together to share our knowledge, experience, and insights. The chapters thus comprise a collection of the expertise and experience of colleagues across a range of professional backgrounds, and who each share a vision for a more just society, globally and locally.

References

Andreotti, V. (2011). (Towards) decoloniality and diversality in global citizenship education. *Globalisation, Societies and Education*, 9(304), 381–397.

Mignolo, W. (2018). The decolonial option. In W. Mignolo & C. Walsh (Eds.), *On Decoloniality: Concepts, Analytics, Praxis*. Durham and London: Duke University Press.

Zuberi, T., & Bashi, V. (1997). A theory of immigration and racial stratification. *Journal of Black Studies*, *27*(5), 668–682.

Acknowledgements

Writing this book has been an accomplishment of partnerships, networking, and teamwork among educators who have a shared commitment to global justice in the different avenues of our work.

As co-editors, we are firstly grateful to the great team of chapter authors, as without them we would not have the book to publish. We are grateful to Sandra Austin, Alice Feldman, Cecelia Gavigan, Elaine Haverty, Paula Murphy, Conall O'Caoimh, Rom Olusa, Laura O'Shaughnessy, Aoife Titley, and Lisa-Maria Whiston.

In addition to the chapter authors we are indebted to a number of individuals who assisted and supported us in different ways.

The idea for this book arose from the collaborative project: *Just Connections, Just Trade: A Teaching Resource about Africa* (www.mie.ie/justtrade). We wish to acknowledge the educators and Proudly Made in Africa (PMIA) staff involved in producing that resource. We particularly want to thank the teachers and students who were part of the Just Trade research study which was the stimulus for this publication.

Liz Morris and John O'Toole read and commented on a number of chapter drafts which is greatly appreciated.

We would like to thank Alice Feldman for her advice along the way and for sharing her knowledge of decoloniality with us.

We would like to thank colleagues at Proudly Made in Africa: director of PMIA, Vikki Brennan, and Feena Kirrkamm for their support; also Professor Maeve Houlihan, Dr Penelope Muzanenhamo, Killian Stokes, and all colleagues at UCD College of Business and other business schools for the work we do together to embed the teaching of Africa in business curricula in Ireland.

We would like to thank colleagues in Marino Institute of Education for their support, particularly Professor Anne O'Gara for her enthusiasm and backing in the early stages of writing and Dr Teresa O'Doherty for her encouragement along the way; to Dr Emer Nowlan for her advice and assistance; and to Mairéad Corcoran who helped with formatting the final draft.

We acknowledge the support of our families, especially Breda O'Toole, mother of Barbara, who never failed to enquire, inspire, and encourage. Sincere thanks to Geraldine Murray, who was endlessly patient and supportive with the entire process from start to finish; through all the speed bumps and highs and lows of the journey.

Lastly, we are grateful to the Routledge team for not only taking an interest in publishing the book, but also for supporting us throughout the process of putting together and producing this publication.

Barbara O'Toole, Ebun Joseph, and David Nyaluke

Contributors

Sandra Austin completed her undergraduate studies in microbiology at Trinity College Dublin in 1989 and spent most of the next two decades as a cardiovascular research scientist in Ireland and the USA, receiving a PhD (pharmacology) in 2001 from the National University of Ireland. From 2006, she retrained as a horticulturist and spent two years working at the Eden Project, Cornwall, UK, and a further three years as co-ordinator of Grow Your Own Future, a horticultural training and accreditation programme for lone parents in Dublin. From 2013 to 2016 she was a lecturer in primary science at St. Patrick's College of Education, Dublin, and completed her Master of Education degree while working there. Austin was national co-ordinator for the RDS STEM Learning Project, a programme of professional development for primary teachers, from 2015 to 2016. Since 2016, she has been lecturer in Social, Environmental and Scientific Education at Marino Institute of Education, Dublin.

Alice Feldman is a lecturer at University College Dublin in the School of Sociology. Alice's scholarship centres on the intersections of art, research, and education. In both her research and teaching she uses arts-informed and collaborative methods to explore the de/colonial dynamics of critical pedagogy, creative agency, and collective mobilisation as they play out in these necropolitical times. Feldman received a PhD in 1998 from the School of Social Transformation (formerly Justice Studies) at Arizona State University, which focused on indigenous peoples' sovereignty and religious freedom movements. Over the past two decades, she has also worked in research, advisory, and volunteer capacities with a number of civic, community, and other organisations in Ireland involved in anti-racism, migration, and interculturalism. She has recently launched a new master's programme on Race, Migration, and Decolonial Studies and a collaborative project on decolonising the curriculum with scholars in Ireland and Africa.

Cecelia Gavigan has been teaching for over ten years in an Educate Together primary school in a diverse community in north County Dublin. She completed her B.Ed. in St. Patrick's College, Drumcondra, in 2008 and a Master's in Equality Studies (MSc) in University College Dublin in 2013. She has been heavily involved in the development of resources to promote equality and human rights in the classroom including 'Different Families, Same Love' (an educational resource that celebrates family diversity); 'We Belong Together' (a teaching guide to LGBT+ inclusive books); and 'Qatar 2022: Fair or Foul?' (an Amnesty resource on migrant workers' rights). She also acted as an advisor on 'All Together Now' (a resource focused on preventing homophobic and transphobic bullying) and the 2019 Show Racism the Red Card teaching pack. She is a committee member of the Strengthening the Practice of Intercultural Education in Primary Schools (SPIEPS) project and is the current Chairperson of the INTO LGBT+ Teachers' Group.

Elaine Haverty is assistant principal of St. Catherine's Primary School in Cabra, Dublin. She holds a Master's in Education Studies (Intercultural Education) from Marino Institute of Education in Dublin. She has worked as a researcher in the area of development education and has co-presented findings of the research study based on the *Just Trade* pilot programme at a number of national and international conferences.

Ebun Joseph is a Race Relations Consultant and Module Coordinator of the first Black Studies course in Ireland. She holds the position of Career Development Consultant at the Royal College of Surgeons in Ireland. She worked with Business in the Community Ireland for over nine years as a Training & Employment Officer supporting immigrants from over 73 different nationalities in accessing the labour market. She is also a Teaching Fellow at Trinity College Dublin's MPhil in Race, Ethnicity, and Conflict. Joseph has a Master's in Education from Maynooth University in Adult Guidance and she is an accredited Counsellor. She focused her PhD dissertation, titled 'Racial Stratification in the Irish Labour Market', on workforce experiences. Her research interests include critical race theory, race and racial stratification. Joseph is a prolific conference speaker with regular TV appearances. She is also an author and Chairperson of the African Scholars Association in Ireland.

Paula Murphy is a primary school teacher at Esker Educate Together National School in Dublin. She completed a Master's in Education Studies (MES) in Intercultural Education at Marino Institute of Education, Dublin, in 2014, and has worked as a teacher in Ireland, France, and Japan. She has lectured on undergraduate programmes in Marino Institute of Education and in Dublin City University, with a specific focus on intercultural education/ethical education.

David Nyaluke is the Proudly Made in Africa Fellow in Business and Development, based at University College Dublin College of Business working to incorporate the teaching of Africa and just and sustainable models of trade and business between Africa and rest of the world. Prior to joining UCD and Proudly Made in Africa, David was a teaching fellow of International Development Studies at Kimmage Development Studies Centre and Maynooth University, focusing on the role of business, NGOs, and state in development and on Africa and the international system. David holds a PhD from Dublin City University where he investigated the trajectories of political and development transformations of African states from independence into the twenty-first century. He is currently the vice chairperson of the African Scholars Association and Co-coordinator of ASAI-ConcernWorldWide Mandela Global Development Inter-university Debate Competition. David nurtures interest in extracurricular activities promoting student engagement in active local and global citizenship.

Conall O'Caoimh is a freelance worker in international development, specialising in trade and livelihoods and projects relating to strategic planning, policy, training, and consortium building. He founded Proudly Made in Africa (PMIA), an Irish and UK registered not-for-profit organisation. PMIA's mission is to build a channel into European markets for African-made value-added goods. O'Caoimh is a member of the board of Trócaire and was Chair of the Debt and Development Coalition at the time of the Jubilee Campaign. O'Caoimh has worked extensively in Development Education, volunteer engagement, and the media. He received ministerial appointments to the National Trade Advisory Forum and the National Consultative Committee on Racism and Interculturalism. He has degrees in Economics and Politics and in Liberation Theology, an MA in Development Studies, and a Higher Diploma in Philosophy and in Community Leadership. O'Caoimh is also a practising artist working as a sculptor in ceramics and other media, and exhibits his work on a regular basis, and is an enthusiastic gardener.

Oluromade (Rom) Olusa has a background degree in Social Science, HDip in Social Policy, and Master's in Social Work. She is presently a PhD candidate in University College Dublin. Olusa is a professionally qualified social worker and has experience working in community development, homelessness, and primary care. Olusa's research interests are in the areas of social work with black and ethnic minorities, social work practice education, post-colonial narratives, and social justice. As a practice educator and researcher, she has interests in delivering quality social work education and contributing to social work and social justice knowledge and policy. She currently works as a primary care social worker with Health Service Executive (HSE) in Ireland. She is a member of Irish Association of Social Workers and currently serves as a member of the Advisory Board of School of Social Policy, Social Work and Social Justice, University College Dublin.

Laura O'Shaughnessy has been teaching for 12 years and is Deputy Principal of an Educate Together Primary School in Dublin, where she is also co-ordinator for teaching English as an Additional Language (EAL) across the school. Laura completed her B.Ed. in St. Patrick's College, Drumcondra, Dublin, and a Master's in Education Studies (Intercultural Education) in Marino Institute of Education in 2014. She has been involved in the provision of continuous professional development in the area of intercultural education with staff groups in multi-ethnic schools across Ireland.

Barbara O'Toole is a senior lecturer at Marino Institute of Education in Dublin (MIE), where she lectures in intercultural education and global justice education. She is a director of Lóchrann, the centre for intercultural education at MIE, director of the Master in Education Studies (Intercultural Learning and Leadership), and course leader for the Professional Master of Education initial teacher education programme for primary teachers. Her current research interests include intercultural education, teacher education, and decolonial perspectives on global justice education. O'Toole completed her Doctorate in Education at St. Patrick's College, Dublin (now DCU), in 2012, focusing on the area of minority languages in schools. She is a member of the management committee of the DICE Project, an Irish Aid–funded programme which supports the embedding of development education and intercultural education into initial teacher education in Ireland.

Aoife Titley is the DICE Lecturer (development education and intercultural education) in the Froebel Department of Primary and Early Childhood Education, Maynooth University. Prior to joining the Froebel Department as a lecturer, she was also the Programme Manager of the DICE Project, a national strategic programme funded by Irish Aid which supports the embedding of development education and intercultural education into initial teacher education in Ireland. In addition to research on sending programmes (international service learning) in Ireland and India, her other main area of interest is the diversification of primary teaching in Ireland. Her doctoral research focuses on the real and perceived barriers to initial teacher education for young people from minoritised ethnic backgrounds within a critical participatory action research framework.

Lisa-Maria Whiston is a primary school teacher who has been based in Dublin city centre for the past 12 years. She studied Arts in University College Dublin (UCD), primary school teaching in Hibernia College, and completed her Master's in Education Studies (Intercultural Education) in Marino Institute of Education, Dublin, in 2014. Lisa helped implement the Just Trade project with her sixth class in 2016.

Part 1

Setting the context

1 Approaching critical pedagogies in education

Barbara O'Toole, David Nyaluke, and Ebun Joseph

Introduction

We are tempted to start this book with a bold declaration: "Africa is not a country", or "Africa is more than a single story of starvation and poverty". In so many ways, the Africa many of us hear about in the West is far removed from the continent that Mansa Musa hailed from or that Nobel Laureate Wole Soyinka so eloquently writes about. Instead, the West presents a picture of a people in need, a people to be saved, a continent that needs 'development' and 'development workers': the innumerable partial perspectives that ignore the wealth of cultures, resources, traditions, and knowledges of the African continent and its people. What do we need to know when we work with people from the continent? How do we, as educators, teach about the continent of Africa? What is our relationship with the people, products, and epistemologies of the African continent?

Here we present you with some basic facts: Africa is a continent comprising 54 countries, a population of 1.216 billion people, and an estimated 2,000 languages; with a landmass of 30.37 million km^2, it is three times the size of Europe. Imagine an Africa that can fit the physical size of Europe into its landmass three times and has twice its human population. From the traditional Mercator maps of the world, it would be hard to conceive of this as a true statement. What other perspective/s have we been fed from a Eurocentric stance? Two decades into the twenty-first century, typical portrayals of 'Africa' in the Global North still reflect essentialist thinking in the form of poverty and hardship, disease and hunger. It is this terrain of one-sided truths that have formed the stimulus for these chapters.

This book draws together a number of perspectives from educators of African, American and Irish descent living and working in Ireland, who want to question and challenge these fundamental misunderstandings. We come to this project from a range of experiences and professional backgrounds and with the commonality of sharing a vision for a just and more equitable global society. Through the chapters in this volume, we combine our experiences and insights in order to challenge existing educational discourse in Ireland in relation to Africa, which we argue, remains predominantly rooted in deficit perspectives overshadowed by colonial continuities (Heron, 2007). As editors and contributors to this volume, we use a variety of lenses to challenge the dominant narrative. We argue that the subalternisation of Africa and African people, alongside the privileging of Eurocentrism and whiteness, is both rooted in and perpetuated by the colonial matrix of power (CMP) (Mignolo, 2018), dating back to the sixteenth century. At the core of our interrogation of global education is the historical privileging of white over black; thus we bring issues of societal power and race to the foreground of this conversation.

We further contend that educational discourse which uncritically espouses such prevailing messages, impacts detrimentally on a number of levels, including on the experience of the black African diaspora and people of African descent living in Ireland, as well as on majority ethnic (white) thinking and behaviour in this country. The outcome, we argue, is symbolic violence on the one hand, with racialised responses on the other, which together create a cocktail of injustice and discrimination, undermining the possibility of ethical and equal relationship. This book sets out to challenge this discourse and open up different conversations.

Reference is frequently made in chapters to the 'Global South', but in this volume we are focused specifically on Africa. The reasons for this are two-fold. First, the initial impetus for this book was a small-scale study which took place in four Dublin schools in 2016, which tracked changes in children's perspectives towards Africa before and after the implementation of a teaching module entitled *Just Trade*. This work focused on countering stereotypes and on introducing primary school pupils to trade justice and is described in further detail in Chapters 3 and 5 of this book.

Second, recent research on racism in Ireland and on racial stratification in the Irish labour market indicates that some groups are more likely to appear at the bottom of the socioeconomic ladder (Joseph, 2018, 2019). This is not simply an economic positioning but is also a racial positioning, which raises questions about whose voices are heard and who has the right to produce knowledge. It also places a spotlight on the way the socioeconomic environment is organised and experienced (EU MIDIS 11, 2016; Michael, 2017; Joseph, 2018, 2019), particularly at a time when Africans make up 1.2% of the total population of Ireland (57,850) (CSO, 2016), and when Afrophobic discourse continues to be used to interpret the presence of Africans in Ireland, as well as to justify harassment and abuse against them (Michael, 2017). A more recent publication (Joseph, 2019) shows that this group have limited recourse to state resources through paid employment and that Africans record one of the most negative encounters in the labour market: of 'going round in circles' trying to secure employment despite having high levels of education both from their home countries and in their country of settlement, Ireland. Joseph's research (ibid.) shows that workers of black African descent start from a disadvantaged position due to the racial stratum they are assigned on arrival into Ireland.

It is important to note that this is not unique to Ireland but that such patterns also exist in other European countries. Nonetheless, it provides the backdrop to the explorations in the chapters that follow. In summary, we believe that a book such as this is essential in Ireland at this time. It troubles the portrayal of the African continent and African people in Irish education and society; it probes the thinking that enables and perpetuates this situation and then it sets out to challenge it. Each chapter takes a discrete lens on the problem; some of our authors take the classroom as their focus, while others take a more expansive sweep, incorporating societal, economic, and global concerns as their enquiry lens. Trade justice was a starting point for this exploration and is included in this book as both a focus in itself and a springboard to other investigations. Collectively, the chapters present the case that existing societal and educational discourse about the African continent and its people necessitates fundamental transformation. We hope this book challenges thinking and practice and, in the process, stimulates debate in educational spheres and helps to bring about changes that are needed.

Setting the scene

This opening chapter sets the scene for subsequent contributions. It begins with an examination of typical perceptions of 'Africa' in Northern classrooms and contexts. This is followed by an interrogation of 'development education' (DE) as it is currently conceptualised and enacted in Ireland. We argue for a 'critical' form of DE, one grounded in an understanding of political, economic, and historical processes. We draw attention to how discourses created before and during colonialism led to and perpetuate the dominance of Northern/white worldviews. These processes continue to impact on contemporary power dynamics between North and South and find their way into the curricula and pedagogy of Western schools. Challenging processes like these through countering such epistemic blindness is part of the work of these chapters.

The conceptual framework for this introductory chapter, which provides the overall context for the book, draws from postcolonial and decolonial theorists, echoing the views of Stein and Andreotti (2016, p. 230), that "despite the formal decolonisation of much of the world, many elements of colonialism continue to contribute to the production of racial and cultural hierarchies". We make the case here for 'critical' global education, one which involves recognition of historical processes and contemporary inequalities (including economic realities), which encompasses critical and political dimensions of thinking and practice, and which, in the process, impacts on race relations in the local context.

Who we are

As editors, we bring shared experiences of working in Irish education. I, David, am an African from Tanzania. I was born, grew up, and studied in Tanzania to first-degree level, which I obtained at the University of Dar es Salaam (UDSM). With an interest in development and politics, I lived through, observed, and studied the major political and economic changes Tanzania undertook after gaining independence in 1961, facing the national and international challenges of a newly independent state. Since coming to Ireland in the early 2000s for further study, I continued my interest in development and politics and am now the University College Dublin (UCD) Proudly Made in Africa Fellow in Business and Development. I teach about models of trade justice and sustainable development between Africa and the rest of the world. My key research interest is in political-economic history: dissecting beginnings and examining how the social-economic order comes to be established. I am also interested in the independence, resilience, self-reliance, and determination of communities and peoples in regional and global contexts.

I, Ebun, am a black studies lecturer with expertise in race, migration, and labour markets. I have worked with people of migrant descent in Ireland from over 80 different countries in the last 12 years in my role as a career development specialist. I approach this book as a critical race theorist and as a storyteller of black African descent who has a different relationship with race and racism. My contributions come from a cultural sensitivity developed from navigating the racial positioning at the bottom of the racial ladder, often ascribed to persons of black African descent in the labour market without their consent, and from critical scholarship on racial stratification, thus giving me a more race conscious view of contemporary and historical happenings.

I, Barbara, am a White Irish teacher educator who has worked in the area of intercultural education for many years. With a background in primary teaching, I worked in inner London for over a decade before returning to Ireland in the early 2000s. The lens I have taken in contributing to this book is that of a White European who endeavours to hold a critical perspective on race, diversity, and interculturalism, while acknowledging the invisibility, and therefore the unconsciousness, of much of the privilege afforded to my ethnicity and geopolitical positioning.

In editing this volume, we aimed to build upon the work of writers such as Pirbhai-Illich, Pete, and Martin (2017), who, through the exploration of their own positionings, experiences, and 'intersectionalities', created an intercultural third space of questioning and enquiry in which complex issues could be teased out. Such an approach also draws from Iris Marion Young (1997), who offers the ideal of 'asymmetrical reciprocity' as a type of 'communicative ethics'. Based on the notion of asymmetry as two un-identical sides, it examines the process of working across differences. Young argues that adopting the standpoint of another person is neither possible nor desirable: "While people may be in touch and their communication may construct relationships of similarity and solidarity, their positions are nevertheless irreducible and irreversible" (ibid., p. 351). She states that,

> participants in communicative interaction are in a relation of approach. They meet across distances of time and space and can touch, share, and overlap their interests. But each brings to the relationship a history and structured positioning that makes them different from one another, with their own shape, trajectory, and configuration of forces. (ibid.)

In approaching this book, Young's ideal of asymmetrical reciprocity thus presented the possibility of having a conversation across our differences, with those differences offering a fertile ground for exploration of shared ideas in order to generate new thinking. As Treacher and Foster (2004, p. 314) point out, "Similarity can be a foundation from which to explore the complex nexus of difference, and it works the other way too – difference can be a place from which to explore similarities". Young (1997) proposed that suspending assumptions in order to listen to each other, through questioning and openness, along with making efforts to express different perspectives and points of view, becomes a process that can lead to dialogue that recognises our asymmetries and ultimately which can enlarge our thinking.

There are limitations however, to 'asymmetrical reciprocity' in the context of Black and White colleagues working together on a project such as this. The concept falls short of capturing forces stronger than 'asymmetries' that underlie the injustices and inequalities which have created the need for this book in the first place. The implied neutrality of the term can mask the perniciousness of white privilege and white supremacy, because it can elide the structural inequalities which underpin those processes (Leonardo, 2004), instead portraying a benign picture of 'working across differences' which are neutral and uncontaminated by historical baggage and 'colonial continuities' (Heron, 2007). The idea of 'suspending assumptions' rather than having a taken-for-granted premise or starting point is in itself a challenging endeavour, one embedded in issues of race and the need for a race critical consciousness. The very foundation on which this book was premised was that of challenging the epistemic violence through which black African voices have been marginalised in Northern educational discourse. This is complex and sensitive territory. It acknowledges that while there may be certain 'intersectionalities', there are also fundamental differences in black/white experience, and obfuscating these differences would constitute epistemic violence in itself. This raises pertinent questions about who has the right to and power of knowledge production. Whose views are accepted as authentic? Critical race theorists who acknowledge the possibility of different viewpoints strongly encourage Black and Brown authors to write. Delgado (1989, p. 2416) insists that while "there is no single true, or all-encompassing description", we participate in creating the things we see by the very act of describing them. For Bell (2003), these "stories are a bridge between individual experience and systemic social patterns" where "historical and social positionality produces a situation in which Whites and People of Color tend to hear and tell very different stories about race/racism" (Bell, 2003, p. 4). She further argues that stories "draw upon and reflect culturally and historically constructed themes that reverberate, often unconsciously, in individual accounts" (ibid.). Stories of Africa and its people, in the West, are often told by White people. Seeing that literally every area of life, is "experienced differently by Whites and People of Color" (ibid., p. 5), their lived realities will be entirely different, and so their perceptions of the world would differ as well. In working together on this book, our intention was to interrogate and harness all of these complexities in the light of our varied experience in Irish society and in the education system, and, in the process, create a joint thinking space which functioned as a type of overarching investigative methodology. Within this space, we attempted to collaboratively engage with theories and ideas relevant to our argument for more critical and politically-based education, one which challenges epistemic blindness. This is the territory this book traverses.

Perceptions of Africa

In 2003, Sheelagh Drudy stated that despite three decades of 'development education' in Ireland at that time, and in spite of a strong sense of solidarity amongst teachers and students, the dominance of negative images of the South was still in evidence (Drudy, 2003). Ten years after that, Bryan (2013) noted that the predominant outlook on the Global South remained rooted in a 'donor mentality': giving charitable aid to 'starving children'. Similarly, Oberman (2013, p. 33) pointed to the dominance of stereotypical views of African countries among primary schoolchildren in Ireland, stating that their perceptions "were both strongly held and extreme" in terms of associations with poverty, hunger, and deprivation. Do such stereotypes change over time as students become better informed through education? In 2012, a national survey of 1,000 higher education students in Ireland (Suas, 2013) examined "attitudes, knowledge, understanding, activism and learning on global development". Among the questions asked, respondents had to identify the first word that came to mind when they heard the term 'developing countries'. Terms such as 'Third World' (18%), 'Africa' (15%), poor/poorer (12%), 'improving' (5%), and poverty (5%) featured in the percentages indicated. When asked about the effectiveness of different activities, "sending out skilled people to share expertise" was deemed to be an 'effective' action by 82% of this 1,000 student sample.

These kinds of perceptions and responses are not peculiar to Irish students; research carried out by Tallon and McGregor (2014) and Tallon (2012) in New Zealand indicated that discussions with students about development issues "often took on a paternalistic tone" (2014, p. 1415). Similarly, Borowski (2012) reports on a study carried out with primary school pupils in Leeds, which found that children's views about Africa were overwhelmingly of a poor and underdeveloped continent. The 2016 research study which formed the impetus for this volume, aimed to investigate whether teaching a module on trade justice across four primary schools (83 children, 11–12 years old) could counter deficit perspectives about Africa. Four primary school teachers participated in an action research project whereby they implemented a teaching pack about trade justice (www.mie.ie/justtrade) in their classrooms. The lessons were grounded in principles of social justice, emphasising connections between Africa and Ireland in terms of trade links and economic activity, thereby depicting people as active agents in their own lives rather than through the stereotypical portrayals of poverty, starvation, and hopelessness that are endemic in media representations (Goldfinger, 2006; Manzo, 2006; Young, 2012; Downes, 2016). Study findings are detailed in Chapter 5; however, at this point it is important to note that baseline findings echoed the overwhelmingly negative perceptions about Africa described above. The fundamental questions, therefore, which are at the core of this book, are: why are such views so prevalent and so enduring, how are they perpetuated, and how can they be countered?

Chimamanda Adichie, in her well-known 2009 TED talk, The Danger of a Single Story, says that Africa continues to be stereotyped as "a place of beautiful landscapes, beautiful animals, and incomprehensible people, fighting senseless wars, dying of poverty and AIDS, unable to speak for themselves, and waiting to be saved by a kind, white foreigner" (2009). The overwhelmingly negative and stereotypical depictions of Africa, which are omnipresent in media depictions, art, and literature, and in school and academic textbooks (Moloney & O'Toole, 2018), compound this cycle of negativity, and this in turn creates both symbolic violence and racialisation. Tallon (2012, p. 10) states that key messages from NGOs continue to frame the Global South in a state of "passivity and deficit". These kinds of negative depictions, which we return to in later chapters, may result in increased charitable donations to NGOs in the short-term, but they have a profoundly detrimental impact in the longer term. As Jefferess (2012, p. 25) points out, when charity-based actions are proposed as solutions to global poverty, they serve to bypass the "process of investigating how we are inextricably implicated in various conjunctions of power".

Rom Olusa and Cecelia Gavigan examine this in more detail in the context of primary school textbooks in this volume. Likewise, Nyaluke (2014) has drawn attention to negative stereotyping of Africans in European academic literature, "as people who are concerned only with immediate welfare, or as political leaders and people who are masters of disorder" (2014, p. 160), giving examples of the titles of two books about African politics that were published in the 1990s: Bayart's *The State in Africa: The Politics of Belly* (1993) and Chabal and Daloz's *Africa Works: Disorder as Political Instrument* (1999). The ubiquity of such stereotyping inevitably impacts on views of Africa in the Global North, and this is no different in primary school classrooms as in the rest of society.

Troubling 'development education'

'Development education' (DE) has traditionally been the pedagogy through which matters concerning the Global South, including Africa, have been approached in Ireland. The evolution of DE over the decades since the 1950s and 1960s, and its more recent mainstreaming into the formal education sector, has been comprehensively documented (Liddy, 2015; Martin, Titley, & Sleeman, 2016; Mallon, 2018a). DE is described by Cotter (2018, p. 138) as "pedagogy of action for global social justice", and one that has "radical roots":

> Activist, academic and state stakeholders in DE have fought hard to develop an action-orientated, development-focused, human rights-based agenda which works on global themes and in solidarity with the poor and marginalised of societies around the world, including Ireland. (ibid.)

DE in Ireland has been supported over the years by funding from the state through Irish Aid at the Department of Foreign Affairs and Trade, which describes DE as follows:

> A lifelong process which aims to increase public awareness and understanding of the rapidly changing, interdependent and unequal world in which we live. By challenging stereotypes and encouraging independent thinking, development education helps people to critically explore how global justice issues interlink with their everyday lives.
>
> Irish Aid (2016, p. 6)

The term 'development education' is problematic however, not least because of the connotations of modernisation embedded in the term itself, which evokes a binary of 'traditional' versus 'modern' societies. As Gruffydd Jones (2005) points out: "the very notion of 'development' is imbued with directional teleology and a sense of progress" (p. 990). Indeed, Bryan and Bracken (2011, p. 15) found that modernisation theory was the most pervasive perspective on development in secondary schools in Ireland, and that it offered "few if any external 'causes' for the continuing 'underdevelopment' of majority world countries", with the result that a 'development-as-charity' response predominated in schools. Nevertheless, a host of writers have debated the terms 'development' (Kapoor, 2004; Biccum, 2005) and 'development education' (Fiedler, Gill, O'Neill, & Pérez Pinan, 2008; Regan, 2015; Bourn, 2018; Cotter, 2018; Dillon, 2018; Mallon, 2018a, 2018b), and the potential impact of this terminology within the field. Our intention here is not to rehearse these arguments, which as Regan (2015, p. 1) points out, can be "tiring and unproductive", and more importantly, "a distraction from the work itself". We acknowledge that 'development education' has been and continues to be the frame within which teaching about global justice and solidarity takes place in Ireland. We further acknowledge that 'development education' in this country encompasses a spectrum of pedagogical perspectives and practices, ranging from 'soft' to 'critical' (Bryan & Bracken, 2011; Murphy, 2011; Liddy, 2015; Dillon, 2018), with more critical forms having "strong social justice underpinnings" (Cotter, 2018, p. 138).

The kind of education proposed by the authors in this volume is firmly rooted in the 'critical' orientation of DE, drawing strongly from postcolonial/decolonial thinking. As Andreotti (2014, p. 13–14) states, critical education strives to challenge the idea "that meaning is objective and self-evident" so by its very nature it incorporates a questioning and enquiry approach. Bourn (2011) encourages such practices of questioning, of challenging assumptions and stereotypes, and of locating poverty "within an understanding of the causes of inequality" (p. 21). Critical education therefore includes a consideration of how the Global North is implicated in structures of power (Jefferess, 2012). It is rooted in an understanding of how colonialism's "power dynamics have shaped contemporary global inequalities" (Gebrial, 2018, p. 28). As such, it is the antithesis of a 'soft' teaching approach based on the '3 Fs': fundraising, fasting, and having fun (Bryan & Bracken, 2011).

Global justice education

We are loathe to add yet another 'adjectival education' to an already crowded field (Mallon, 2018a), and we also acknowledge the overlap between all of these ideas and approaches; however, the term that we feel best reflects the work that we are carrying out in this volume is 'global justice education'. We believe that this fits best with our aim of combining 'global learning' with 'social justice education', in that we are actively seeking to highlight intersectionalities between education about the wider world, specifically about Africa, with a critical intercultural education in which race is foregrounded and analysed, and we carry this out through a critical and decolonial theoretical lens. Throughout this volume, authors emphasise that teaching about Africa which is *not* grounded in perspectives of ethical and equal relationship, contributes to the ongoing racialisation and marginalisation of African people in Irish society, who are a little over 1.2% (57,850) of the population. Our contention is that unless educational interventions are rooted in thinking informed by critical theoretical perspectives, in which African/Southern voices are foregrounded, and in which an examination of 'race' is centred, the impact on students' worldviews will be negligible. Perceptions of Africa on the part of White students and students of African descent will continue to be informed by thinking predicated on processes of Othering along with assumptions of Northern (white) supremacy. The harm caused by such educational discourse will continue to reverberate in society.

Unlearning from a White perspective

One of the areas examined in this volume is the importance of White Northern educators 'unlearning' stereotypical viewpoints and negative perspectives that subsequently become the lens through which 'Africa' is viewed in the North. These viewpoints then find their way into the education system as 'fact' and impact on all students – Black and White alike. Spivak (2012) speaks about 'learning to learn', implying the necessity of critically engaging with one's own beliefs and worldviews, followed by re-learning which is grounded in critical perspectives (Spivak, 1990, 2012; Stein & Andreotti, 2015). As straightforward as this idea sounds, it is a complicated process with a myriad of potential pitfalls and complexities. Implicit in the idea of 'unlearning' is the importance of 'decentring' oneself from a position of privilege (Di Angelo, 2011, 2018; Stein & Andreotti, 2015) and becoming open to seeing how privilege blinds people to other worldviews (Porter, 2004). The complexity of this process cannot be underestimated. Furthermore, Kitching (2014, p. 176) cautions against the notion of the 'good' White, who, by merely acknowledging his or her white privilege, can be seen as giving back "the cultural, psychological and material wages of white supremacy", thereafter feeling insulated against accusations of racism (Ahmed, 2004). And as Leonardo (2004) points out, the risk of a discourse on 'privilege' is that, once again, it centres discussion on the positioning of Whites rather than on examining the structural issues which have created the problem to begin with: "privilege is the daily cognate of structural domination" (Leonardo, 2004, p. 148). As Leonardo states, White 'confessionals' are useful only insofar as they represent "a discursive strategy to recognise the insidiousness of structural privileges" (ibid., p. 141). In the next section, we begin to unpack the starting point of these structural privileges – by focusing on historical processes through which the idea of 'the West as the World' (Spivak, 1990) became naturalised. It examines how the colonial mindset began and how its legacy continues to impact on worldviews, both North and South. This is the backdrop against which subsequent chapters are written.

Challenging 'The West as the World'

Our project in this book is to challenge, unsettle, and disrupt; therefore, the theoretical frames that have influenced us as editors have included postcolonialism, decoloniality, and Critical Race Theory (CRT). We agree with Andreotti (2011, p. 381) that each theory "will only offer a partial and limited perspective on an issue", particularly in a field as complex as the one we are examining. What our complementary perspectives have in common is the intention to trouble and counter Eurocentric forms of knowledge which are presented as universalities, and in which non-European epistemologies have been framed via European parameters as "inferior, less evolved, primitive, erroneous or eccentric" (Andreotti, 2011, p. 385).

An important element of this work is an examination of how the 'West' became the 'World' from the sixteenth century onwards; this explains the processes through which Eurocentric paradigms of epistemology became established as universalities and as 'totalising claims' (Walsh & Mignolo, 2018). It underscores the long-standing nature of power inequalities in economic and political relationships between North and South, inequalities which, we contend, continue to reverberate and to impact on global and local relations.

Colonial matrix of power: how the 'West' became the 'World'

The decolonial theorist Walter Mignolo (2008, 2018) has explained how the classification system of 'civilisation' was determined by Christian European men in the sixteenth century. These men defined themselves as superior in relation to other groups (the classification criteria being religion, 'purity of blood' in terms of parental origins, and colour). European women and children were excluded from the "locus of enunciation" (Mignolo, 2008, p. 16) and became the point of reference for defining the inferiority of non-Europeans. However, as Maldonado-Torres, Vizcaino, Wallace, and We (2018) explain, European women remained within the dominant racial/cultural category in relation to other groups, on account of their being European and white. White Europeans thus became the "ordering principle" Maldonado-Torres et al. (2018, p. 81) around which all peoples were classified.

> Patriarchy, Christianity, and white blood established the epistemic foundation of modernity and the colonial matrix of power: the justification to convert, appropriate, and exploit, and justified the expendability of human lives that were not needed or that refused to be integrated into the system; a system known today as Western modernity and capitalism grounded in Western Christianity.
>
> Mignolo (2008, p. 16)

The consequence of constructing and promulgating this discourse created a paradigm which in itself facilitated colonialism. It became the 'classificatory lens' by which European administrators would not only see the 'native' (Nayar, 2010), but it also laid the foundations for policies and political administrative measures based on such 'truth' claims. Nayar (2010) concludes that this discourse became the mode of perceiving, judging, and acting upon the non-European, thereby forming the basis for coloniality. In this way, according to Said (1978), to say that Orientalism was a rationalisation of the colonial rule is to ignore the extent to which colonial rule was justified in advance rather than after the fact, with the imperialism project being "impelled by impressive ideological formations that include notions that certain territories and people require and beseech domination ..." (Said, 1994, p. 8).

Postcolonial theorists call our attention to how discourses created before and during colonialism led to and perpetuated the dominance of the Western worldview. They further point to the continuation of many elements of colonialism in various spheres even after former colonies gained their independence (Loomba, 2007). Alongside postcolonial theory, the most recent development on the examination of colonialism and its impact, is decolonial thinking, with leading theorists including Quijano (2000, 2007, 2010), Dussel (1998), Escobar (2004, 2010), Grosfoguel (2007), Mignolo (2008, 2010, 2018), Bhambra, Gebrial, and Nisancioglu (2018) and Walsh (2018). Decolonial thinkers focus on challenging the Eurocentric view of 'modernity' as a progressive and enlightened movement which was developed in Europe in the Middle Ages and expanded worldwide. Rather, modernity is seen as the project of European expansionism and domination with coloniality as its 'dark side', whose totalising (and totalitarian) intent is hidden in messages of salvation, progress, and freedom (Mignolo, 2000, 2018).

Decolonial theorists contend that the 'CMP', instituted in the sixteenth century, was "above all a massive conceptual (epistemic) machine: building and managing knowledge that the actors ruling institutions believed was superior or truer than others" (Mignolo, 2018, p. 172), and that coloniality has been "constitutive, and not a derivative, of modernity" (Mignolo, 2008, p. 22). Consequently, the twin concept of modernity/coloniality inherent in decolonial thinking emphasises that there is no modernity without coloniality: "decolonially speaking, modernity/coloniality are intimately, intricately, explicitly, and complicitly entwined" (Walsh & Mignolo, 2018, p. 4).

How is this relevant to this book? As editors, we contend that one of the by-products of the persistence of the CMP is the ubiquity of stereotypical depictions of Africa in educational discourse in the North and in societal representation. Through the following chapters, we draw attention to how political and economic structures, created before, during, and after colonialism, led to the emergence and perpetuation of the global dominance of a Northern/white worldview with its attendant epistemic violence, eradication of knowledges, and propagation of Eurocentric thinking as 'universal'. As Stein (2018, p. 2) states, "Western ways of knowing and being have not only crowded out other epistemological and ontological possibilities, they have also naturalised dominant political and economic systems, while masking the colonial conditions that make these systems possible". We argue that global justice education must engage with these matters and bring critical and questioning perspectives into classrooms.

Mapping the chapters

What are the necessary components of such a critical education? Each of the following chapters takes a different yet complementary stance on answering this question; we hope that in its totality, this book offers educators fresh and alternative perspectives on some of the theoretical and practical elements of engaging with these matters in classrooms, whether in primary or secondary schools, or in university and teacher education settings. The book is divided into three parts, Part 1 beginning with this introductory chapter which sets out the theoretical framework for subsequent contributions. Chapter 2, by Conall O'Caoimh and David Nyaluke, takes trade justice as its focus, reflecting the initial impetus for this volume, which comprised an educational intervention on trade. The authors interrogate perceptions of Africa and African people in the Global North and examine how those perceptions are used to justify the ongoing extraction of wealth from African countries, in particular through unfair trade practices. O'Caoimh and Nyaluke argue that dominant messages about Africa, embedded in educational and public discourse, serve Northern interests and its attempts to justify its ongoing wealth extraction. So, education that uncritically adopts those messages will serve to perpetuate them. The authors examine efforts by citizens, both in the North and South, to create more just and equal trading relations between Africa and the Global North. They conclude their chapter with a focus on educational interventions that have been designed to teach about the role of trade justice in poverty reduction on a sustainable basis.

Part 2 of the book takes up the theme of educational initiatives, with pedagogical concerns as its primary focus. In Chapter 3, Barbara O'Toole deepens the case for 'unlearning' on the part of Northern educators. She contends that countering dominant educational discourse in relation to the South, specifically Africa, necessitates a process of deconstruction or 'unlearning' of existing views, and that 'learning to learn' requires moving away from positioning that privileges

European epistemology and projects it as universal and neutral. The chapter unravels some of the complexities of unlearning, suggesting that such a process cannot simply involve superficial engagement with one's own thinking and understandings but instead requires deep self-questioning and self-reflexivity, followed by learning grounded in critical perspectives. The chapter examines educational implications of unlearning and pedagogical frameworks that support global justice education.

Chapter 4, by Aoife Titley, synthesises some of the prevailing questions raised by the educational phenomenon of 'sending programmes' or 'international service learning' (ISL). Titley examines and troubles the 'taken-for-grantedness' of the increasing numbers of Northern teachers and student teachers who travel to the African continent in search of 'authentic' global experiences in the form of voluntary, short-term teaching opportunities. Titley draws upon postcolonial thought, Freirean notions of praxis and theories of whiteness to problematise the unequal power dynamics embedded in the mechanisms of sending programmes. She encourages teachers to interrogate the wider historical, social, and educational contexts in which sending programmes operate and to reflect on the prevailing contradictions involved in participation.

Chapter 5 examines research data that emerged from the study carried out by teachers who piloted *Just Trade* in 2016 and is written by four of those teachers: Elaine Haverty, Paula Murphy, Laura O'Shaughnessy, and Lisa-Maria Whiston, along with Barbara O'Toole. The intervention challenged stereotypical views about Africa amongst primary school children, using trade as a lens through which to examine unequal global power structures. The authors reveal the persistence of negative views, particularly in relation to children's perceptions of images of Africa, despite an enhanced understanding of the diversity of the African continent which was evident after the module. They conclude with the view that a trade justice module, despite its value, does not constitute the radical curricular shift that is required in order to address the deficit perceptions towards Africa held by children in Irish classrooms, and that global justice education should begin at a very early stage in children's formal education.

Chapter 6 scrutinises the themes of imagery and messages in greater depth, and in the process, it centres race in the discussion. Using a postcolonial lens along with CRT, the authors, Rom Olusa and Cecelia Gavigan, examine how unequal relations between the Global South and Global North result in a stereotypical construct of what being black means. The authors present a critical review of how white supremacy and privilege is reinforced by deficit portrayals of people from the African continent. They buttress their work with data generated from examining images of the African continent in media, NGO fundraising campaigns, and in educational materials used in Irish primary schools. Their review of how Africa and people of African descent are portrayed in a selection of textbooks used by primary school children in Ireland, is also included in the chapter. Olusa and Gavigan then provide recommendations of ways to tackle and address stereotyping and deficit portrayals of children and peoples of Africa.

The final contribution to Part 2, Chapter 7 by Sandra Austin, argues that the ability to think and engage critically with global justice education is greatly enhanced when a culture of inquiry exists in the classroom and where participatory pedagogies are the norm. The focus of this chapter is on the translation of critical thinking into meaningful action. How we teach is as important as what we teach. Local actions may change global thinking. Sandra Austin examines how learning through inquiry can empower children to think and act more positively from a position of understanding. She espouses the view that moving teachers towards a critical pedagogy in the classroom and encouraging debate, dialogue, and critical literacy will empower learners to make informed choices and to recognise their capabilities their capabilities and competence, while supporting their agency, participation, and action.

Part 3 returns to a broader theoretical debate, beginning in Chapter 8 with Alice Feldman's interrogation of 'knowledge justice as global justice'. Here she examines how the legacies of Anglo-European colonialism, modernity, and Eurocentrism have been responsible for creating a hegemonic system of knowledge which has been reproduced as a 'universal' way of understanding, knowing, and being in the world. These 'universals', Feldman argues, were neither natural nor inevitable. They required the elimination of diverse knowledges during the course of Western empire-building and imperial expansion. Extending the principle that there can be no justice without cognitive justice, the fundamental premise of Feldman's argument is that *knowledge justice* is a matter of *global justice*. We also see in this chapter how processes at work in unjust trade relations are replicated in the maintenance of epistemic hegemony, whereby the knowledges of African scholars are largely extracted in the form of 'raw data' for the benefit of the North, and subsequently imported into African countries as 'concepts and theories'. 'Wealth extraction' is broader than export of raw materials; Alice Feldman shows how it also concerns scholarship and intellectual labour. She examines how anti-colonial, anti-apartheid, and post-independence movements created the ground for Rhodes Must Fall (#RMF); the chapter closing with reflections on the idea of knowledge justice as a matter of global justice and the implications of #RMF for the Irish context.

Chapter 9, from Ebun Joseph, centres 'race' in the examination of global justice education, and in the process, brings the investigative lens directly onto Irish society. Joseph's chapter highlights that the issues presented by each of the authors in this volume are not abstract reflections but have direct impact on the lived experience of African people living in the Global North. Joseph argues for a CRT perspective in global justice education that includes a comprehensive understanding of racial stratification, its operation, and effects. She contends that when global education and global justice educators do not centre or acknowledge race, they skim the surface without impacting transformative learning.

In Chapter 10, Barbara O'Toole, Ebun Joseph, and David Nyaluke conclude the volume by drawing together many of the conceptual threads of the book; we respond to ideas raised, and signpost further praxis suggestions for education. We trouble 'intercultural education', the main platform and policy perspective used to address the challenges of modern European multicultural societies. We argue for a robust conceptualisation of intercultural education, one which incorporates historical and geopolitical dimensions of study along with an examination of contemporary societal power issues. Intercultural education must move beyond celebratory and utilitarian practices; it must challenge manifestations of racism and injustice, both locally and globally. In the final chapter, we emphasise the intersectionality of intercultural education and global learning, contending that such critical pedagogy (i.e. *global justice education*), has the potential to challenge and disrupt dominant educational discourse in relation to North and South, as well as to counter racial stratification and racist ideologies in the local sphere. We trace the evolution of Ireland's 'white' identity in the nineteenth and twentieth centuries, demonstrating how a very particular and context-specific black/white dichotomy operates in Ireland. The chapter, and the volume, concludes with ideas for moving forward with and supporting the work of critical pedagogies in education.

References

Adichie, C.N. (2009). The danger of a single story. [Online] TED.com. Retrieved from https://www.ted.com/talks/chimamanda_adichie_the_danger_of_a_single_story

Ahmed, S. (2004). Declarations of whiteness: The non-performativity of anti-racism. *Borderlands e-Journal*, 3(2).

Andreotti, V. (2011). (Towards) decoloniality and diversality in global citizenship education. *Globalisation, Societies and Education*, 9(304), 381–397.

Andreotti, V. (2014). Critical literacy: Theories and practices in development education. *Policy & Practice: A Development Education Review*, 19, 12–32.

Bayart, J. (1993). *The state in Africa: The politics of the belly*. London: Longman.

Bell, L.A. (2003). Telling tales: What stories can teach us about racism. *Race, Ethnicity and Education*, 6(1), 3–28.

Bhambra, G.K., Gebrial, D., & Nisancioglu, K. (2018). Introduction: Decolonising the university? In G.K. Bhambra, D. Gebrial, & K. Nisancioglu (Eds.), *Decolonising the university*. London: Pluto Press.

Biccum, A. (2005). Development and the 'new' imperialism: A reinvention of colonial discourse in DFID promotional literature. *Third World Quarterly*, 26(6), 1005–1020.

Borowski, R. (2012). *Media influences on young people's perceptions of Africa*. Leeds University Centre for African Studies, University of Leeds. Retrieved from https://lucas.leeds.ac.uk/wp-content/uploads/sites/61/2014/01/Africa-UK-Journalism-Conference-Paper.pdf

Bourn, D. (2011). Discourses and practices around development education: From learning about development to critical global pedagogy. *Policy & Practice: A Development Education Review*, 13(Autumn), 1–29.

Bourn, D. (2018). Global citizenship education: A critical introduction to key concepts and debates. *Policy & Practice: A Development Education Review*, 27(Autumn), 199–203.

Bryan, A., & Bracken, M. (2011). *Learning to read the world? Teaching and learning about global citizenship and international development in post-primary schools*. Dublin: Irish Aid.

Bryan, A. (2013). Initial reflections. In Suas (2013). National Survey of Third Level Students on Global Development Report. Dublin. Retrieved from http://www.suas.ie/sites/default/files/documents/Suas_National_Survey_2013.pdf

Chabal, P., & Daloz, J. (1999). *Africa works: Disorder as political instrument.* Bloomington, IN: Indiana University Press.

Cotter, G. (2018). Nailing our development education flag to the mast and flying it high. *Policy & Practice: A Development Education Review*, 27(Autumn), 127–141.

CSO. (2016). Census 2016, profile 7, migration and diversity. Irish Central Statistics Office. Retrieved from http://www.cso.ie/en/

Delgado, R. (1989). Storytelling for oppositionists and others: A plea for narrative. *Michigan Law Review*, 87(8), 2411–2441.

Di Angelo, R. (2011). White fragility. *International Journal of Critical Pedagogy*, 3(3), 54–70.

Di Angelo, R. (2018). *White fragility: Why it's so hard for White people to talk about racism.* Boston, MA: Beacon Press.

Dillon, E. (2018). Critical history matters: Understanding development education in Ireland today through the lens of the past. *Policy & Practice: A Development Education Review*, 27(Autumn), 14–36.

Downes, L. (2016). *Imaging global perspectives: Representations of the global south in a higher education environment.* Retrieved from http://www.diceproject.ie/research/papers-reports/

Drudy, S. (2003). Seminar conclusions. In A. Dolan, D. O'Grady, C. Regan, V. Duffy, & N. Keating (Eds.), *Research report and seminar proceedings on the extent and effectiveness of development education at primary and second level.* Dublin: Development Cooperation Ireland.

Dussel, E. (1998). Beyond eurocentrism: The world-system and the limits of modernity. In F. Jameson & M. Miyoshi (Eds.), *The cultures of globalization* (pp. 3–31). Durham: Duke University Press.

Escobar, A. (2004). Beyond the third world: Imperial globality, global coloniality and antiglobalization social movements. *Third World Quarterly*, 25(1), 207.

Escobar, A. (2010). Modern knowledge otherwise: The Latin America modernity/decoloniality research program. In D. Walter & A. Escobar (Eds.), *Globalization and the decolonial options* (pp. 33–64). London: Routledge.

EU MIDIS 11. (2016). *Second European Union minorities and discrimination survey – Main results.* Retrieved from http://fra.europa.eu/en/publication/2017/eumidis-ii-main-results

Fiedler, M., Gill, B., O'Neill, C., & Pérez Pinan, A. (2008). *Global dimensions: A guide to good practice in development education and intercultural education for teacher educators.* Dublin: DICE Project.

Gebrial, D. (2018). Rhodes must fall: Oxford and movements for change. In G.K. Bhambra, D. Gebrial, & K. Nisancioglu (Eds.), *Decolonising the university.* London: Pluto Press.

Goldfinger, D. (2006). *Development pornography: Images of the Global South.* The Democracy and Governance Network. Retrieved, 5 May 2017, from http://www.comminit.com/democracy-governance/content/development-pornography-images-global-south

Grosfoguel, R. (2007). The epistemic colonial turn. *Cultural Studies*, 21(2–3), 211–223.

Gruffydd Jones, B. (2005). Africa and the poverty of international relations. *Third World Quarterly*, 26(6), 987–1003.

Heron, B. (2007). *Desire for development: Whiteness, gender and the helping imperative*. Ontario: Wilfrid Laurier University Press.

Irish Aid (2016). *Irish Aid development education strategy 2017 to 2023*. Dublin: Irish Aid.

Jefferess, D. (2012). The "Me to We" social enterprise: Global education as a lifestyle brand. *Critical Literacy: Theories and Practices*, 6(1), 18–30.

Joseph, E. (2018). Whiteness and racism: Examining the racial order in Ireland. *Irish Journal of Sociology*, 26(1), 46–70.

Joseph, E. (2019). Discrimination against credentials in Black Bodies: Counterstories of the characteristic labour market experiences of migrants in Ireland. *British Journal of Guidance Counsellors*, 47(4), 524–542.

Kapoor, I. (2004). Hyper-self-reflexive development? Spivak on representing the Third World 'Other'. *Third World Quarterly*, 25(4), 627–647.

Kitching, K. (2014). *The politics of compulsive education*. Oxford: Routledge.

Leonardo, Z. (2004). The colour of supremacy: beyond the discourse of 'white privilege'. *Educational Philosophy and Theory*, 36(2), 137–152.

Liddy, M. (2015). The neglect of politics and power analysis in development education. In R. Reynolds, D. Bradbery, J. Brown, K. Carroll, D. Donnelly, K. Ferguson-Patrick, & S. Macqueen (Eds.), *Contesting and constructing international perspectives in global education*. Rotterdam: Sense Publishers.

Loomba, A. (2007). *Colonialism/postcolonialism*. London: Routledge.

Maldonado-Torres, N., Vizcaino, R., Wallace, J., & We, J.E.A. (2018). Decolonising philosophy. In G.K. Bhambra, D. Gebrial, & K. Nisancioglu (Eds.), *Decolonising the university*. London: Pluto Press.

Mallon, B. (2018a). *DICE literature review: The impact and evaluation of development education in Irish primary schools*. Dublin: DICE.

Mallon, B. (2018b). Illuminating the exploration of conflict through the lens of global citizenship education. *Policy & Practice: A Development Education Review*, 27(Autumn), 37–69.

Manzo, K. (2006). An extension of colonialism? Development education, images and the media. *The Development Education Journal*, 12(2), 9–12.

Martin, M., Titley, A., & Sleeman, S. (2016). The DICE Project in Ireland: Development education and intercultural education. In H. Hartmeyer & L. Wegimont (Eds.), *Global education in Europe revisited: Strategies and structures, policy, practice and challenges*. Munster/New York: Waxmann.

Martin, F., Pirbhai-Illich, F., & Pete, S. (2017). Beyond culturally responsive pedagogy: Decolonising teacher education. In F. Pirbhai-Illich, S. Pete, & F. Martin (Eds.), *Culturally responsive pedagogy: Working towards decolonisation, indigeneity and interculturalism* (pp. 235–256). London: Palgrave Macmillan.

Michael, L. (2017). Anti-Black Racism: Afrophobia, exclusion and global racisms. In J. Schweppe, A. Haynes, & S. Taylor (Eds.), *Critical perspectives on hate crime: Contributions from the island of Ireland* (pp. 275–299).

Mignolo, W. (2000). *Local histories/global designs: Coloniality, subaltern knowledges, and border thinking*. Princeton, NJ: Princeton University Press.

Mignolo, W. (2008). Preamble: The historical foundation of modernity/coloniality and the emergence of decolonial thinking. In S.A. Castro-Claren (Ed.), *Companion to Latin American literature and culture*. London: Wiley-Blackwell.

Mignolo, W. (2010). Introduction: Coloniality of power and decolonial thinking. In D. Walter & A. Escobar (Eds.), *Globalization and the decolonial options* (pp. 1–21). London: Routledge.

Mignolo, W. (2018). The decolonial option. In W. Mignolo & C. Walsh (Eds.), *On decoloniality: Concepts, analytics, praxis*. Durham & London: Duke University Press.

Moloney, C., & O'Toole, B. (2018). 'Windows and mirrors' or closed doors?' Representations of diversity in early years' textbooks. *Irish Teachers' Journal*, 6(1), 55–72.

Murphy, C. (2011). *Towards an African perspective: Exploring challenges and considerations for development educators*. Africa Centre Research Report. Dublin: Africa Centre.

Nayar, N. (2010). *Post-colonialism: A guide for the perplexed*. London: Bloomsbury.

Nyaluke, D. (2014). The African basis of democracy and politics for the common good – A critique of the neopatrimonial perspective. *Taiwan Journal of Democracy*, 10(2), 141–164.

Oberman, R. (2013). From research to resource: Critical literacy and global citizenship education in Middle Primary School. *Proceedings of the Irish Association for Social, Scientific and Environmental Education (IASSEE) Annual Conference 2013* (pp. 29–39).

Porter, L. (2004). Unlearning one's privilege: Reflections on cross-cultural research with indigenous peoples in South East Australia. *Planning Theory and Practice*, 5(1), 104–109.

Quijano, A. (2000). Coloniality of power, eurocentrism and Latin America. *Nepantla: Views from South* (1)3, 533-580.

Quijano, A. (2007). Coloniality and modernity/rationality. *Cultural Studies*, 21(2–3), 168–178.

Quijano, A. (2010). Coloniality and modernity/rationality. In D. Walter & A. Escobar (Eds.), *Globalization and the decolonial options* (pp. 22–32). London: Routledge.

Regan, C. (2015). Development education: Roots and values. Development Education.ie Blog, 13 March 2015. Retrieved, 14 December 2018, from https://developmenteducation.ie/blog/2015/03/development-education-roots-and-values/

Said, E. (1978). *Orientalism*. London: Penguin.

Said, E. (1994). *Culture and imperialism*. London: Vintage.

Spivak, G. (1990). *The post-colonial critic: Interviews, strategies, dialogues*. New York: Psychology Press.

Spivak, G. (2012). *An aesthetic education in the era of globalisation*. Cambridge, MA: Harvard University Press.

Stein, S., & Andreotti, V. (2015). Complicity, ethics and education: Political and existential readings of Spivak's work. *Critical Literacy: Theories and Practices*, 9(1), 29–43.

Stein, S., & Andreotti, V. (2016). Post-colonial insights for engaging difference in educational approaches to social justice and citizenship. In A. Peterson, R. Hattam, M. Zembylas, & J. Arthur (Eds.), *The Palgrave international handbook of education for citizenship and social justice*. London: Palgrave Macmillan.

Stein, S. (2018). Beyond higher education as we know it: Gesturing towards decolonial horizons of possibility. *Studies in Philosophy and Education*, 38(2), 143–161

Suas (2013). *National survey of third level students on global development report*. Dublin. Retrieved from http://www.suas.ie/sites/default/files/documents/Suas_National_Survey_2013.pdf

Tallon, R. (2012). The impressions left behind by NGO messages concerning the developing world. *Policy & Practice: A Development Education Review*, 15(Autumn), 8–26.

Tallon, R., & McGregor, A. (2014). Pitying the Third World: Towards more progressive emotional responses to development education in schools. *Third World Quarterly*, 35(8), 1406–1422.

Treacher, A., & Foster, A. (2004). Regarding difference: respecting others. *Organisational and Social Dynamics*, 4(2), 311–324.

Walsh, C. (2018). The decolonial for: Resurgences, shifts and movements. In W. Mignolo & C. Walsh (Eds.), *On decoloniality: Concepts, analytics, praxis*. Durham and London: Duke University Press.

Walsh, C., & Mignolo, W. (Eds.) (2018). *On decoloniality: Concepts, analytics, praxis. Durham and* London: Duke University Press.

Young, I.M. (1997). Asymmetrical reciprocity: on moral respect, wonder, and enlarged thought. *Constellations*, 3(3), 340–363.

Young, O. (2012). *African images and their impact on public perception: What are the Human Rights implications?* Northern Ireland: African and Caribbean Support Organisation.

2 Learning about Africa and global justice

The contribution of trade justice education in schools and universities

Conall O'Caoimh and David Nyaluke

Introduction

This chapter examines how Africa and African people are portrayed in the Global North, where those perceptions come from, and how they are used to justify the ongoing extraction of wealth from that continent, in particular through unfair trade practices. Ending unjust practices requires changing the perceptions that justify and underpin them.

The chapter argues that the dominant messages about Africa serve Northern interests and its attempts to justify ongoing extraction of wealth from the continent. Those messages are embedded in the dominant culture of the North, and permeate education and public discourse; so, education that uncritically adopts those messages will serve to perpetuate them. The chapter looks at efforts by citizens, both in the North and South, to create more just and equal trading relations between Africa and the Global North. It also examines educational initiatives designed to challenge the dominant discourse.

This chapter has been co-authored by Conall O'Caoimh and David Nyaluke. I, Conall, am a practitioner involved for 25 years in development education and advocacy in relation to global justice. I grew up in an Ireland that was transitioning from being highly monocultural to multicultural and rooted in agriculture without significant processing. I studied liberation theology in Brazil and volunteered with the popular movement for housing there. My work has focused on advocacy for debt cancellation and trade justice with a focus on the impact of trade rules on sub-Saharan African countries. In 2007, I founded Proudly Made in Africa (PMIA), an organisation that supports African producers to achieve greater justice in their trade with other countries. This role regularly brought me to visit and work closely with many African producers seeking to export processed products.

I, David, am an African from Tanzania. I am a development and politics researcher and currently the UCD-PMIA Fellow in Business and Development, teaching on models of trade justice and sustainable development between Africa and the rest of world, as already introduced earlier in this book in Chapter 1.

In this chapter, we speak of 'African countries' and 'African states', and the period under consideration spans 60 years. There are 54 states in the continent of Africa, with much diversity therein. Likewise, we use collective terms such as 'Western'/'Northern' and 'colonial powers'. Several European states held formal colonies in Africa. Others, including the USA and Soviet Union, wielded significant influence without formal colonial structures. Ireland did not have colonies but many Irish people served in British colonial administrations. The reader should understand that there is much diversity among the actors; the chapter speaks of *trends*, and there are clearly many outliers and exceptions from those trends. It is beyond the scope of this chapter to describe each of these.

Emerging from colonialism

There is a dominant discourse about Africa, prevalent in much media and popular discourse, that typically might be expressed something like this:

> In the 1960s, colonialism 'ended' in the 'decade of independence'. Aid was generously given through the decades to support these countries to develop and modernise.
>
> But, corrupt local leaders thwarted development by robbing public coffers and mistreating their people. Add population increases, a series of famines and wars and the high hopes of the 1960s were dashed.
>
> On the economic side, Africa is resource rich but much of it is plundered by corrupt local elites and anonymous western companies.
>
> Western charities worked against this tide to support development. Missionaries were followed by development workers and organizations, and slowly progress is being made.

Few of those statements are technically untrue, yet together they paint a false picture. The statements reflect a discourse that serves Western interests in many respects. This discourse supposes that the original sin of colonialism is washed away by decades of generously giving aid and sending development workers to help African countries to 'catch up'. It also attributes blame for problems in Africa to African leaders and African people themselves.

That perspective is well-represented in Robert Calderisi's *The Trouble with Africa* (2007), where he justifies colonialism and lists the benefits it brought. Quoting a 1950s British author, Basil Davidson, Calderisi says:

> They ['Africans'] underestimate their historical need for the revolutionary stimulus of other and more advanced cultures. ... The supplying of this revolutionary stimulus may be the only moral and material justification for colonial conquest: but is a real one. ... Another benefit of imperialism is the former colonial powers' continued interest in Africa. ... Like the slave trade, the impact of colonialism is also beginning to grow stale.
>
> Calderisi (2007, pp. 22–25)

He asks why so many good people accept bad government:

> I believe the answer has three parts: culture, corruption and political correctness ... Africa is now responsible for most of its own problems and that outsiders can help only if they are more direct and demanding in their relations with the continent. ... Africans criticize Western double standards, but African hypocrisy is just as deep. Are Africans really in a position to teach morality to anyone. ... First they should stop feeling sorry for themselves.
>
> Calderisi (2007, pp. 7, 77, 95, 229)

Such a perspective collects all the diverse peoples of Africa under one stereotype, as passive, dependent, and subordinate to the Eurocentric world. It obscures questions of justice and facilitates ongoing injustice to African people and countries. It contributes to what a group of UK and African NGOs jointly argue is "a perverse reality in which ... wealthy governments celebrate their generosity whilst simultaneously assisting their companies to drain Africa's resources" (Anderson, 2014).

Much of European discourse on Africa to date has been dominated by the fallacious understanding of African development, which clears the West of the role it has played in weakening African economies and in deepening poverty there. This discourse seeks to lay the blame with what it portrays as malevolent local leaders, deficient culture, and people who would not embrace opportunities offered to them through aid. So strong are these currents that in recent years Stanford academics James Fearon and David Laitin, among others, have argued that the USA should take on 'neotrusteeship' or 'postmodern imperialism' in relation to perceived 'failing' states, including in Africa (Easterly, 2006). This perspective also permeates education about Africa. Much of the leading Western academic literature on Africa goes under supremacist titles such as *The White Man's Burden* (Easterly, 2006) or *The State They're In* (Lockwood, 2005).

The narrowness of that analysis also restricts the options for action by young people. It funnels them towards ethical consumerism as the automatic response. This may give them an easy conscience but without them examining the system that created and perpetuates global inequality (Gaynor, 2016). Critical social analysis of the legacy of colonialism in Africa leads to a widening of options for young people to bring both their energy and their creativity to acting in solidarity with others across the world. We return to education later in the chapter.

Power dynamics

The power imbalance between Northern countries and Africa started with enslavement: The forced movement of Africans to the Americas. It was followed by colonialism, whereby colonial powers defeated the armed resistance of African people who, hitherto, had lived in their own independent and prosperous communities. To achieve this, the colonialists employed the 'divide and rule' technique (Illife, 1979), favouring one local group over others, which, as Meredith (2005, p. 5) explains, best served their purposes, because "only a thin white line of control existed". The colonial powers could also extract the resources they wanted without having to actively govern or develop the countries. By 1960, four centuries after the Portuguese arrival in Mozambique, as much as 93% of the population were illiterate and only 13% of children went to school (Abrahamsson & Nilsson, 1995). Tanzania, at independence, had a population of nine million people, yet there were as few as 44 medical doctors and less than 50 rural health centres, in a country where 85% of the population was in rural areas (Nyaluke, 2013).

The Africans who encountered the invading colonialists resisted the invasion and upon defeat of their resistance acquiesced to colonial rule, mostly resorting to non-violent resistances and subversive activities to the regime (Raum, 1965; Illife, 1979). In later centuries, however, using all forms of mobilisation, African people defeated colonialism, leading to one of the largest independence movements in history: achieving the sovereignty of more than 47 territorial holdings in a space of four decades, largely non-violently. The long history of struggle for independence in Africa is a fascinating story, in terms of political mobilisation, subversive activities and resistance against colonialism, local and international connections, and trans-continental movements such as Pan-Africanism, political oratory, and leadership. These matters are beyond the scope of this chapter. Many are at the heart of works by great African writers such as Chinua Achebe, Ngugi Wa Thiong'o, Okot p'bitek, Wole Soyinka, Peter Abrahams, Ayi Kwei Armah, and many others.

Yet, winning independence did not end Western power over newly formed African governments. Nor did it end the unfair exploitation of African resources. Across the decades, old and new mechanisms (aid, debt, war, trade rules) were employed to ensure the new African states continued to serve Western interests. Both Easterly (2006) and Lockwood (2005) describe how European powers departed the colonies, leaving African leaders to take over. In most cases, European colonialists ensured they struck good relations with independence movement leaders so that these leaders would continue to favour Western interests. Particularly strong in the minds of Western powers was the Cold War, which pitted the USA/European states on one side of the axis, against the Soviet Union and its satellite states, and China and Cuba, on the other. Western powers were keen to keep African states on their side, thereby continuing to benefit from access to African resources and markets. Independent Africa thus became a battleground between East and West.

The role of aid

Instead of establishing just and mutually beneficial trading relationships, European countries chose to run aid programmes, ostensibly to help countries to develop, but also to ensure that African leaders who favoured relations with the West would continue to hold power, so that these leaders would not turn to the East. Even so, the notion of Western 'goodness' and 'generosity' dominated discourse, neatly obscuring the underlying political and power dynamics involved.

This instrumentalisation of aid frustrated whatever chance it had of benefiting local development. Examples abound of ex-colonial powers giving aid to African rulers who were clearly corrupt and abusive of their own people. For example, Bokassa in the Central African Republic, while enriching himself and his circle, was underwritten by the French with financial and military support (Meredith, 2005). Félix Houphouët-Boigny, who held the presidency of Côte d'Ivoire for 33 years (1960–1993), was also backed by the French. Britain acted similarly with Daniel Moi in Kenya (Keane, 2009). And, Meredith (2005, p. 550) says of Samuel Doe of Liberia: "What is remarkable about Doe's career as a tyrant was the support he enjoyed from the United States government".

Similarly, Van de Walle (2001) argues that France favoured authoritarian regimes like those in Cameroon, Cote d'Ivoire, and Togo, with sharp increases in aid in the early 1990s seemingly intending to help vulnerable leaders there to survive the democratisation wave. Not only was the aid used to reward loyal African leaders and their states, it was also used to punish those that did not accept the wishes of Western powers. When Guinea decided by referendum in 1958 not to take part in France's proposal of a post-colonial Franco-African Community, "De Gaulle's reaction to Guinea's vote was swift and vindictive … all French aid was terminated" (Meredith, 2005, p. 68).

Economic colonialism

The economics of colonialism did not stop when colonial rulers departed their villas. Even more so today, commodities are taken from poor countries and brought to the North where they are processed and where wealth is generated. A group of UK and African NGOs issued a report in 2014 arguing that 'sustained looting' by Western governments and companies leads to the extraction of resources each year six times the value of what is given in aid. This 'looting' happens through debt repayments, tax avoidance, and transfers of profits by multinationals (Anderson, 2014). Furthermore, 'The Scramble For Africa' epitomised in the 1885 'Berlin Conference' that divided Africa among European colonial powers, is, according to Carmody (2011), being repeated today as Africa becomes a more important source for commodities and a growing market for international goods and services. In addition to the traditional competitors of European and US powers, Carmody (2011) outlines how China, Russia, and Brazil have joined in this new struggle for domination in Africa.

It is also important to take into account that newly independent African nation-states faced a triple challenge (Nyaluke, 2014). They had to build effective government machinery, maintain, and continue to cultivate democratic political legitimacy of a unified polity, and rebuild viable economic bases. Success stories against all odds can be found. For example, Botswana managed its mineral wealth by investing its earnings in infrastructure, education, and health (Meredith, 2005), and per capita income grew steadily through the 1970s and 1980s. Côte d'Ivoire was called a 'miracle' for its sustained growth during the first two decades after independence. Malawi, though under the dictatorship of Hastings Banda, became the paradigm for small landlocked states. Kenya grew steadily, driven by agricultural output, some of which was processed into finished goods, e.g. the garment industry that emerged, providing manufacturing jobs there and supplying the region.

Despite these successes, the key economic challenge for Africa is that a very high proportion of resources and commodities leave the continent without local producers benefiting from the wealth generated by those resources. In the international trade system set up since colonialism, Africans still largely produce and sell raw material (minerals and crops) to the North, and more recently China. Meanwhile, Africa is the ***market*** for manufactured goods: African raw material is bought back as expensive manufactured product, a mode of economy which ensures that technology and industries are further developed elsewhere, while they lag behind in Africa. The United Nations Conference on Trade and Development (UNCTAD) *State of Commodity Dependence 2014* report illustrates how for most regions of Africa, commodities still comprise over 80% of total exports (UNCTAD, 2015).

The debt trap

Much of the aid which newly independent African countries received was not given as grants but as loans that had to be repaid with interest (Concord Europe, 2018). Many of these countries thus built up significant debts to their 'donors'.

With the collapse of commodity prices following the oil shock of the 1970s and the oscillation of prices ever since, many African countries were plunged deeper into debt. The West rescued its commercial banks in a series of programmes that came to be known as '*Brady Bonds*' after the US Secretary of the Treasury at the time who proposed the escape route for banks. These programmes rescued Western bondholders but not the African borrowers. In order to get new loans, many bankrupt African countries had to accept the International Monetary Fund (IMF) into their countries, and with them came 'conditions' and 'structural adjustment programmes' through the late 1980s and early 1990s (Bierman & Wagao, 1986; Lockwood, 2005). These required that countries 'restructure' and 'liberalise' their economies. This included cutting state spending on public services; introducing 'user fees' in education and hospitals; selling off state assets (e.g. Zambia's copper mines) to international bidders; reducing the role of the state in the economy; devaluing currencies; and accepting demands that they liberalise or open up their economies to imports from the rest of the world. In many cases, the effective government of these African countries was not the elected president but instead the IMF and World Bank who dictated a very broad range of public policy. Lockwood (2005, p. 49) argues that this process "... undermined normal democratic politics by making governments upwardly accountable to donors, rather than to their own people".

Through the 1990s, many African countries struggled with debt burdens, and many remained in arrears. Eventually, in 2005, a package of debt cancellation was introduced. However, as many countries were in arrears, some found that in order to receive such cancellation they actually had to increase their debt repayments.

Once again, the tardy and inadequate action on African debt cancellation was presented in Western media and political discourse as benevolence on the part of the West. The reality is that it was mostly paid out of aid budgets. Meanwhile, Tony Blair and Bono were presented in the media as the heroes of debt cancellation. In fact the true burden of debt had been borne by Africans such as the many parents who struggled to put their children through education despite school fees being introduced so debts could be paid to Western banks, and the many African girls who were taken out of school as the family struggled to pay for the boys.

The fundamental underlying problem leading to indebtedness is that Africa was, and continues to be, leached of its resources. Farmers and miners have consistently been paid poorly for their produce. Commodities leave the continent in a raw state, without stimulating jobs for factory workers and for support industries if processing and manufacturing had happened locally (UNCTAD, 2015). Were this problem addressed, African nations would be well able to repay their borrowings.

Production, trade, and livelihoods

Trade justice involves many technicalities. However, fundamentally, it concerns how people work and earn to provide for themselves and their families. The core issue at stake in trade justice is how ordinary African people can earn a decent livelihood from their work. If we understand the fundamentals of this in the economic and trade relations between North and South, that is then the basis of acting justly and in solidarity with people who are exploited in global trade and economic relations.

In the 1980s and 1990s, many African farmers saw their incomes shrink due to the liberalising of markets, the end of state support, the collapse of currencies, and the growth of competition from other developing countries. Meredith (2005) estimates the loss of earnings by African states, due to falling commodity prices from 1986 to 1988, to be $50 billion. Added to this was the issue of 'escalating tariffs' that meant that you could sell, for example, raw cocoa into Europe tax free, but if you sold chocolate it would be taxed at a 100% rate of import duty. EU 'tariff peaks' could be as high as 252% in the case of meat (Oxfam, 2005). These policies trapped African countries in the production of low-value cash crops for export. They also reduced the incentive for investment in the development of value chains in African countries.

It made great sense to advise Uganda to grow coffee as a cash crop. European demand for coffee was growing fast, with a boom in coffee prices between 1976 and 1978 (Meredith, 2005). But coffee plants take several years to reach maturity, so Uganda had to borrow money to survive while it matured its coffee-growing sector. However, the same international organisations which advised

Uganda to increase its coffee exports also advised many other countries likewise. Hardly surprising that by the 1980s there was a glut of coffee supply and, as a result, between 1986 and 1989 the price for coffee beans collapsed by 55% (Meredith, 2005), leaving farmers in penury and governments in debt. Still the loans had to be repaid. To earn the same amount, farmers had to produce more, which further increased supply and again depressed the price.

Soon, young industries such as garment making in Kenya and Nigeria shrank to a fraction of their earlier size, as the enforced opening up of trade meant cheaper industrial products displaced locally made ones. Similarly, many agricultural sectors were seriously damaged as the EU 'dumped' its 'mountains' of subsidised produce, undermining local farmers. Goodison (2002) has researched the impact on Southern African countries caused by the EU offloading its subsidised 'mountains' of beef, dairy, sugar, and tinned tomato products on regional markets. This temporary convenience for the EU caused South African, Namibian, and Botswanan farmers to lose markets that they traditionally supplied and led to the closure of tomato canning, sugar refineries, and meat processing factories in those countries.

WTO rules allowed Europe to subsidise its exports of crops but did not allow African states to protect their farmers from these imports. When a country joins the WTO, it must register its current levels of subsidies and in future only reduce them. When the EU countries joined, their levels of subsidy were very high. When the African countries joined, they had almost no subsidies. So the EU and the USA could continue to subsidise their farmers, but the African countries (starting from close to zero) could not introduce any subsidies. This led to disastrous consequences in Malawi when crops failed in 2002–2003 and they could not give farmers recovering from famine a sack of seeds and two sacks of fertiliser, as to do so would constitute a subsidy (Harrigan, 2007).

When European powers did agree to structure trade relations in such a way that would also benefit African countries – the results have been positive. For example, under an EEC preferential trade agreement and more specifically the Sugar Protocol of the Lomé Convention of 1975, Mauritius was allowed to sell a significant quantity of sugar into the otherwise closed EEC market. This 'preference' was utilised by Mauritius, helping to propel it to 'middle-income country' status (Zafar, 2011).

Trade justice

Many people in the North and South could see the unfairness of how African countries were treated in trade, and how these practices increased poverty. Various campaigns emerged to call for 'trade justice' to enable African producers escape the 'commodity trap': They could sell raw commodities to the North without taxes, but if they processed those resources into finished products and tried to sell the products in wealthy countries, very high levels of tax were imposed.

Furthermore, Western companies could patent the traditional herbal knowledge of African countries, turn it into tablets, and make vast profits without payment to communities who developed that knowledge. At the same time, African countries had to respect pharmaceutical companies' patents and were not allowed to copy essential HIV/AIDS medicines, while a pandemic killed many people. African countries had to allow Western companies to bid for government contracts, but when was an African company going to be competing to build a hospital in Europe?

Trade rules needed to change to level the playing field. Thus, many specific campaigns were started, collectively known as the Trade Justice Movement, and are increasingly being led by activists from Africa, Latin America, and Asia (see www.TWN.my). These organisations research the impact of trade rules and engage in public education to raise awareness of the need for change. The movement focuses on mobilising citizens and on putting pressure on politicians to make these changes. It also connects to issues of tax justice and climate justice. Some call for 'reparations' to compensate for damage caused by slavery, colonialism, and post-colonial exploitation.

Alternative trade organisations

There was also a desire among many Western citizens to trade honestly with the South. They sought a way around unfair trade structures. Thus, many 'just trading' initiatives emerged in different countries of Europe, North America, and Japan. One of the earliest was organised by Oxfam as far back as 1958 in response to the devastation caused by floods in Hong Kong. It initiated selling hand-made products to help local people earn a livelihood.

Similar initiatives began in other countries and under various titles, many including the words 'fair', 'just', 'equitable', or 'direct'. Initially the focus was on craft products and on a narrow range of commodities. A fair price was central to the initiatives. Coffee became a flagship product in part because of its value, its ease of transport, its prevalence, and its symbolism arising from the collapse of coffee prices in the 1980s.

What these '***alternative trade organisations***' had in common was the directness of the link they created between producer and consumer. They varied in their origin, products, emphasis, standards, directness, and their quality. These pioneering initiatives remained a tiny part of the overall trade of developing countries but were important in that they were generating new models of trading and constituted a response to a situation many saw as unjust.

FairTrade

It was clear that standardisation was needed in order for the movement to make a scale difference to producers in the South. Eventually many of these merged into what is known as the 'Fairtrade' label that is prevalent today (www.Fairtrade.org.uk). The FairTrade label has very clearly defined standards and processes so that it signifies a guarantee to the consumer; these are independently audited to ensure compliance. FairTrade also supports local development initiatives selected by the community or trade union. Those standards include very precise requirements in relation to

- Minimum price guarantee
- Labour standards
- Environment standards
- Community development, with 1-person-1-vote

The FairTrade label has many strengths. It gives a guaranteed minimum price to producers, so if world commodity prices fall, the producer still gets the guaranteed minimum. This is a huge incentive to farmers in many sectors. FairTrade has been successful in organising 1.6 million farmers into cooperative structures and into certification processes so that consumers know standards are being implemented (www.Fairtrade.org.uk).

However, solutions need to work at a global scale and be capable of including many millions of farmers. In 2015, 41% of people in sub-Saharan Africa were living in extreme poverty, defined as living on less than $1.90 per day (data.WorldBank.org). Ten per cent of the world population is living in this degree of extreme poverty (data.WorldBank.org). For ethical trade initiatives to bring scale change, they need to be capable of reaching these vast numbers of people. Such scale unavoidably entails dilution of the 'directness' that was central to the early ethical trade initiatives, and has led to deep collaboration with large corporations. It is understandable that FairTrade will dedicate its available resources to growing in that direction so as to include more farmers.

Though initiated by consumers, FairTrade's key stakeholder is the farmer, organised in a cooperative or trade union. This will leave it less attentive to the interests of other groups in developing countries – particularly urban dwellers who could benefit from employment in processing the resources that FairTrade helps to export. But something is lost in that choice. The corporations want the raw material to be processed in their factories in the North. This is still within the colonial model of Africa exporting its resources as bulk raw materials. FairTrade has brought the ethical trade movement a great distance, but there is further to go, particularly as African capacity to produce high-quality goods accelerates.

Moving up the value chain

Through the early post-colonial decades, circumstances militated against making processed products in the South, and it remains very challenging today. In sub-Saharan Africa, electricity outages cause businesses to lose three months' work time each year (World Bank Group, 2017). If it must also purify its own water and import its packaging directly, then the cost of production rises and will leave the final product uncompetitive (Foster & Briceño-Garmendia, 2010). Poor transport infrastructure increases the cost of transport and delays delivery times resulting in lost orders (Calderon & Serven, 2010; OECD, 2011). Then add a policy environment that is unsupportive, a currency that fluctuates widely, and high taxes on the product when it reaches Northern markets. The result is that many African countries remain trapped in raw commodity exporting. However, a shift is beginning.

A number of factors have converged in recent decades to lead to positive changes. Principal among these is the end of the Cold War; Africa is no longer a battleground for West–East tensions. This has enabled de-escalation of many of the conflicts that plagued the continent and enabled peaceful transfers of power following elections. Educational attainment continues to increase (Graetz et al., 2018). Women are progressively becoming empowered (Berger, 2016). Civil society organisations are maturing and expanding civil dialogue. Further, gradual improvements in infrastructure and agricultural methods have reached a critical point (World Bank Group, 2018). Many actors played roles in this process, in particular, national governments together with local and international development agencies. The African diaspora also made a huge contribution, as their remittances are now almost as large as total aid received (Nsiah & Fayissa, 2013). A critical mass of emigrants returned with international experience and qualifications (Semhar Araia, 2012).

As urbanisation accelerated, the cost of bringing products and services to people reduced and became more affordable. In the growing cities, an African middle-class has emerged, and processing industries have grown to supply the local market. Mobile technology has also transformed many aspects of commerce in rural areas. Mobile money transfer first took hold in Kenya as early as 2007 (O'Caoimh, 2017). It reduces the cost and increases the transparency of many forms of business, even for the small farmer selling crops to traders. Within two years of the introduction of Safaricom's mobile money transfer system in Kenya, 'M-Pesa', 10% of the country's GDP was being transferred through the system (Mbiti & Weil, 2011).

Some modifications in trade rules have also incentivised investment in processing of resources locally, but not without a sting in the tail. Since 2007, most countries in Africa, particularly the poorer countries, are allowed to send processed products to Europe and the USA without meeting the 'escalating tariffs' that previously trapped them in commodity production. However, in response they have been required to open up their markets to European products and services, a factor that will prevent the development of some industries.

Further, the flows of trade have changed in recent decades with the progression of globalisation. The West has exported most of its manufacturing to Asia, particularly China. And so, a growing proportion of African raw materials are exported to China for processing into goods that then go to the West. Accordingly, the role of China has grown significantly in Africa and posed a challenge to European hegemony there and to its model of aid and development. Chinese investment in Africa has risen from less than 1% of total foreign direct investment in Africa in 2004 to over 6% in 2015 (Brautigam & Diao, 2017). Chinese involvement has brought rapid improvements in infrastructure and in productive capacity, particularly in extractives and manufacturing. African academics question whether Chinese extraction of raw materials, its impact on the environment, and its holding of land is reminiscent of traditional forms of colonialism (Asongu & Aminkeng, 2013; Manji & Marks, 2007). Fourteen per cent of sub-Saharan foreign debt is now owed to China (Schneidman & Wiegert, 2018). While problematic on many levels, Chinese involvement has certainly accelerated growth in many African economies in a way that European involvement did not.

In response to these changes, innovative ways are emerging for broader movements of citizens to respond to the multi-layered injustices of trading relationships between North and South. These are mostly at an early stage of development and have yet to achieve significant scale, but they indicate the direction of travel. The following sections outline some ways of both 'moving up the value chain' and 'capturing more value'; each represents one dimension of how the trading relationship can become just. Justice is not only about fair trade; it includes 'fair made'.

Value addition in Africa

As the African processing sector grows, new producers are reaching the standards required by Northern retail distributors and supermarkets. With the right supports in place to export such products, they can generate jobs and make a real contribution to reducing poverty (Brouder & Tulej, 2015). Instead of exporting raw commodities, the opportunity opens up for African countries to process their resources and to capture more of the value in their products. This creates new prospects for justice in African trade.

One of the current authors, Conall O'Caoimh, was involved in starting Proudly Made in Africa (PMIA) in 2007, in Ireland and the UK, an organisation which supports African producers to sell their products in European markets. In that role, he worked closely with many producers in this emerging processing sector.

Through detailed examination of value chains, PMIA has learned a number of criteria that best indicate that social benefit will arise from a product. These include being based on locally grown farm products; processed at source; creating jobs for both women and men; including a range of skill types; respect for workers' rights, good care for the environment; sourcing other inputs from other local companies; and fulfilling its tax obligations (PMIA, 2012). The sectors PMIA found that best achieve this and have opportunities for creating millions of jobs are the food and garment sectors. In this way, the greatest opportunities arise to benefit a large number of local people – farmers, workers, suppliers, businesses, and so on.

Alongside these social criteria, PMIA's sourcing criteria hold that the product must be high quality; demand must exist for it in the export market, and the producer must fulfil all market requirements, including price, delivery times, reliability, consistency; in other words, the full set of commercial viability factors.

PMIA has encountered value chains where for example, teabags generate twice the local earnings compared with export of bulk tea leaf; quality roasted coffee generates about three times more than exporting raw coffee beans. Chocolate earns for the country between three and four times more compared to the export of raw cocoa beans (MIA Chocolate, 2019). Garments stimulate the local economy many times more compared with the export of raw cotton – depending on the quality of the garment, this can readily pass fifteen times more than the value of the raw cotton (O'Caoimh, 2016). Clearly, significant opportunities arise for alleviation of poverty through incomes earned from processing raw materials at source. Many other benefits derive from the presence of processing industries:

> This growth in the manufactured and processing sector in Africa has the potential to drive up income levels and growth. Research has shown that for every job created in agro-processing, 2.8 indirect jobs are created in support leading to multiple benefits: higher incomes; increased food security; community development; capacity building and higher skills; less food waste; and the empowerment of women.
>
> Brouder and Tulej (2015, p. 9)

Furthermore, skilled jobs are created, and such jobs are part of the formal sector where payment of taxes, social insurance, and pensions lead to long-term benefits to workers and the wider community. Skills are transferred. Factories purchase supplies and services from other local companies, further distributing gains. Taxes earned by local governments enable provision of public services and reduced dependence on aid. Successful local companies can create a large-scale impact beyond their immediate participants. They give confidence to other local producers that they too can manufacture products. They change the perception of what is possible.

When people in the North wish to purchase products ethically and support just relations with Africa, these products offer new opportunities for meaningful action for justice. They contribute to reducing the economics of colonialism.

Control of brand value

The capacity to process products at source is not yet developed in many Africa regions to meet the level required by Northern supermarkets and retailers. Rather than stay trapped in exporting raw materials, a number of African producers have created innovative business models to get around the limitations. With support from Twin Trading, a UK-based organisation, a number of companies have been started where African farmers control the processing of their product in Europe and its marketing to European consumers.

In these novel businesses, the farmers' cooperative is a joint owner in the European company that owns the consumer-facing brand. Leading examples are Cafédirect, Divine Chocolate, and Liberation Nuts. These companies do not own any factories, nor do they have a warehouse. Each is a vehicle for farmers to capture more of the value in their resources. Typically, the company buys FairTrade-certified raw materials (e.g. raw coffee beans) from farmers in the coop. They outsource to a European factory to process the farm produce into a quality-finished product ready for supermarkets. The company promotes the product in the market and convinces supermarkets and other retailers to purchase product. When orders come in they instruct the factory to deliver produce to the supermarket. They also build awareness of the product among consumers (O'Caoimh, 2016).

In this innovative model, the resources still leave the African country as raw material, but the African farmers gain control of part of the value chain beyond their farms. They control the processing and marketing, even though these functions are outsourced. At the end of the day, the farmers earn profit from processing and marketing of their resources, not just the pittance gained from sale of raw material.

Divine chocolate

The Ghanaian farmers' cooperative Kuapa Kokoo grows cocoa beans that are FairTrade certified. Most of its produce is sold as raw beans to large chocolate companies. But Kuapa Kokoo have themselves also become a chocolate brand through starting up Divine Chocolate. The cooperative owns 47% of the shares of Divine. Forty-seven per cent is owned by Twin Trading and the remaining 6% is owned by Triodos, an 'ethical bank' that lent the money to start the company (Scott, 2006).

Divine has an office in London where it engages in marketing of its brand of chocolate. As orders come in from supermarkets, Divine purchases raw cocoa beans from the Kuapa coop. These are outsourced to be processed at a chocolate factory in Germany, and the Divine Chocolate bars are delivered into supermarkets throughout Europe.

The profits of the company are shared among stakeholders, with Kuapa Kokoo receiving 47% of profits. In this way, it captures more of the value inherent in its cocoa beans.

As each vehicle matures, Twin Trading can sell its shares in the company to start new vehicles for other African farmers to gain control of their value chains. Already Twin Trading raised money to start Liberation Nuts through selling its shares in Cafédirect. While the nuts are processed at a factory in the UK, the farmers of the NASFAM cooperative in Malawi earn dividends from the sale of Liberation Nuts in the same way as for Kuapa Kokoo.

A similarly innovative approach was used by The *Good African Coffee Company* based in Uganda. Initially UK supermarkets liked the coffee but doubted the reliability of the roasting process in Uganda. So Good African outsourced their coffee roasting to Bewley's, an Irish company. Bewley's would roast and package the coffee under the Good African brand. This then sold in the UK supermarkets. When, after three years, the UK supermarkets knew Mr. Rugasira better, they trusted for the coffee to be roasted in Uganda. With this creative solution

Good African overcame the barrier to selling value-added goods into Europe. This story is described in the autobiography of the entrepreneur behind it, *A good African story: How a small company built a global coffee brand* by Andrew Rugasira (2013).

These innovative market structures enable African producers to control more of the value chain. They represent other dimensions of shifting away from colonial patterns of trade. They also provide additional opportunities for people living in the North to support just trading, both in their own purchasing decisions and as activists who help fashion new ways of overcoming the injustices of the trade system and the legacy of colonialism.

Harrar coffee – A brainwave

Coffee first grew in Ethiopia. Harrar is one of the regions in Ethiopia with a distinct variety of coffee that is valued by coffee drinkers. Coffee brands have for years sold Harrar coffee at a higher price than other coffees, yet the farmers of Harrar have not received that extra income.

'Light Years IP' is a UK NGO that set out to overcome this challenge; the 'IP' in its name stands for 'intellectual property'. Light Years IP works with African communities and governments to win back control of Southern intellectual property and ensure that groups in the North who commercialise it have to pay a royalty to the rightful owners of the IP in the South.

Light Years IP worked with the coffee farmers of Ethiopia, the coffee exporters association, and the Ethiopian government to address this 'capture' of their intellectual property. Through the use of legal skills they registered the 'geographical designation of origin' of Harrar coffee. Today Harrar coffee enjoys the same protection through its intellectual property as Champagne wines do. Nobody anywhere in the world can sell coffee under the name of Harrar without a royalty being paid to the farmers of Harrar. As a result, the price that Harrar farmers earn for their raw coffee beans has increased significantly (O'Caoimh, 2017).

Educational implications

The history of Northern countries' involvement in the Global South, with their enslavement projects in Africa, followed by colonialism and the extraction of resources, through to independence (Rodney, 1972) and the post-independence period (Bond, 2006), has demonstrated that injustice takes many forms: political, cultural, and military. This chapter has focused on economic injustices: The continued costs of Northern extraction of Southern resources without proper recompense.

The role of educators includes challenging the discourse about Africa that permeates Northern society and Northern education, including the neo-colonial perspectives outlined in this chapter. Educators must take stock of the language they use and the assumptions that underlie their teaching. They must present perspectives wider than those of the dominant culture and equip children and young people with skills to source information and weigh up evidence from many sources. As proposed in this volume, education about trade can introduce a political and critical dimension to enquiry, by encouraging students to investigate below the surface of global power structures and to challenge colonial assumptions (Bryan & Bracken, 2011). In this way, trade justice education helps to counter the 'declawing' or 'softening' of development education as it is often approached in Northern classrooms (Bryan, 2011).

Through lessons on trade, including the importance of 'value chains', students can learn about structural ways in which poverty can be combatted (O'Caoimh & Mallon, 2013). This kind of work challenges the stereotypical misunderstanding of poverty in African countries as being primarily caused by in-country factors or lack of 'modernisation' (Andreotti, 2014); it demonstrates Northern dominance in maintaining unjust trading arrangements whereby value added is stripped from African countries. It requires that students (re)consider "their prior knowledge of facts relating to trade relationships between Ireland and partner African countries" (O'Caoimh & Mallon, 2013, p. 9). In the process it takes people in the North "out of the territory of beneficence and into the realm of justice" (Dobson, 2006, p. 172). This is potentially powerful learning which can have a major impact on student perceptions.

This chapter has featured the work of PMIA, an NGO which, alongside its activist work, has experience of introducing education about trade into the secondary school curriculum in Ireland (O'Caoimh & Mallon, 2013). This intervention is in the form of a business module designed for Transition Year[1] students, developed in collaboration with teachers and in accordance with the National Council on Curriculum and Assessment (NCCA) guidelines. It is applicable in subjects ranging from business; Civic, Social and Political Education (CSPE); religious education; and geography. It teaches students about Ireland's relationship with particular African countries – Ethiopia, Lesotho, Tanzania, Mozambique, Uganda, and Zambia. Students find out more about these countries, and about how they are linked to Ireland by trade. They consider perspectives of residents of these countries and examine how individuals have/can overcome barriers to forming successful businesses. In examining the role of business in development, students explore the options available in seeking ways to combat poverty through trade.

Teaching trade justice in the university

PMIA also works with students at tertiary level, namely, in the School of Business at University College Dublin (UCD), through a Fellowship in Business and

Development, taught by one of the current authors, David Nyaluke. The Fellowship envisages a future where all business schools in Ireland will incorporate a global view on the role of trade justice in stimulating and sustaining development in African countries. The programme works with business educators to support them with the integration of a focus on Africa into their teaching and research, with the aim of informing students' perceptions of Africa as a place to do business in and with, and of teaching about the role of trade justice in poverty reduction on a sustainable basis.

A key outcome of the Fellowship has been the broadening of career options for people wishing to engage in creating social change. Often when people wish to contribute to reducing poverty they have looked in the direction of charities and development organisations. Through PMIA's engagement in global education at university level, many students undertake a broader spectrum of career paths motivated by a desire to build a more just world. These included business, innovation, and technology disciplines, with some students motivated by examples such as Divine Chocolate. David has also noticed a reduction in deficit and charity-based perspectives that the students bring with them: Perceptions shift once students get up-to-date information on developments in Africa and on justice-based perspectives on engaging with African countries, through trading connections based on parity of esteem and on equitable relations.

However, we believe that young people should not have to wait until university to learn about just ways of understanding and engaging with countries of the South, specifically Africa. Programmes such as the PMIA Fellowship and other interventions by NGOs in the education system, while effective, cannot sustainably solve the problem of students not learning justice perspectives about Africa. This kind of education must begin at a much younger age. It must be mirrored in media messaging, so that notions of deficit are not reinforced in wider social spheres.

Conclusion

The dominant discourse about Africa and African people includes assumptions and judgements that portray the Global North as generously assisting former colonies to graduate to maturity, even though, according to the discourse, they have continually 'faltered' and not put to good use the assistance offered to them. Such messages have served and continue to serve Northern interests. It is not simply a question of the legacy of past colonialism, because economic patterns of colonialism have persisted to this day and continue to enable the extraction of African resources.

Trade is at the core of the economic relation between North and South. Bringing justice to this relation is an essential component of decoloniality, along with ceasing the patterns of political, cultural, and military interference. Aid has been utilised by the North to both justify and distract from their continuing interference in African countries. Education has often carried the messages of the beneficence of aid without paying attention to the underlying unjust economic relation. Changing that discourse requires re-examination of the economic ties, historically and in recent decades. Therefore, education for global justice must, by definition, include trade justice; seeking to understand that economic relationship and how to change it.

List of Acronyms

IMF	International Monetary Fund
NGO	Non-Governmental Organisation
OECD	Organisation for Economic Co-operation and Development
OPEC	Organization of the Petroleum Exporting Countries
PMIA	Proudly Made in Africa
UNCTAD	United Nations Conference on Trade and Development
WB	World Bank
WTO	World Trade Organization

Note

1 Transition Year is an optional one-year programme that takes place after the Junior Certificate year in most schools in Ireland

References

Abrahamsson, H., & Nilsson, A. (1995). *Mozambique, the troubled transition: From socialist construction to free market capitalism*. London: Zed Books.

Anderson, M. (2014, July 15). Aid to Africa: Donations from West mask '$60bn looting' of continent: UK and wealthy states revel in their generosity while allowing their companies to plunder Africa's resources, say NGOs. *The Guardian*. Retrieved, 18 March 2019, from https://www.theguardian.com/global-development/2014/jul/15/aid-africa-west-looting-continent

Andreotti, V. (2014). Critical literacy: Theories and practices in development education. *Policy & Practice: A Development Education Review*, 19, 12–32.

Asongu, S., & Aminkeng, G. (2013). The economic consequences of China–Africa relations: Debunking myths in the debate. *Journal of Chinese Economic and Business Studies*, 11(4), 261–277.

Berger, I. (2016). *Women in twentieth-century Africa – New approaches to African history*. Oxford: Blackwell.

Bierman, W., & Wagao, J. (1986). The quest for adjustment: Tanzania and the IMF – 1980–1986. *African Studies Review*, 29(4), 89–103.

Bond, P. (2006). *Looting Africa: The economics of exploitation*. London: Zed Books.

Brautigam, D., & Diao, X. (Eds.). (2017). *Chinese investment in Africa: How much do we know?* PEDL Synthesis Series. Retrieved from: https://pedl.cepr.org/sites/default/files/PEDL_Synthesis_Papers_Piece_No._2.pdf

Brouder, A., & Tulej, S. (2015). *Africa making it: A UK business perspective*. London: Forum for the Future and Proudly Made in Africa.

Bryan, A. (2011). Another cog in the anti-politics machine? The de-clawing of development education. *Policy and Practice: A Development Education Review*, 12(Spring 2014), 1–14.

Bryan, A., & Bracken, M. (2011). *Learning to read the world? Teaching and learning about global citizenship and international development in post-primary schools.* Dublin: Irish Aid.

Calderisi, R. (2007). *The trouble with Africa: Why foreign aid isn't working.* Yale: Yale University Press.

Calderon, C., & Serven, L. (2010). Infrastructure and economic development in sub-Saharan Africa. *Journal of African Economies*, 19(1), 13–87.

Carmody, P. (2011). *The new scramble for Africa.* Cambridge: Polity Press.

Concord Europe. (2018). *Aidwatch report 2018: EU aid – A broken ladder.* Brussels: CONCORD. Retrieved from https://concordeurope.org/aidwatch-reports/

Dobson, A. (2006). Thick cosmopolitanism. *Political Studies*, 54(1), 164–184.

Easterly, W. (2006). *The white man's burden.* Oxford: Oxford University Press.

Foster, F., & Briceño-Garmendia, C. (2010). *Africa's infrastructure a time for transformation.* Washington, DC: World Bank.

Gaynor, N. (2016). Shopping to save the world? Reclaiming global citizenship within Irish universities. *Irish Journal of Sociology*, 24(1), 78–101.

Goodison, P. (2002). *The impact of the EU Beef Regime on Southern Africa: A review of the experience and arising issues.* Brussels: European Research Office.

Graetz, N., Friedman, J., Osgood-Zimmerman, A., Burstein, A., Biehl, M., Shields, C., ..., Hay, S. (2018). Mapping local variation in educational attainment across Africa. *Nature International Journal of Science*, 55(7694), 48–53. Retrieved, 20 March 2019, from https://www.nature.com/articles/nature25761

Harrigan, J. (2007). Food insecurity, poverty and the Malawian Starter Pack: Fresh start or false start? *Food Policy*, 33, 237–249.

Illife, J. (1979). *A modern history of Tanganyika.* Cambridge: Cambridge University Press.

Keane, J. (2009). *The life and death of democracy.* New York: W.W. Norton & Company.

Lockwood, M. (2005). *The state they're in: An agenda for international action on poverty in Africa.* Bradford: ITDG Publishing.

Manji, F., & Marks, S. (Eds.). (2007). *African perspectives on China in Africa.* Capetown, Nairobi/Oxford: Fahamu, Networks for Social Justice.

Mbiti, I., & Weil, D. (2011). Mobile banking: the impact of M-pesa in Kenya. Working paper no.17129 of the National Bureau of Economic Research(NBER), Massachusetts. Retrieved from https://www.nber.org/papers/w17129.pdf

Meredith, M. (2005). *The state of Africa: A history of the continent since independence.* New York: Simon & Schuster.

MIA Chocolate. (2019). *Social impact report 2017–18.* London: MIA Foodie.

Nsiah, C., & Fayissa, B. (2013). Remittances and economic growth in Africa, Asia, and Latin American-Caribbean countries: A panel unit root and panel co-integration analysis. *Journal of Economics and Finance*, 37(3), 424–441.

Nyaluke, D. (2013). *The basis of democracy and regime legitimacy in African states: The case of Tanzania.* PhD thesis, Dublin City University, Dublin, Ireland.

Nyaluke, D. (2014). The African basis of democracy and politics for the common good: A critique of the neopatrimonial perspective. *Taiwan Journal of Democracy*,

O'Caoimh, C., & Mallon, B. (2013). *A business studies and development education transition unit learning activities resource.* Dublin: Value Added in Africa, Proudly Made in Africa.

O'Caoimh, C. (2016). Developing value chains to benefit smallholder farmers. Paper presented at *the Gorta/Self-Help Africa Workshop*, Nairobi.

O'Caoimh, C. (2017). *Alliances with the private sector: Mapping Irish NGO involvement*. Dublin: Dóchas.

Organisation for Economic Cooperation and Development (OECD). (2011). *Estimating the constraints to developing countries' trade: A taxonomy of the binding constraints to trade expansion of landlocked countries, small and vulnerable economies, and commodity exporters*. Retrieved from http://www.oecd.org/dac/aft/47428944.pdf

Oxfam. (2005). *Rigged rules and double standards: Trade, globalisation and the fight against poverty*. Boston, MA: Oxfam International.

Proudly Made in Africa. (2012). *VAA criteria for sourcing of products*. Unpublished paper.

Raum, O. (1965). German East Africa: Changes in Africa tribal life under German administration 1892–1914. In V. Harlow, E. Chilver, & A. Smith (Eds.), *History of East Africa* (Vol. 2). Oxford: Oxford University Press for the Colonial Office.

Rodney, W. (1972). *How Europe underdeveloped Africa*. Dar es Salaam: Tanzania Publishing House.

Rugasira, A. (2013). *A good African story: How a small company built a global coffee brand*. London: The Bodley Head.

Schneidman, W., & Wiegert, J. (2018). *Competing in Africa: China, the European Union, and the United States*. Brookings Institute. Retrieved from https://www.brookings.edu/blog/africa-in-focus/2018/04/16/competing-in-africa-china-the-european-union-and-the-united-states/

Scott, N. (2006, November/December). Ethical indulgence. *Ethical Consumer Magazine*, (103), 20–34.

Semhar Araia. (2012, January 12). Defining the diaspora's role and potential with Africa (a response to 'What's diaspora got to do with it?'). *African Arguments*. Retrieved from https://africanarguments.org/2012/01/12/defining-the-diasporas-role-and-potential-with-africa-a-response-to-whats-diaspora-got-to-do-with-it-by-semhar-araia/

United Nations Conference on Trade and Development (UNCTAD). (2015). *State of commodity dependence 2014*. New York: United Nations.

Van de Walle, N. (2001). *African economies and the politics of permanent crisis, 1979–1999*. Cambridge: Cambridge University Press.

World Bank Group. (2017). *Migration and remittance data*. Washington. Retrieved, 28 June 2019, from http://www.worldbank.org/en/topic/migrationremittancesdiasporaissues/brief/migration-remittances-data

World Bank Group. (2018). *State of electricity access report*. Washington, DC: World Bank Inc.

Zafar, A. (2011). Mauritius: An economic success story. In P. Chunan & M. Angwafo (Eds.), *Yes African can: Success stories from a dynamic continent*. Washington, DC: World Bank Inc. Retrieved from http://siteresources.worldbank.org/AFRICAEXT/Resources/258643-1271798012256/YAC_Consolidated_Web.pdf

Part 2

Pedagogical perspectives

3 'Unlearning' in global justice education

Barbara O'Toole

Introduction

This chapter takes up one of the ideas from Chapter 1, which is that global justice education in the North, specifically with Africa as its focus, necessitates first, a process of 'unlearning' by White educators, followed by learning that is grounded in critical social justice perspectives (Spivak, 1990; Andreotti, 2007; Spivak, 2012; Stein & Andreotti, 2015). The chapter looks at research evidence which demonstrates that descriptions of Africa found in classrooms in the Global North overwhelmingly depict Africa and Africans in situations of deficit and poverty, and in positions of dependence on the benevolence and charity of White Northerners. As long as perceptions such as these remain in place, ethical and reciprocal engagement between North and South will remain unlikely, if not impossible.

Who is this chapter written for? Research into the demographics of entrants into initial teacher education (ITE) in Ireland reveals the overwhelming homogeneity of pre-service teachers, in terms of being predominantly White, settled, female, Catholic, and middle class (Keane & Heinz, 2016). Moreover, between 57.7 and 66.5% of White Irish respondents in that study reported having 'a little experience' with ethnic groups different to their own and between 18.5 and 19.1% reporting having 'none at all' (ibid., p. 517). These figures raise a number of concerns. One of these is to do with the task facing teacher education in this context, in terms of developing and supporting educators' understanding of difference and diversity, including in relation to the Global South. This chapter draws attention to the self-reflexivity required on the part of White educators in order to carry out the perspectival shift necessary to successfully engage with social justice pedagogies in classrooms. It is written from the standpoint of a White teacher educator who endeavours to engage in such self-reflexivity, so it comes from the position of being an 'insider' in this work while also acknowledging the challenges and 'blind spots' inherent in such positioning.

In this chapter, I attempt to unravel the complexities of engaging in unlearning; for example, Stein and Andreotti's comment (2015, p. 32) that "one cannot escape one's rootedness in structural relations by disavowing them" suggests that a process of unlearning cannot simply involve a superficial engagement with one's own thinking and understandings, but instead requires deep self-questioning and self-reflection. The chapter examines what might be involved and the forms such 'unlearning' and 're-learning' might take for White educators. Given that this volume is premised on the contention that global justice education *can* effect change through challenging the dominant discourse, I explore the application of 'unlearning' in classroom contexts, along with implications for teacher education in the context of global concerns.

Part 1: why 'unlearning'?

Why is 'unlearning' necessary in the North? The very idea of '*un*learning' in itself requires examination, suggesting as it does that there is an inherent flaw not just in what is 'seen', but more fundamentally, in prevailing 'ways of seeing' Africa in the North. It suggests that predominant knowledge about and perceptions of Africa are grounded in positioning that is, typically, fundamentally faulty. This is indeed my argument in this chapter. Drawing on the work of writers such as Said (1985, 1993), Spivak (1988, 1990, 2012), Kapoor (2004), Andreotti (2006, 2007, 2011, 2016a, 2016b), and Stein and Andreotti (2015), I propose that in order to unravel prevailing views and perceptions, a process of 'deconstruction' (unlearning) is first required, followed by 'learning to learn' which is grounded in critical social justice perspectives. These are not new ideas, but as the chapter demonstrates, they need to be reiterated in the light of ongoing evidence from classrooms which reveals the persistence of Eurocentric thinking and beliefs about Northern/white superiority, alongside perceptions of African poverty, dependence, and lack of agency. My contention, using evidence from classrooms, is that predominant ways of 'seeing' Africa continue to be rooted in deficit perspectives and modernisation thinking. This problem can only be addressed when global justice education in Northern classrooms becomes deeper and more critical, involving deconstruction of existing views (unlearning), followed by global learning informed by African perspectives and African voices, and which addresses issues of power and politics in age-appropriate ways. I argue that a predominance of 'soft' approaches to global learning, which eschews deeper and more politically oriented investigation, will continue to keep children's and young people's views of the African continent and African people entrenched in deficit thinking.

As noted in Chapter 1, a risk of enjoining Northern educators to examine and unlearn their own privilege is that it once again centres the discussion on the positioning of Whites, and in the process, can obscure structural issues underpinning discrimination, and downplay the importance of resistance (Leonardo, 2004). Second, such an exploration may paradoxically insulate White people *against* self-awareness because it may create an illusion that acknowledgement is an end in itself ("I acknowledge White privilege; therefore my work is done"), thereby shielding people from ongoing self-reflexivity. The 'good' White (Kitching, 2014) declares their privilege, feels exonerated and 'off the hook'. The purpose of this chapter is to highlight the complexities and the lifelong nature of this kind of work. There are no quick fixes.

Privileging the West: the historical connection

In the *Guardian* newspaper on Saturday, 14 April 2018, a review by Claire Armistead of the book *Packing my Library: An Elegy and Ten Digressions* by Alberto Manguel contained the following:

> .... he recalls the syphilitic knight Pedro de Mendoza, who sailed to South America in 1536 under instructions from Charles 1 to set up a Spanish colony, taking with him not only 13 ships and 2,000 men, but "seven volumes of medium size bound in black leather" ***which were to become the continent's first library.*** (italics added)

Armistead went on to say that the books in this "founding library ... communicate an eclectic generous conception of what a new city should be" (2018, p. 15). Apart from the assumption that a 'new city' in a subjugated colony can in any way be 'generous' when the human cost is considered, this brief extract captures many problematic presumptions. First, the 'epistemic blindness' (Martin, Pirbhai-Illich, & Pete, 2017) of much of Northern discourse in relation to the South comes across, discourse which presupposes an absence of scholarship when it is not *European* scholarship. There is no suggestion that the explorers might have expanded their own learning through engaging with the "knowledge structures, cultures and intellectual agendas" (Richardson, 2018, p. 236) of these civilisations. Said (1985, p. 44) stated: "a certain freedom of intercourse was always the Westerner's privilege; because his was the stronger culture, he could penetrate, he could wrestle with, he could give shape and meaning ... " Along with the presumption of the right to penetrate rather than to learn from, the Manguel extract echoes what Stein and Andreotti (2015, p. 33) describe as "the universal claims of Western thought and the unexamined authority of the Western subject", whereby the scholarship of the South is (un)seen and (un)heard through Northern frames of reference, becoming obliterated through the nexus of Eurocentric knowledge and power. Moreover, the example draws a connective line of thought from the 1500s to the present day, underscoring the deep rootedness and long-standing nature of binary ways of framing the world since the inception of the colonial matrix of power, with the projection of European epistemology as "universal, unmarked and neutral" (Andreotti & De Souza, 2008, p. 24), in which the knowledge of the South became subjugated and the voices of its citizens silenced, a process which Andreotti (2011, p. 384) describes as the "subalternisation of non-European knowledges".

While this highlights the necessity for educators to promote alternative approaches to global learning, it also underlines the complexity and challenge of such a task, given that the privileging of Northern epistemology has been such a long-standing and totalising phenomenon, with the delegitimising of other forms of knowing and being (Stein, 2018b) stretching back to the sixteenth century (Mignolo, 2008; Walsh, 2018). The challenge facing Northern educators concerned with these matters is immense. And, before looking at educational approaches which might facilitate the kind of deconstruction and unlearning that is required, it is important to review evidence from classrooms in order to underline the extent of the problem.

What research is telling us: evidence from classrooms

Research from Northern classrooms consistently demonstrates the predominance of negative stereotyping and deficit perspectives, beliefs which reflect perceptions of European superiority (Scheunpflug, 2011) along with ideas about lack of agency, and silence, in the South. This has been illustrated by Oberman, Waldron, and Dillon (2012), Borowski (2012), Oberman (2013), Tallon (2012), Tallon and McGregor (2014), Simpson (2016), Oberman and Waldron (2017), Lawson (2018), amongst many others. It also emerged in the *Just Trade* study which was the impetus for the current volume, and which is described in further detail in Chapter 5.

Although the studies referenced here mainly comprise small-scale qualitative research, the findings from all are remarkably similar. Participants' views about Africa are predominantly deficit, focusing on 'charity' as the solution to world hunger and scarcity, and seeing the African continent in essentialist terms as ubiquitously poverty-stricken. In all the studies reviewed when researching this chapter, none revealed findings in which children and young people's views, at baseline, reflected perceptions of parity of esteem between North and South. None of the evidence pointed to balanced and nuanced perceptions of African countries and the lives of African people. Instead, findings overwhelmingly indicated that children and young people perceived the Global North in the role of benevolent donor towards the 'impoverished' South, as well as being the source of modernisation, progress, and development. Oberman et al. (2012, p. 45) note the persistence of negative views in spite of an educational intervention, where stereotypical ideas "tended to dominate children's perceptions of African countries and African people even when they were exposed to positive images as part of the research process". And, in studies which investigated the *causes* of global poverty, views typically reflected modernisation beliefs, along with a perception that in-country problems such as war and food scarcity are at the root of poverty, with typically, charitable aid being seen as the solution to these problems (Simpson, 2017; Lawson, 2018).

The *Just Trade* study, introduced in Chapter 1, set out to investigate whether a module that challenged stereotypes about Africa and which examined trade justice, could impact on children's views about the continent. The study began with baseline activities, adapted from Reading International Solidarity Centre (Allum et al., 2015), which were implemented before the trade module was taught and then returned to on completion. One of these activities asked: "What would you see in a country in Africa?", requiring pupils to write or draw their answers. Typical responses depicted a continent dominated by exotic animals, hot weather, and overwhelming poverty and hunger. 'Disease' also featured strongly in perceptions, while predominant views of the 'built environment' consisted of "mud huts" or "houses made of straw".

Findings from this research study, which are partially reported here and returned to in Chapter 5, are not unique. Borowski (2012) recounted very similar findings in his Leeds-based study, while the work of Reading International Solidarity Centre (Allum et al., 2015) has highlighted that these are fairly typical responses in this kind of activity. The results of these and other comparable studies have enormous implications for educators. First, as Oberman et al. (2012, p. 50) point out, children's understandings of the world are strongly influenced by "learning outside the classroom", particularly through the dominance of fundraising campaigns which utilise imagery of impoverished and desperate people (Borowski, 2012). This makes an educator's job more difficult, because preconceptions are already in place even before very young children start school, and these ideas must then be countered in classrooms. This has implications for curriculum design, ITE, and continuous professional development (CPD). And, as already noted, the depth of the negative perceptions means that they sometimes remain in place despite educational interventions which are designed to challenge them. Finally, the evidence raises questions about the predominant type of global learning that currently takes place in schools, given that deficit views continue to be so entrenched. Clearly, something in current educational approaches is falling short.

The 'pedagogic authority' of textbooks

This problem may be compounded by the impact of the textbooks which are generally available in schools. Written texts are not created in a neutral space, and the cultural context in which they are written cannot be underestimated.

Chapter 1 gave examples of two academic texts identified by Nyaluke (2014, p. 160),[1] which portrayed Africans as either hungry or chaotic: "in neither case are Africans portrayed as having the potential to be political actors who may be motivated by ideals and a sense of the common good". Classroom resources for younger students can be even more problematic, because, as Tallon (2012, p. 9) notes, such materials come with "the authority of the teaching environment", thereby potentially giving them considerable status and power in students' eyes. According to Mc Daid (2011), teachers have 'pedagogic authority' based on their institutional legitimacy as school authority and can impose the selection of meanings by virtue of that authority. This involves what is included and what is omitted from classroom discourse. While Mc Daid's (2011) study focused on recognition of students' first languages in schools, this argument can also be made in relation to the knowledge, information, and perspectives deemed to be legitimate in the school environment: namely, from textbooks used in classrooms. Indeed, Bryan and Bracken (2011b, p. 119) note that while textbooks do not "solely determine what is taught" in schools, they are often relied upon "as the authoritative and definitive sources of knowledge". Those writers examined texts and curricular resources in use for the purposes of 'development' education in secondary schools in Ireland and found a prevalence of modernisation theory, which "attributes few if any external 'causes' for the continuing 'underdevelopment' of majority world cultures" (ibid.). They also found the 3Fs approach (fundraising, fasting, and having fun) to be pervasive, leading to a trend whereby global activism initiatives were underpinned by a development-as-charity perspective. Their investigation highlighted the predominant representations of the South in selected texts: "numerous photographs of bedraggled shanty towns, overcrowded classrooms and polluted environments" (Bryan & Bracken, 2011a, p. 117).

While textbooks may not be used to the same extent in primary schools, the 'pedagogic authority' of the teacher could be even stronger in that context, with younger and more impressionable children and with typically a stronger pupil/teacher relationship than in second level. Primary school texts in Ireland have similarly been examined by Bennett (1995) and Waldron (2005, 2013), with Waldron taking history texts as her focus. She notes that educators must be alert to the power of textbooks "to define children's experiences of history ... a message that denies both the constructed and the partial nature of historical knowledge and the power of dominant interests and narratives to determine the story" (2013, p. 58). Moloney and O'Toole (2018) investigated representations of diversity in texts widely used in early years' classrooms in Ireland and found stereotypical and essentialist portrayals of African countries as impoverished, overwhelmingly rural, and with a need for assistance from the Global North. As Andreotti (2014, p. 23) states, these kinds of portrayals reinforce views that the North leads the way "in terms of economic development to those lagging behind".

Active unlearning: 'learning to learn'

The kind of depictions described above reflect the prevailing 'modernisation' and Eurocentric approach endemic in many educational materials, with people of the South portrayed as a "helpless mass" (Jooste & Heleta, 2017, p. 46), dependent on the superior knowledge and experience of those in the North. Consequently, it is hardly surprising that classroom research demonstrates that deficit perceptions of Africa are deeply entrenched and that such views can persist in spite of interventions that aim to challenge them (Oberman et al., 2012). It is clear that the content of textbooks needs to be reviewed, ensuring that Southern voices and Southern perspectives are included, and that depictions are nuanced and fair. However, a deeper approach must also be taken; the problem will not be resolved simply by re-writing textbooks: interrogating the concept of 'learning to learn' may also help to identify alternative ways of approaching global justice education, and of moving from a charity to a rights-based approach.

The argument at the heart of this chapter is that, given the persistence and deep rootedness of negative portrayals of Africa in the media and in dominant discourse, including in education systems in the North, *unlearning* must form a key part of critical approaches to global learning. This argument has been made by a number of writers. Simpson (2016, p. 4), for example, proposes that in order to achieve 'deep learning' in relation to social justice issues, "learners must engage in active unlearning", such is the extent and depth of the reach of stereotypical messages about 'Other' in Western societies. Part of this work involves unlearning 'the charity mentality', so that learners can then begin to reconstruct their knowledge about the South through the lens of social justice. Active unlearning thus requires deep and meaningful engagement which places demands on White educators. It means suspending my belief "that I am indispensable, better, or culturally superior; it is refraining from always thinking ... that I have the solutions; it is resisting the temptation of projecting myself or my world onto the Other" (Kapoor, 2004, p. 641). Unlearning means "stopping myself from always wanting to correct, teach, theorise, develop, colonise, appropriate, use, record, inscribe, enlighten ... " (ibid.).

Martin, Pirbhai-Illich, and Pete (2017, p. 237) use the term 'decolonisation of minds', which they argue means confronting whiteness and white privilege by "turning the gaze ... towards those whose assumed normalcy and neutrality support their narratives of 'doing good' while hiding themselves from their complicities in ontological and epistemological violences". Furthermore, Andreotti (2007, p. 74), drawing on the work of Gayatri Spivak, sets out propositions for countering the dominant discourse and for establishing an "ethical relation to the Other", the first of which involves deconstruction or a 'negotiation from within', whereby people engage in a critique of the "representations as they inhabit them". The core of unlearning involves the recognition and undoing of the epistemic violence of colonialism, whereby European epistemology is projected as universal and neutral and which "implies, specifically, a reversal of information and knowledge production so that they flow from South to North, and not always in the other direction" (Kapoor, 2004, p. 642).

Part 2: pedagogical implications

From these descriptions, it is clear that learning to unlearn represents a significant undertaking and poses weighty questions for White educators. For example, how can such ideas be translated into classroom practice? What are the pedagogical implications of 'unlearning' given the demands it makes upon existing constructs and worldviews, including active 'deconstruction' of some of those worldviews? How can a requirement to confront white privilege be scaffolded? What are the implications for teacher education in supporting such in-depth work?

There are numerous examples of educational interventions that have endeavoured to challenge Eurocentric discourse about the South and engage students in critical examination of world issues; however, according to Scheunpflug and Mehren (2016, p. 216), there is an absence of systematic studies on the actual teaching and learning processes involved and insufficient research "on the conditions characterising the instructional setting which promotes (such) learning processes". Consequently, these authors state that in order to have robust and generalisable findings, "data has to become more comprehensive". In the absence of systematic research, the concept of a 'pedagogical framework' for global learning can be a useful starting point in considering the above questions (Bourn, 2015; Blackmore, 2016). Such frameworks may point to overarching principles that need to form part of pedagogical approaches that have active unlearning at their core.

Bourn (2015, p. 102), for example, introduces a pedagogical framework based around four principles:

- Global outlook
- Recognition of power and inequality in the world
- Belief in social justice and equity
- Commitment to reflection, dialogue, and transformation

He states that, together, these principles "form a framework that emphasises the importance of processes of learning" (ibid., p. 103) and make connections between theory and practice of global learning. In this context, a 'global outlook' consists of more than an awareness of world issues, but includes moving to a mindset of social justice and solidarity, along with a sense of global responsibility. 'Recognition of power and inequality in the world' includes an understanding of historical forces such as colonialism and imperialism, and their implications at social, cultural and economic levels. 'Belief in social justice and equity' relates to the wish to see a more just and equal world where all people have their voices heard and where learners begin to "question and re-think their own views about the world, the reasons for inequality and power differentials" (ibid., p. 114). Finally, 'commitment to reflection, dialogue and transformation' incorporates "notions of critical thinking, reflection, dialogue and engagement that could lead to some form of personal transformation" (ibid.). This kind of learning may be unsettling to the learner and bring them to question their assumptions and beliefs, as well as their own relationship with the world.

Blackmore (2016) puts forward a framework for what she describes as 'critical global citizenship education pedagogy' which consists of four interrelated dimensions:

- Critical thinking
- Dialogue
- Reflection
- Responsible being/action

Here, the 'critical thinking' dimension involves exploring and making explicit historical and contemporary manifestations of power, along with questioning historical causes of contemporary issues. 'Dialogue' concerns engaging with difference and alternative perspectives: "whether difference in the form of theoretical knowledge or everyday experiences lived by different people" (ibid., p. 42) and comprises a means of learning '*from*' and '*with*' rather than learning '*about*' others. Blackmore places emphasis on "reflection and a focus on examining the self and one's own assumptions, knowledge and implication" (ibid., p. 44). 'Reflection' includes an increasing awareness of "connections between oneself and others, and the wider socio-political and natural environment" (ibid.), and by its nature, can consist of an encounter with 'difficult knowledge'. Finally, 'responsible being/action' is the point at which action can take place as a result of critical thinking, dialogue, and reflection. Transformative actions are those directed towards "challenging existing political and social structures" (ibid., p. 45).

There is a two-fold reason for detailing these pedagogical frameworks here, in the context of examining 'unlearning'. First, the idea of a framework containing *guiding principles* suggests that a social justice approach to global issues can underpin one's pedagogy, regardless of the subject or topic at hand. It moves global justice education out of curricular silos and into the arena of the philosophical perspective underpinning one's entire teaching, suggesting that it can permeate a teacher's practice across the curriculum and into the whole school. This echoes Stein's (2018a, p. 10) view that "perhaps our role as educators is not to transfer any particular set of skills or values", but instead to "prepare young people to face the storms that characterise these complex, uncertain times with an internal groundedness in the face of unpredictable weather .... "

Second, these examples highlight demands made upon teachers and learners when engaging in pedagogy which incorporates critical thinking and self-reflection. The self-reflective and self-interrogatory aspects of these frameworks draw attention to the complexity of teaching and learning processes in global justice education, which aim to engage in critical (re)examination of world issues. This complexity includes the kinds of strategies an educator might use to encourage reflection, dialogue, and critical thinking; it also encompasses the nature of the learning environment that needs to be in place for such investigation to take place. More fundamentally however, it implies openness and receptivity on the part of the White educator to the 'unknown-ness' of what might emerge in explorations into complex world issues, where people are required to recognise and unpack their privilege. The nature of this type of engagement is that it must displace white Northern knowledges from their central positioning, and in the process, open people to the possibility of being changed by new perspectives. This is 'learning to learn', and it brings teacher education, and indeed, the nature of the teaching/learning experience itself, into the spotlight.

Teacher education

The research study which was the stimulus for the current volume consisted of implementing a module on trade justice across four primary schools in Ireland, with audit activities at baseline and endline to determine if children's perceptions of Africa changed as a result of the intervention. Lessons aimed to encourage pupils to investigate below the surface of global power relationships, specifically between trading partners in the North and South (see Chapter 5). Another core element involved challenging Eurocentric portrayals of the world through examining stereotypes and countering negative portrayals of Africa. *Just Trade* (and there are many other similar projects in existence) set out to challenge the dominant narrative of poverty and hardship in African countries and to present more nuanced and equitable depictions of Africa and its people.

Nonetheless, as Scheunpflug and Mehren (2016, p. 215) state: "global learning in schools is strongly influenced by those teaching it". In other words, regardless of its inception, once a module has been designed and disseminated, its success is subsequently reliant on the skills, expertise, and dispositions of teachers who choose to implement it. While teaching materials can be honed and improved according to feedback from piloting and/or research, the expertise and disposition of participating teachers is harder to regulate and predict. In the absence of structured CPD, the risk is that some teachers may take easier options rather than engage on a deeper level with thorny global topics. Social justice concepts can be challenging and can necessitate ongoing support and CPD for teachers.

Indeed, Oberman et al. (2012, p. 52) report on a collaborative initiative undertaken in Ireland in 2011, which resulted in a global citizenship education programme for three-to-six-year-olds, "developed through an iterative process of research, practice and critical reflection" (ibid., p. 56). Pedagogies included poem and story, puppets and props, and teacher-in-role methodology as ways to explore alternative perspectives and to enable children to make emotional connections with storybook characters. It also aimed to address a deficit perspective on Kenya through highlighting similarities in people's daily lives in Ireland and Kenya (Bourn, 2015). However, Oberman et al. (2012, p. 52) report that some educators 'didn't want to upset' children by depicting poverty, which they felt might "take away from the colourful and happy portrayal of Kenyan life depicted" in lessons. And on the other hand, some educators focused mainly on poverty, thereby reinforcing essentialist views of Africa, while others used materials as a stimulus for cross-curricular work but "did not explicitly explore issues of social justice" (ibid., p. 45). In essence, merely creating materials does not necessarily facilitate unlearning; by their nature, such materials are at one remove from the people who designed them, so it is possible that any 'disruptive' intention that was present at design phase can be diluted on implementation. The role of teachers in global justice education is critical.

Teacher education (pre-service and in-service) in matters of global justice must involve more than a fact-based cognitive approach; it must engage White teachers at a deeper level of attitudes, assumptions, and beliefs, i.e. a process of active unlearning grounded in the kinds of pedagogical frameworks presented by Bourn (2015) and Blackmore (2016). This is not saying that many White teachers do not engage in deep critical inquiry; rather, it is to reinforce this notion for those who already do and to bring it to the fore for all educators. Teacher education in global learning requires critical reflection, learning to (un)learn, and then bringing these fresh perspectives into the classroom and school, a process which Bourn (2016, p. 71) sums up in the phrase "moving from a charity mentality to one of social justice".

Simpson (2017) reports on a CPD programme in England specifically designed around 'unlearning', in that sessions aimed to move teachers' practice from charity towards social justice. This initiative was part of the Global Learning Programme (GLP) in the UK, a Department of International Development (DfID)-funded programme of support, which was the main mechanism for supporting teachers in promoting global learning in schools in the UK from 2013 to 2018 (Bourn, 2016; McCloskey, 2016; Huckle, 2017). Simpson's programme had a number of stages, beginning with unearthing and unsettling teachers' fundamental assumptions about the Global South. Teachers were encouraged to bring previously unconscious worldviews into conscious awareness and to evaluate those assumptions against current experiences and against the experiences of others. Finally, they were encouraged to reframe their beliefs about the world, the aim being that teachers would make changes in their practice based on their new understandings. Evidence from the intervention indicated that teachers' perceptions and practice *were* impacted upon through the CPD, with Simpson reporting: "those initial interventions which shook the foundations of their own assumptions or constructed knowledge had a subsequent significant impact on their personal perspective and openness to 'new' ideas or concepts" (2017, p. 105).

This kind of intervention, based on experiential learning in the form of participative and self-reflective methodologies, could support the kind of in-depth unlearning that can move White teachers away from "charitable concepts of development towards deeper, more critical forms of inquiry into the underlying causes of local and global inequality and injustice" (McCloskey, 2016, p. 158). This requires the kind of critical self-reflexivity which necessitates White Northern educators keeping their structural positionality to the fore of their awareness and working to bring blindspots into conscious awareness. D'Arcangelis (2015, p. 269) maintains that in order to achieve this, self-reflective processes must take a 'double turn', "moving towards and away from the self in continual succession". Such a process may help to avoid falling into the trap of 'colonial continuities' (Heron, 2007, p. 7), through which Northern educators feel authorised and entitled to intervene for the benefit of 'Others' or feel vindicated as 'good Whites' (Kitching, 2014), thereby remaining immune, as they see it, from processes of racialisation and Othering.

Risks and opportunities in learning anew

A feature of the *kind* of exploration that would seem to be a necessary part of the process of unlearning, is, therefore, an element of 'disruption' and 'unsettling', or what Kerdeman (2003) describes as "being pulled up short". However, Dunne (2015, p. 30) points to what she terms "the great stability" in the beliefs and attitudes of pre-service and practising teachers, because these views have not been challenged with evidence to the contrary. Yet this chapter is premised on the necessity of providing the kinds of 'disrupting' experiences that can create dissonance and challenge existing views. The pedagogical frameworks put forward by Bourn (2015) and Blackmore (2016) include self-reflection, critical thinking, and dialogue; implicit here is the notion of receptivity to new ideas and experiences whilst challenging one's existing ideas and assumptions about the world and one's place in it as a White Northern educator. Similarly, Stein and Andreotti (2015) underline the importance of moving oneself away from holding a central positioning and becoming open to the new possibilities that arise from ethical engagement: "the idea would be neither to deny difference, not to appropriate and therefore sublate it, but rather to engage with it in such a way that *one might be changed by it in unexpected ways*" (Stein & Andreotti, 2015, p. 35, italics added).

In my experience as a teacher educator, the 'triggers' or prompts to such unsettling that I have found useful, typically comprise experiential learning methodologies (e.g. moving debates, group work, simulations) followed by discussion and debate to tease out issues raised. Interrogation of media images of the Global South using Compass Rose-type activities (see Chapter 5) has been another means of provoking thought and generating conversation and debate. In relation to trade justice, 'Bean to Bar' activities, alongside the juxtaposition of figures showing Irish government aid against money spent by Irish consumers on African products (€72 per capita on aid vs 42c spent on products – O'Caoimh & McGauley, 2011) usually startles people into a new awareness about trade vs aid imbalances and prompts new understandings. Such activities can also deeply resonate with teachers and student teachers who are already questioning and are already engaged in self-reflexive processes.

Listening to Southern voices and the perspectives of the African diaspora is also an important dimension of unlearning. Borowski (2012, p. 5), for example, describes an initiative where African postgraduate students delivered 'activity days' in local primary schools in Leeds, using approaches which challenged the dominant narrative about Africa: "direct contact with someone from Africa can dispel the stereotypical perceptions young people have about the continent".

These kinds of approaches can place demands on those engaged in them, both learners and educators. Indeed, in this context, *all* those involved are essentially learners, given the challenges to Northern assumptions, to Eurocentric thinking and to white privilege that are inherent in experiential methodologies. According to Salzberger-Wittenberg, Henry and Osborne (1983), and French and Simpson (2000, 2003), the act of learning begins, by definition, from a place of *not knowing*. These writers explore processes of learning and teaching through a psychoanalytic lens, drawing on the work of W.R. Bion and Melanie Klein. They propose that learning, by its very nature, represents a risk to the individual, because in order to learn, one must suspend belief and assurance that one already knows, and one must be open to the uncertainty that comes from not knowing. Salzberger-Wittenberg et al. (1983, p. 57) identify the kinds of anxieties that can accompany the learning process: "fear of confusion and chaos in the face of unsorted 'bricks' of experience, helplessness in the face of not knowing, fear of inadequacy, fear of being judged [as] stupid in comparison with others". French and Simpson (2003, p. 182) state that learning arises from a capacity to tolerate such anxieties and from being able to remain "at the edges between knowing and not knowing". Similarly, Salzberger-Wittenberg et al. (1983, p. 58) propose that "real learning and discovery can only take place when a state of not knowing can be borne long enough to enable all the data gathered by the senses to be taken in and explored until some meaningful pattern emerges". By definition therefore, the 'edge' of knowing is an uncomfortable place to be. It calls upon an individual to suspend her or his prior certainty and assumptions, remaining open to the possibilities of new insights and fresh perspectives. Being on the 'edge' of one's knowing requires a 'disposition' to stay with discomfort rather than retreating into self-protective positions or quick solutions; or "well-worn defensive routines" (French & Simpson, 2000, p. 63). The disposition which French and Simpson describe as "a state of mind, a way of being, a way of attending to experience" is that which enables an individual "to bear the experience of encountering the edge" (2000, p. 68), and ultimately of being open to learning. For educators, the paradox is that of creating a safe space for learning, whilst simultaneously disrupting certainties, challenging existing worldviews, and facilitating new understandings and perspectives.

This exploration about the nature of learning is expressly pertinent to global justice education in the North, particularly for White educators. In that context, the recognition of "self-implication", including the acknowledgement of white privilege and Northern complicity, can represent "difficult knowledge" (Blackmore, 2016, p. 44) which can challenge learners' worldviews, identities, and their previously held 'truths'. Di Angelo (2011, 2018), for example, describes 'White Fragility' as the state "in which even a minimum amount of racial stress becomes intolerable, triggering a range of defensive moves" (2011, p. 54). How can educators support learners in the challenging stages of unlearning, "when they face the uncertainty, fear, anger and possible paralysis that comes in the early stages of the renegotiation of (and disenchantment with) epistemic privilege?" (Andreotti, 2011, p. 393). Remaining with the attendant discomfort is an essential part of the learning processes. A key feature of global learning for Northern educators must involve bringing unseen assumptions to conscious awareness and processing the ensuing discomforting and potentially revelatory insights. It is precisely in this territory of risk and uncertainty that the possibility arises of learning something new and unexpected (Blackmore, 2016). Remaining on the edge of knowing, and tolerating 'unknowing', is what enables real learning to take place.

Todd (2003) takes this a stage further. Drawing on the work of Melanie Klein, she examines the distinction between learning *from* as opposed to learning ***about*** the Other. She states that it is anxiety over encountering difference "that both leads to the possibility of learning and presents learning with its fiercest form of resistance" (ibid., p. 11). This is because, in gaining new insight, the individual risks losing a sense of coherence and place in the world: "Precisely because the Other is seen to be that which disrupts its coherency, the subject tumbles into uncertainty, its past strategies for living challenged by the very strangeness of difference itself" (ibid.). The disruption that constitutes a necessary component of unlearning can in itself produce resistance and defensiveness. Consequently, within this territory of uncertainty and riskiness, teaching itself becomes "a delicate engagement", because the emphasis is no longer on specific strategies or methodologies, but rather on "an attentiveness to the exposure and riskiness that students face in their everyday experiences of learning" (ibid., p. 36). The implication is that teachers must be attuned to the inherent disruptiveness of the learning experience, both for themselves and for their students. And, when the content of one's teaching relates to global justice issues, the stakes are high indeed; as Stein (2018b, p. 12) reminds us: decentring oneself and suspending one's preconceptions "can result in an unexpected and potentially disruptive rearrangement of knowledge".

Conclusion

The kind of pedagogical engagement required in critical global justice education places high demands on teachers and students. What is at stake, in terms of the kind of unlearning and re-learning that is involved for a White Northern educator, concerns one's relationship with oneself, including the disruption of one's coherence and certainty. It also includes one's relationship with 'Other', including the awareness of self-implication, the call to reciprocity and mutual learning, and the challenge to ethically frame one's activist responses. Global justice education, when approached in ways outlined in this chapter, necessitates negotiating complex material which may touch on sensitivities and evoke a range of emotional responses. White teacher educators who are committed to social justice have no choice but to engage at this level, both with themselves and with their students. Teacher education has the capacity to reaffirm one's privilege or disrupt one's certainty (Kerr & Andreotti, 2017). This chapter is part of the growing conversation about how the latter can be achieved.

Note

1 Bayart's *The State in Africa: The Politics of Belly* and Chabal and Daloz's *Africa Works: Disorder as Political Instrument.*

References

Allum, L., Dral, P., Galanská, N., Lowe, B., Navojsky, A. Pelimanni, P …, Skalická, Z. (2015). *How do we know it's working?. Book 2, Tracking changes in pupils' attitudes.* Reading, UK: Reading International Solidarity Centre (RISC).

Andreotti, V. (2006). *Critical literacy in global citizenship education.* Retrieved from https://www.academia.edu/194048/Critical_Literacy_in_Global_Citizenship_Education_2006_

Andreotti, V. (2007). An ethical engagement with the Other: Spivak's ideas on education. *Critical Literacy: Theories and Practices,* 1(1), 69–79.

Andreotti, V., & de Souza, L.M. (2008). Translating theory into practice and walking minefields: Lessons from the project Through Other Eyes. *International Journal of Development Education and Global Learning,* 1(1), 23–36.

Andreotti, V. (2011). (Towards) decoloniality and diversality in global citizenship education. *Globalisation, Societies and Education,* 9(304), 381–397.

Andreotti, V. (2014). Critical literacy: Theories and practices in development education. *Policy & Practice: A Development Education Review*, 19, 12–32.

Andreotti, V. (2016a). Global education and social change. In H. Hartmeyer & L. Wegimont (Eds.), *Global education in Europe revisited: Strategies and structures, policy, practice and challenges* (pp. 199–203). Munster/New York: Waxmann.

Andreotti, V. (2016b). The educational challenges of imagining the world differently. *Canadian Journal of Development Studies*, 37(1), 101–112.

Armistead, C. (2018, April 14). Book review. *The Guardian*. Retrieved from www.guardian.com

Bennett, J. (1995) Primary school textbooks and the implementation of the Primary School Curriculum in the Republic of Ireland, 1971–1993. *Irish Educational Studies* 14(1), 129–142.

Blackmore, C. (2016). Towards a pedagogical framework for global citizenship education. *International Journal of Development Education and Global Learning*, 8(1), 39–56.

Borowski, R. (2012). *Media influences on young people's perceptions of Africa*. Leeds University Centre for African Studies, University of Leeds. Retrieved from https://lucas.leeds.ac.uk/wp-content/uploads/sites/61/2014/01/Africa-UK-Journalism-Conference-Paper.pdf

Bourn, D. (2015). *The theory and practice of development education*. Oxon and New York: Routledge.

Bourn, D. (2016). Teachers as agents of social change. *International Journal of Development Education and Global Learning*, 7(3), 63–77.

Bryan, A., & Bracken, M. (2011a). *Learning to read the world? Teaching and learning about global citizenship and international development in post-primary schools*. Dublin: Irish Aid.

Bryan, A., & Bracken, M. (2011b). 'They think the book is right and I am wrong': Intercultural education and the positioning of ethnic minority students in the formal and informal curriculum. In M. Darmody, N. Tyrell, & S. Song (Eds.), *The changing faces of Ireland: Exploring the lives of immigrant and ethnic minority children*. Rotterdam: Sense Publishers.

D'Arcangelis, C.L. (2015). *The solidarity encounter between indigenous women and white in a contemporary Canadian context*. PhD thesis, University of Toronto. Retrieved from https://tspace.library.utoronto.ca/bitstream/1807/71428/3/D'Arcangelis_Carol_Lynne_201511_PhD_thesis.pdf

Di Angelo, R. (2011). White fragility. *International Journal of Critical Pedagogy*, 3(3), 54–70.

Di Angelo, R. (2018). *White fragility: Why it's so hard for White people to talk about racism*. Boston, MA: Beacon Press.

Dunne, C.M. (2015). *Becoming a teacher of Irish: The evolution of beliefs, attitudes and role perceptions* (unpublished PhD thesis). Trinity College, University of Dublin, Dublin, Ireland.

French, R., & Simpson (2000). Learning at the edges between knowing and not knowing: 'Translating' Bion. *Organisational and Social Dynamics*, 1(1), 54–77.

French, R., & Simpson, P. (2003). Learning at the edges of knowing and not knowing: 'Translating' Bion. In R.M. Lipgar & M. Pines (Eds.), *Building on bion: Branches* (pp. 182–203). London and New York: Jessica Kingsley.

Heron, B. (2007). *Desire for development: Whiteness, gender and the helping imperative*. Ontario: Wilfrid Laurier University Press.

Huckle, J. (2017). Becoming critical: A challenge for the Global Learning Programme. *International Journal for Development Education and Global Learning*, 8(3), 63–84.

Jooste, N., & Heleta, S. (2017). Global citizenship versus globally competent graduates: A critical view from the South. *Journal of Studies in International Education*, 21(1), 39–51.

Kapoor, I. (2004). Hyper-self-reflexive development? Spivak on representing the Third World 'Other'. *Third World Quarterly*, 25(4), 627–647.

Keane, E., & Heinz, M. (2016). Excavating an injustice?: Nationality/ies, ethnicity/ies and experiences with diversity of initial teacher education applicants and entrants in Ireland in 2014. *European Journal of Teacher Education*, 39(4), 507–527.

Kerdeman, D. (2003). Pulled up short: Challenging self-understanding as a focus of teaching and learning. *Journal of Philosophy of Education*, 37(2), 293–308.

Kerr, J., & Andreotti, V. (2017). Crossing borders in initial teacher education: Mapping dispositions to diversity and inequity. *Race, Ethnicity and Education*, 22(5), 647–665.

Kitching, K. (2014). *The politics of compulsive education: Racism and learner-citizenship.* Oxon and New York: Routledge.

Lawson, H. (2018). *Primary pupils' attitudes towards and understandings of poverty* (Research Paper No. 19). London: Development Education Research Centre, Institute of Education.

Leonardo, Z. (2004). The colour of supremacy: beyond the discourse of 'white privilege'. *Educational Philosophy and Theory*, 36(2), 137-152.

Martin, F., Pirbhai-Illich, F., & Pete, S. (2017). Beyond culturally responsive pedagogy: Decolonising teacher education. In F. Pirbhai-Illich, S. Pete, & F. Martin (Eds.), *Culturally responsive pedagogy: Working towards decolonisation, indigeneity and interculturalism* (pp. 235–256). London: Palgrave Macmillan.

McCloskey, S. (2016). Education for social change: The Global Learning Programme in the North of Ireland. *Policy and Practice: A Development Education Review*, 23(Autumn), 139–161.

Mc Daid, R. (2011). GLOS, VOCE, VOICE: Minority language students reflect on the recognition of their first languages in Irish primary schools. In M. Darmody, N. Tyrell, & S. Song (Eds.), *The changing faces of Ireland: Exploring the lives of immigrant and ethnic minority children*. Rotterdam: Sense Publishers.

Mignolo, W. (2008). Preamble: The historical foundation of modernity/coloniality and the emergence of decolonial thinking. In S.A. Castro-Claren (Ed.), *Companion to Latin American literature and culture*. London: Wiley-Blackwell.

Moloney, C., & O'Toole, B. (2018). 'Windows and mirrors' or closed doors?' Representations of diversity in early years' textbooks. *Irish Teachers' Journal* 6(1), 55–72.

Nyaluke, D. (2014). The African basis of democracy and politics for the common good – A critique of the neopatrimonial perspective. *Taiwan Journal of Democracy*, 10(2), 141–164.

Oberman, R., Waldron, F., & Dillon, S. (2012). Developing a global citizenship education programme for three to six year olds. *International Journal of Development Education and Global Learning*, 4(1), 37–60.

Oberman, R. (2013). From research to resource: Critical literacy and global citizenship education in middle primary school. *Proceedings of the Irish Association for Social, Scientific and Environmental Education (IASSEE) Annual Conference 2013*, St Patrick's College (DCU), Dublin, pp. 29–39.

Oberman, R., & Waldron, F. (2017). 'They should be grateful to God': Challenging children's pre-conceptions of the Global South through human rights education. *Policy and Practice: A Development Education Review*, 25(Autumn), 9–33.

O'Caoimh, C. & McGauley, P. (2011). *Evidence and opportunity: Ireland's trade programme with its development programme countries in Africa*. Dublin: Value added in Africa.

Richardson, W.J. (2018). Understanding Eurocentrism as a structural problem of undone science. In G.K. Bhambra, D. Gebrial, & K. Nisancioglu (Eds.), *Decolonising the university*. London: Pluto Press.

Said, E. (1985). Orientalism re-considered. *Cultural Critique*, 1, 89–107.

Said, E. (1993). *Culture and imperialism*. London: Vintage.

Salzberger-Wittenberg, I., Osborne, E., & Henry, G. (1983). *The emotional experience of learning and teaching*. London: Routledge & Kegan Paul.

Scheunpflug, A. (2011). Global education and cross-cultural learning: A challenge for a research based approach to international teacher education. *International Journal of Development Education and Global Learning*, 3(3), 29–44.

Scheunpflug, A., & Mehren, R. (2016). What do we know about global learning and what do we need to find out? A summary of empirical evidence. In H. Hartmeyer & L. Wegimont (Eds.), *Global education in Europe revisited: Strategies and structures, policy, practice and challenges* (pp. 205–223). Munster and New York: Waxmann.

Simpson, J. (2016). *A study to investigate, explore and identify successful 'interventions' to support teachers in a transformative move from a charity mentality to a social justice mentality*. Global Learning Programme Innovation Fund Research Series: Paper 2. London: Development Education Research Centre.

Simpson, J. (2017). 'Learning to unlearn' the charity mentality within schools. *Policy and Practice: A Development Education Review*, 25(Autumn), 88–108.

Spivak, G. (1988), Can the subaltern speak? In C. Nelson & L. Grossberg (Eds.), *Marxism and the interpretation of culture*. Basingstoke: Macmillan Education.

Spivak, G. (1990). *The post-colonial critic: Interviews, strategies, dialogues*. New York: Psychology Press.

Spivak, G. (2012). *An aesthetic education in the era of globalisation*. Cambridge, MA: Harvard University Press.

Stein, S., & Andreotti, V. (2015). Complicity, ethics and education: Political and existential readings of Spivak's work. *Critical Literacy: Theories and Practices*, 9(1), 29–43.

Stein, S. (2018a). Rethinking critical approaches to global and development education. *Policy & Practice, A Development Education Review*, 27(Autumn), 1–13.

Stein, S. (2018b). Beyond higher education as we know it: Gesturing towards decolonial horizons of possibility. *Studies in Philosophy and Education*. Retrieved from http://doi.org/10.1007/s11217-018-9622-7

Tallon, R. (2012). The impressions left behind by NGO messages concerning the developing world. *Policy & Practice: A Development Education Review* 15, 8-26.

Tallon, R., & McGregor, A. (2014). Pitying the Third World: towards more progressive emotional responses to development education in schools. *Third World Quarterly*, 35(8), doi:10.1080/01436597.2014.946259.

Todd, S. (2003). *Learning from the other. Levinas, psychoanalysis, and ethical possibilities in education*. New York: SUNY Press.

Waldron, F. (2005). A nation's schoolbooks wield a great power: How the Romans are depicted in Irish history textbooks. In C. Morgan (Ed.), *Inter- and intracultural differences in European history textbooks* (pp. 257–290). Bern: Peter Lang.

Waldron, F. (2013). The power to end history? Defining the past through history textbooks. *Inis*, 39(Summer), 54–59.

Walsh, C. (2018). The decolonial for: Resurgences, shifts and movements. In W. Mignolo & C. Walsh (Eds.), *On decoloniality: Concepts, analytics, praxis*. Durham and London: Duke University Press.

4 Africa as pedagogical playground

Problematising sending programmes for teachers

Aoife Titley

Introduction

Teaching in an increasingly unequal and globalised world

Every January, the annual Oxfam report on global inequality brings a stark reminder of the unjust world we have created for ourselves. In 2019, we were confronted with the news that 26 billionaires now own the same wealth as half the planet (Public good or private wealth? Oxfam, 2019), and that rather than improving, global inequality is becoming even more pronounced. The increasing gap between the rich and poor in our world contributes to the denial of human rights, widespread poverty, and insecure political climates. In a progressively more globalised and interconnected world, there is a tendency to look to formal education to enhance our knowledge, values, and understanding of such complex global justice issues. Teachers are often seen as crucial changemakers and key actors through which transmission and engagement in learning for global social change can take place (Bourn, 2016).

Do teachers really appreciate the politically charged nature of global education? How are teachers making sense of new global interdependencies? If we want teachers to become transmitters of global knowledge, what type of global experiences are they having that might influence their thinking? As development education (DE) "comes in from the cold" (Honan, 2005, p. 20) and becomes more mainstreamed, an increasingly wide range of pedagogical responses have emerged. In a formal education context, these include school projects, integrated learning, immersion, linkage and twinning schemes, and child sponsorship. In recent years, there have also been increasing numbers of Irish teachers travelling to the Global South in search of adventure and more 'authentic' global experiences. It has now become easier than ever for teachers to avail of voluntary, short-term teaching opportunities in African countries. International service-learning (ISL) or sending programmes can sometimes be regarded as the 'face' of DE in Ireland and the perceived benevolence of this 'voluntourism' warrants further unpacking.

Author positionality

> The master's tools will never dismantle the master's house
>
> Audre Lorde

As a White, middle-class and settled woman, it is necessary to begin this chapter by scrutinising my own positionality and the ideas, values, tools, and assumptions that I bring to this discussion. As an 'insider' in DE and intercultural education, I strive to regard reflexivity as both a goal and a pedagogical approach of my work. However, Blasco (2012) argues that while reflexivity is a crucial skill for global educators, the self is not always self-accessible and doubts that the "self-accessible self can supposedly engage in the same constructive forms of reflexivity irrespective of the temporal and special contexts it inhabits" (p. 475). Bearing this potential limitation in mind, it is nonetheless important to engage with my own "cultural situatedness" (ibid., p. 476) in this regard.

To begin with, it is important to note that I have participated in sending programmes in Zambia, Uganda, and India over the last number of years and continue to be involved in the facilitation of orientation for student teachers and debriefing sessions for return volunteers. I have found my involvement in these programmes to be motivating, inspiring, and affirming, but equally troubling, disquieting, and uneasy. It is heartening to see many researchers who write in this area similarly struggle with such contradictions and address their misgivings through their writing. Sharpe and Dear (2013) having reflected on points of discomfort in their own work admit to being left with a "more encumbered view of ISL practice" (ibid., p. 49) and Crabtree (2008) also confesses to feeling "intellectually and ideologically conflicted about ISL work" (p. 19).

My own experiences overseas, as well as my professional involvement in DE have challenged me to reflect on the tensions and complexities which arise when a Northern teacher spends time in a Southern context. At times, one could wonder whether it might be easier to disassociate from sending programmes altogether. But the fact remains that these opportunities exist, and teachers will continue to be drawn to them for a myriad of reasons. The hope is that by interrogating these programmes through lenses of power, privilege, pedagogy, and praxis, I will become more intentional in my understanding of the wider historical, social, and educational contexts in which they operate, and that these reflections will inform the wider debate.

Parameters of chapter

Many researchers of ISL have called for more rigour in this area (Whitley, 2014). Generally, as a field of study it is relatively under-theorised, and in an Irish context, this lack of research is even more marked. Despite many Irish universities, higher education institutions, and non-governmental organisations (NGOs) being involved in sending programmes, and despite the wide availability of statutory funding from Irish Aid,[1] in-depth analysis of the impact of such programmes is virtually non-existent.

This chapter draws upon post-colonial thought, Freirean notions of praxis, and theories of whiteness to begin problematising the unequal power dynamics embedded in the mechanisms of sending programmes. This chapter will focus on in-service and pre-service teacher education in Ireland, and the teachers who participate in short-term, immersive educational placements in an African context. The aim is not to make a definitive judgement about sending programmes as a signature pedagogy of global justice education, but rather to synthesise some of the prevailing contradictions involved, in the hope of contributing to the wider conversation about their sustainability in an Irish context.

Contextualising sending programmes

Definition of sending programmes

The most common terminology emerging from the literature is that of 'international service learning' (ISL). Bamber and Pike (2013) understand ISL as a pedagogical approach which combines student learning in a formal context, with engagement with an overseas community. Social justice, citizenship, and commitment to global justice tend to feature as among the main motivators for many of these programmes (Crabtree, 2008). One of the most accepted definitions derives from Bringle and Hatcher (2011):

> A structured academic experience in another country which students a) participate in organised service activity that addresses identified community needs; b) learn from direct interaction and cross-cultural dialogue with others; and c) reflect on the experience in such a way as to gain further understanding of course content, a deeper understanding of global and intercultural issues, a broader appreciation of the host country and discipline and an enhanced sense of their own responsibilities as citizens, locally and globally. (p. 19)

'International service learning', 'global service learning', or 'international citizen service' (Birdwell, 2011) are not descriptions typically associated with the dominant Irish models. The inclusion of the word 'service', by its very nature conjures up notions of working 'for' rather than 'with' communities. It reinforces stereotypical thinking in relation to the supposed helplessness and dependency of the host population. This is explored in greater depth later in the chapter. In addition, it can be argued that it has a more layered meaning in the context of consumerism (Bamber & Pike, 2013) and capitalism. For the purposes of this chapter, except in deference to the original context where ISL might have been used, I will use the term 'sending programme'. This represents a more accurate term for the Irish system, which adopts a structured, one-way system of travel to host countries for student teachers, newly qualified teachers, and teachers on summer placements. We send, but we do not receive.

Theoretical and conceptual underpinnings

Whitley (2014) traces the foundational theory of service-learning back to the work of Dewey, Kolb, and Freire, and their theses around how meaningful learning happens when students are actively involved in their own education and can engage in diverse environments without traditional classroom power dynamics.

However, it is Mezirow's (1978) *Transformative Learning Theory* which is the favoured theoretical framework for ISL as a powerful learning experience (Bamber & Hankin, 2011; Whitley, 2014).

Mezirow (1978) believes that people are "caught in their own history and reliving it" and this can impact their potential perspective growth (p. 101). He argues that that critical learning requires students to examine their own assumptions in relation to new knowledge, leading to the construction of fresh meanings. Reflection and dialogue serve as the basis for action (Crabtree, 2008).

At a more conceptual level, the theme of 'reciprocity' in sending programmes can be understood as a relational concept which describes the desire for relationships to be both respectful and mutually beneficial. Many authors acknowledge it as a guiding philosophy driving their work in this area (Sharpe & Dear, 2013; Bamber, 2016). Reciprocity alludes to an approach of mutuality, where partners (both 'providers' and 'recipients') are respected for contributing in different but equal ways. This idea of collaboration and the mutual benefit of both giving and receiving is a supposed mitigator of inequalities that have the potential to exist within the frameworks of sending programmes. The constraints to this ethos of reciprocity will be unpacked later in the chapter.

Development education

DE is an active, dynamic, and participatory educational process which aims to deepen people's understanding of global inequality and the interconnectedness of people and events around the world. For an educational experience to have a DE focus, it should attempt to usurp a dominant worldview by incorporating multiple perspectives, link the local and the global, foster solidarity, scaffold critical thinking, and promote action towards a more just world. DE questions political and unequal power relations between developing and developed nations and encourages us to consider our own complicity in global injustices.

> It represents the enduring capacity of education to raise the learner beyond his or her physical environment, extend their imagination to new horizons, attain new forms of cultural expression, overcome societal inequalities and embrace humanisation above the 'otherness' of materialism.
>
> McCloskey (2014, p. 1)

For the most part, sending programmes in an Irish context operate under the banner of DE. In particular, they focus on the idea of action; and the hope that after engagement with DE and sustained critical reflection, people will be empowered, not to mention compelled, to act for a more just and equal world. As a result, short-term immersion visits to the Global South are often unproblematically presented as an output of DE programmes. The notional benefits of sending programmes in the context of action will be revisited over the course of this chapter.

The case for sending programmes

It has been argued (Loughran, 2007, p. 64) that learning about teaching requires a pushing of the "boundaries of practice" in order to encourage seeing from a variety of vantage points, with discomfort presented as an important attribute for both learning and risk-taking. When young teachers spend time in the Global South, it can certainly be the case that going outside of their comfort zone in this way can result in a profound or transformative experience. The literature points to innumerable personal and professional competencies which can be cultivated as a result.

Continuum of skills

In the area of emotional intelligence for example, empathy and compassion (Ryan, 2012) are often regarded as positive by-products of participation in sending programmes. The experience has the potential to support young teachers' supposed move from thinking about themselves, to thinking about others. Personal growth can also accrue from increased resilience, confidence, and self-esteem (Bamber & Hankin, 2011). In particular, the motivation for self-challenge (Ryan, 2012) and how it can be tied to perseverance (Strage et al. in Whitley, 2014) and self-reliance (Birdwell, 2011) are often referenced in this context. Overall, there can be many moments of self-discovery; for example, Kiely (2004) points to how participants can often see their more vulnerable, or even less flattering side as a result of these experiences.

Exposure to diversity in an immersive context can enhance intercultural competence and cross-cultural learning. Appreciating different cultures, understanding diversity, potentially learning a new language (Nussbaum, 2010), and challenging stereotypes (Bamber & Hankin, 2011) all contribute to a bank of cultural skills.

Sending programmes can arguably contribute to social change, as they encourage return participants to reflect on their attitudes, values, and beliefs. Crabtree (2008) argues that volunteers rethink their lifestyle and their place in the world, sometimes even questioning previously held notions about consumerism, materialism, and individualism in Western societies. Participants may experience a process of consciousness-raising, whereby they develop more open-mindedness, critical thinking, respect for other viewpoints, and even greater appreciation of complexity. Bamber and Hankin (2011) argue that this shifting of worldviews can support participants in understanding the nature of power and unequal relationships. Kiely (2004) found that students in his study experienced profound changes in their worldview in at least one of the following dimensions: political, moral, intellectual, personal, spiritual, and cultural. This idea of "transforming forms" results in a dynamic shift in how they see themselves (ibid., p. 8).

Interestingly, Bamber and Pike (2013) go even further and pronounce ISL experiences as having the potential to "evince distinctly aesthetic and even spiritual dimensions" (p. 535) enacted through participation with "the lives and worlds of those living in other countries" (p. 536). Kiely (2004) similarly talks about the potential for spiritual development as a result of first-hand engagement with resource-poor communities. Participants in his study reported a renewed spiritual base and new ways of looking at "larger life forces" or "the human spirit" (ibid., p. 14).

At a more professional level, returning participants have reported enhanced levels of resourcefulness in relation to their teaching, reporting that their experience made them more aware of their resources, less reliant on technology, and more conscious of making better use of the natural environment (Ryan, 2012). Further professional competencies such as consensus building, leadership skills (Whitley, 2014), and commitment to volunteering can enhance their belief in themselves as change agents – a popular motivation for many young and idealistic teachers.

Enactment of global citizenship

Developing powerful teacher education is complex and multifaceted. Darling-Hammond (2013) maintains that in spite of evidence that teachers benefit from learning about their craft, it is also true that many teachers feel underprepared for the challenges they face in their work and as a result it is the *type* of teacher education they receive that matters. This is certainly the case when it comes to the enactment of meaningful global justice education. It is well-documented that teachers often lack confidence in the area of global education (Bourn, 2012), not to mention outright resistance to delivering DE in the classroom (McCormack & O'Flaherty, 2010).

There is a school of thought which believes that sending programmes can contribute to the delivery of higher quality global citizenship education in the Irish classroom. For example, the Réalt programme[2] believes that participation in their African programme will produce more experienced and well-rounded educators:

> (*participation*) ... increases the likelihood that development and intercultural education will be competently and sensitively addressed in schools through participants' enhanced personal understanding and increased pedagogical skill.
>
> Réalt Project (2012, p. 8)

Through experiential learning, preparation courses, and ongoing education partnerships, it is often argued that sending programmes produce global citizens with heightened awareness of global development issues (Baily, Regan, & Lyons, 2010). Nussbaum (2010) speaks about the need for an 'openness to the world', and this is echoed in the findings of Bamber and Hankin (2011) whose students identified their appreciation of a more extended citizenship role at both local and global levels (2011).

From a Southern perspective, this idea of enactment also bears weight. Perold, Mavungu, Cronin, Graham, Muchemwa, and Lough (2011) report how many Southern NGOs would like to see return volunteers set up international social networks between stakeholders and challenge "entrenched perceptions of the power relations between North and South" (p. 10). The hope is that these experiences in the South will contribute to the development of skills, values, and attitudes which will be infused through critical global education in the Irish curriculum upon their return.

Mapping the disconnect between theory and practice

An uncritical reading of sending programmes would have us believe they are unproblematically dynamic, benevolent, and mutually beneficial educational opportunities. However, in the same way that meeting people from diverse backgrounds does not automatically result in reduced racism, travel, immersion, and experience in the Global South do not, on their own, inevitably produce a global citizen, let alone a competent global justice educator. It is now necessary to examine the mismatch between the theory and practice of sending programmes, or as Sharpe and Dear (2013) describe it, "the contradictions between the rhetoric and reality of ISL" (p. 49).

The very nature of transformation is that it takes time, and this is not always possible in the context of sending programmes which are typically fleeting in nature, lasting often for just a matter of weeks. During initial transition teacher participants, for many of whom it is their first overseas experience, often contend with high levels of intensity (Niehaus & Crain, 2013), culture shock, sickness, and unfamiliarity with food (Sharpe & Dear, 2013). Notions of temporality permeate through how these programmes are constructed and established. In a university context, for example, few overseas placements are adequately staffed or even supervised. As a result, participants lose the opportunity for observation or feedback (Whitley, 2014), despite such placement support being linked with positive outcomes during evaluation (Birdwell, 2011).

Pre-departure and orientation

Meaningful sending programme experiences require comprehensive orientation and reorientation. Participants with enhanced preparation have a better chance of experiencing positive outcomes (Whitley, 2014). There are however significant inconsistencies when it comes to how orientation for sending programmes is approached. When preparation sessions do take place, sessions can often be superficial, focusing more on issues of health and safety than critical reflection on motivations, expectations, or personal complicity in unequal power relations.

It is important to note that within the university system, there is a wide diversity of approaches to sending programmes. Many universities offer supporting modules for such initiatives, either in mandatory or elective formats. Some are interdisciplinary and well-integrated into the curriculum; some are stand-alone and delivered by outside agencies. In other instances, there are no formal support structures for student learning. Martin and Griffiths (2012) argue that in order for any such international visits to be effective, they need to be underpinned by post-colonial theory and run as courses "designed to enable learners to move away from the neo-colonial tendency of the North to exploit the South for their own emotional and knowledge gains" (p. 919).

But critical reflection and academic rigour are not a given, and consequently many volunteers are not adequately prepared for their placement experiences in any meaningful way. Preparatory priorities of logistics rather than 'unlearning' reveal assumed superiority and self-importance which will be elaborated on in a later section. In a Southern context, Perold et al. (2011) point to how host organisations in the South have only indirect relationships with sending organisations in the North, and this is symptomatic of unbalanced partnerships which characterise the sending programme industry. Host organisations in the South had further criticisms about the preparation of volunteers prior to their arrival, in particular in relation to language briefings, cultural context, and the Eurocentric nature of orientation sessions (Perold et al., 2011).

These uneven relationships between sending and receiving stakeholders can result in mixed expectations. Perold et al. (2011) found that the supply-driven nature of international voluntary service skews the relationship between sending and host organisations and can often result in host organisations in the South not receiving people with skill-sets they requested or required. This can often be the case with very young volunteers of school or college age, who require a lot of support before they can do their job, especially during short-term placements. In Mozambique and Tanzania for example, Perold et al. (2011) found that in a supply-driven context, host organisations are less able to seek out their preferred sending partners, which puts them at a disadvantage in sourcing international volunteers with the skills appropriate for their organisations' development.

Debriefing and the action gap

Another important issue with sending programmes is the 'action gap', whereby return volunteers struggle to make sense of their experience and find it difficult to enact their new learning upon arriving home. The case for sending programmes consistently points to the transformative potential of these overseas experiences. Yet returning participants can find it difficult to name the benefit they accrued from the experience or merely identify one thing that has changed in their actions as a result. Kiely (2004) coined the term 'chameleon complex' to illustrate the inability of some returning participants to translate their 'emerging global consciousness' into action and come to terms with the constraints that exist for them upon their return home. In the long-term, this involved being able to communicate their experience to friends and family while also trying to challenge dominant cultural norms they were now rethinking and questioning. In an Irish context, student teachers are warned of similar possibilities after the initial thrill of arriving home:

> You may feel alienated and disorientated. It can often be hard to settle back into the life we live here while all the while thinking of the struggle of those we left. You may find that you cannot share your experiences from abroad

> with anyone else. Friends and family will listen with interest initially, then out of politeness, but eventually they will have heard enough.
>
> DICE Project (2010, p. 29)

Inadequacies similar to the preparation sessions can also be seen in debriefing as well. These workshops are not always mandatory and are often poorly attended. But the debrief is sometimes even more crucial than orientation, in that it provides space for teachers to share experiences, discuss feelings, unpack current thinking, and make suggestions for future iterations of the project. Debriefing can too often focus on evaluating practical or logistical components to the overseas placement, without providing participants with a space to reflect on more multi-layered aspects to their involvement. It is important to note, that in an Irish context, even if quality debriefing has occurred, teachers return to their privileged career path in schools which are often very conservative by nature. Questioning cultural superiority, colonial mindsets, or the merits of capitalism are unlikely to continue or be supported in these contexts.

Power

Most White Northern participants arrive at their engagement with DE from an ethnocentric place, taking European 'superiority' for granted and believing that their perspective is best. When it comes to global justice issues, they are often locked into a binary mentality of 'powerful giver' versus 'grateful receiver'. These paternalistic notions of cultural superiority, operating within the context of an assumed African homogeneity, can contribute to a climate of exploitation and dependency – to the extent that sometimes the job of a Northern teacher in the Global South can be regarded synonymously with aid worker (Andreotti, 2006). This section looks at how hierarchies of power, representation, and perceived educative superiority play out both ideologically and materially in the context of sending programmes.

Sending programmes: a neocolonial mission?

> Where colonialism left off, development took over.
>
> Kothari (1996)

It is impossible to problematise sending programmes without engaging with their imperial roots. Colonialism positioned Africa as the 'Dark Continent' which was so 'primitive' it was in need of Northern support and expertise. In an education context, such notions of cultural superiority can become conflated with intellectual or pedagogical superiority, and Martin and Pirbhai-Illich (2015) concede that ISL can often take on neocolonial outlooks as a result. They remind us that "while the intentions of ISL are usually to make a positive difference to the communities in receipt of the service, the actions themselves often unwittingly reinforce the status quo, due to a lack of understanding of the socio-political and historical factors that affect the server-recipient relationship" (p. 135).

From a Southern perspective, it is essential to foreground this point. Perold et al. (2011) argue that international voluntary service is not an isolated activity that can be evaluated in a vacuum. Moreover, it needs to be considered as a process embedded within the history of relations between the Western world and the African continent (Perold et al., 2011). Sending programmes exist in a post-colonial age. But in the Irish context, Bryan (2013) encourages us not to forget Ireland's own history of imperialism and allow the "narrative of Irish innocence" to be so readily accepted (p. 10). The racialisation of Africans through the Irish Missionary Movement, the supposed benevolence of the 'penny for the black babies' fundraising campaigns and Irish people's involvement in slave plantations in the Caribbean are just some examples she cites as evidence of Irish complicity in colonial-style oppression (Bryan, 2013).

In an education context, stereotypical representations of Africans as "poor, incapacitated, weak, lazy, unresourceful and dependent" (Perold et al., 2011) fuel the *raison d'être* behind sending programmes. In the hierarchy of teachers, Northern teachers are viewed as superior, regardless of qualifications or experience. In fact, it can actually happen that many Northern teachers usurp or replace local teachers for the duration of their stay. Freire (1970) believes that for learning to be meaningful, the learner has to be in a position to co-create knowledge along with the teacher. This is not possible in sending programmes, where Northern teachers are often unfamiliar with the national curriculum, not educated in relevant pedagogical approaches, and potentially unequipped to facilitate meaningful teaching and learning with large class sizes. The quality of teaching by Irish teachers in an African context is rarely critiqued. The assumed superiority is taken for granted and emblematic of the great distance that can develop between teacher and learner that Freire warns us about. Positioning the Irish teacher, sometimes only newly qualified or not-quite qualified, as the 'expert' in this context, and expecting the Black African teacher to reposition themselves as a 'spectator' in their own classroom is yet another example of the power imbalances which characterise this neocolonial mission. Furthermore, it sends out a dangerous message to pupils in that classroom, about how the voices of transient visitors are to be privileged in the hierarchy of teacher role models.

Othering

Sociological theories of 'othering' have been fundamental to many theoretical shifts in thinking about cultural superiority, through post-colonial and decolonial theory, gender studies, critical race theory. First conceptualised by Edward Said (1978), and then coined as a term by Spivak (1988), 'othering' is typically understood as how minoritised groups are positioned as 'different' or 'other', in ways which highlights and reinforces this difference. Othering is a process by which we clearly differentiate between 'us' and 'them' and use these hierarchies to position ourselves where we think we belong. Particular groups are differentially categorised and constructed as intrinsically different or inferior from the rest of the general population and therefore as something that could potentially pose a threat to the rest of 'us'. Said (1978) argues that the West creates an 'opposite' as a mechanism through which to understand the construction of their own collective identity. This is particularly relevant in the context of racial identity.

Lentin and McVeigh (2002) argue that 'race' or ethnicity cannot be 'known' in the same way as class or gender:

> Ethnicity is quintessentially dialectical because it never *is* except when it *is not*. In other words, ethnicity is about constantly (re)negotiating and maintaining boundaries, and about inclusion and exclusion, where inclusion always excludes and differentiates between who is allowed and who is not allowed to belong to the collectivity. (ibid., p. 15)

'Othering' therefore classifies and defines 'us' in terms of who we are not. It invites us to think in the most fundamental of terms, as there can be no sense of self without the 'Other'. As such, relational understandings are established. Through participation in sending programmes, individuals can become classified as either 'normal' or 'other'. This idea will be elaborated on later in the chapter.

From prior knowledge to fixed knowledge

According to literature outlined previously, sending programmes have the potential to challenge White students, push them out of their comfort zones, and disrupt their worldview. Unfortunately, a potentially unintended consequence is that while there may be some in the cohort who experience such consciousness-raising, there are others whose existing viewpoints and stereotypical ways of thinking are reinforced. The experience can highlight power inequalities for a discerning participant, but it can reify these inequalities for another. In the previous section we saw how the process of 'othering' is both complex and multidimensional. Southern populations are constructed by Northern teachers as 'other' in relation to their assumed underdevelopment, cultural inferiority, and deficit educational standards. Othering centres the 'normality' of the White teacher's experience, and as a result, their overseas experience can compound what they think they already know. This 'them/us' binary is already so entrenched it denies legitimacy to the 'Other' as an equal knowledge holder/producer. Pre-existing stereotypes of 'they are poor, but happy', become 'authentic knowledge' as a result of personal overseas experience. When participants return, they may take on the role of 'expert' or have this role foisted upon them by others in their school, because they have met the 'Other' first-hand.

Stein and Andreotti (2015) take a critical stand on 'voluntourism'. They directly link it to the epistemic violence which is at the heart of the North–South divide, and central to the ongoing project of 'Othering' the Global South, saying that when:

> students from the Global North are centred as dispensers of universal knowledge and values, benevolent purveyors of education, and innocent

heroic protagonists, and those in the Global South are framed as lacking in education and ability, incapable of self-determination and necessarily eager to receive help, such programmes reproduce existing hegemonies and global power disparities. (ibid., p. 36)

Privilege

We have seen how many sending programmes take place in countries with complex histories and hitherto racialised populations. We have also seen how the literature on ISL is an underdeveloped field. Freire (1970) asks us to name the word and name the world – but we have yet to do this in a real way about sending programmes in an Irish context. A stark omission in the literature relates to how superficially the privilege of participants is referenced. Teachers participating in sending programmes tend to be socially, economically, and culturally mobile. They have the privilege to access the supports of the sending programmes, the finances to be able to travel, or at least the social capital to be able to fundraise the money needed.

Earlier in this book, Spivakian notions of 'unlearning' were introduced. Spivak argues that in order to have an 'ethical' encounter with the 'Other', you have to first unlearn your privilege (1988). In a Freirean approach to 'naming' the problem, I would suggest that sending programme providers in an Irish context should explicitly name this privilege as 'whiteness' and embolden prospective participants to reflect on their racial identity as a precursor to participation.

Whiteness and education

According to Hall (1997), identity is not essentialist, but rather strategic and positional. Identities are never single or unified but are constructed through a relation to the 'Other'. Dominant groups rarely allow themselves the opportunity to engage with their ethnic identity. At this point, it is necessary to examine the demographics of teachers in Ireland, in the context of hegemonic privilege. The evidence clearly reveals significant commonalities among pre-service teachers in Ireland, in that they tend to be overwhelmingly White, female, settled, Catholic, and middle-class (Keane & Heinz, 2016). In 2014, 95.8–96.2% of undergraduate primary entrants claimed only Irish nationality and a further 2.8–3.5% of undergraduate primary student teachers claimed Irish nationality plus a secondary non-Irish nationality (Keane & Heinz, 2016, p. 9). This is very revealing, showing an overwhelming majority (approximately 99% at upper level of the data) identifying as 'White Irish' based on census categorisations. What is more revealing is student teachers' limited exposure to diversity. Leavy's (2005) study of pre-service teachers found that where 59% had little or no 'exposure' to Irish Travellers, 65% had never met a refugee or an asylum seeker and 20% had never even had a conversation with someone who was not Irish. More recent statistics do not show much improvement. Approximately 60% of White Irish primary entrants to primary initial teacher education reported having little experience with ethnic groups different to their own and approximately 20% reported having none at all (Keane & Heinz, 2016).

Solomon, Portelli, Daniel, and Campbell (2006) argue that whiteness is often constructed in the everyday life of multiracial educational institutions as neutral or invisible. Many privileges which are bestowed on White people are not immediately seen (the so-called invisible knapsack analogy from McIntosh, 1989) or acknowledged. Not only is it invisible, when it is discussed, it can result in discomfort among White teachers and teacher candidates (Solomon et al., 2006), particularly when they are asked to consider the "possibility of alternative interpretations" of history, or societal interactions (p. 149). Picower (2009) argues that whiteness is operationalised in a variety of ways and that White people often respond to discussions or challenges by relying on 'tools of whiteness'. These tools (such as defensiveness or denial) might be emotional, ideological, or performative, but have the unified outcome of protecting dominant understandings of racial power in society (Picower, 2009).

Typically, White, middle-class, and privileged teachers have little or no understanding of their own culture or racial identity (Ladson-Billings, 2001). Whitaker and Valtierra (2018) argue that teachers have never been pushed to explore their own identity and that for many White teachers, having 'students of colour' is the first time they confront their own whiteness (p. 11). In the context of ITE, most White pre-service teachers have little understanding or awareness of discrimination, particularly racism, and their often-limited experience with communities of colour means they have not had to put in the time understanding their own racial identity (Sleeter, 2008).

Whiteness and cultural superiority are taken for granted in education spaces and rarely critically discussed or problematised. It is important to note that whiteness in this sense is not just about skin colour. It is about structural ideologies of racial dominance and systems of privilege and power (Ladson-Billings, 2001), where privilege can result in unequal access, opportunities, and outcomes.

In the context of sending programmes, it can be argued that participants rely on these 'tools of whiteness' in order to maintain their stereotypical thinking or avoid feeling overwhelmed at the level of inequality they see. This is very significant in the Irish context, as many teacher participants have not even had the space to explore their own racial identity, let alone trouble or disrupt it. They may have a superficial understanding about how global economic systems are set up to disprivilege countries in the Global South, yet they are unlikely to have reflected on how they themselves benefit from those same structures. Before they bring their 'invisible knapsack' as luggage to the Global South, there is a real need for teacher participants in sending programmes to create 'post-colonial learning spaces' (Fiedler, 2007) where they can understand their racial identity in the context of power, privilege and othering, and historical oppression. Supporting this learning within a framework of global justice education is where teacher education should focus its attention.

'White saviour' and 'hero' narratives

Dominant development discourses often focus on the helplessness of people in the South and the need for individuals in the North to act for change (Bryan & Bracken, 2011). As a result, paternalistic narratives of 'I just want to help them', often drive the supply and demand of sending programmes. In this sense, charity can be understood as one of the performative tools of whiteness that Picower (2009) talks about. As Simpson (2016) argues, this centring of responsibility of the North towards the South "as a seemingly kind and benevolent master, but a master nonetheless" (p. 2) feeds into binary thinking of giver/receiver. She suggests that this 'master' mentality has not really changed from colonial times but becomes repackaged in the mainstream through things like Band Aid, Comic Relief or similar initiatives (Simpson, 2016). White people are 'good people', working for the betterment of needy, helpless Africans. This 'White Saviour' mindset positions White people as protagonists in the story of development and centres their experience as a result. It is in this context that the supposed driving concept of 'reciprocity' becomes nearly impossible to achieve. Hero narratives or what Freire terms as an 'assistencialist' mindset towards poverty (1970) contribute to distorted assumptions and negative stereotypes of people in the Global South. Centring the white experience is essentially an acknowledgement that there is nothing to be learnt from the locals in this context.

Furthermore, the 'White Saviour' trope does a disservice to the diversity of volunteering models and the strong traditions of volunteering for social change which exist in many African countries. Service and volunteering have been part of African social life since pre-colonial times (Rankopo, Osei-Hwedie, & Moroka, 2007) and are a growing phenomenon. In Botswana for example, the 'botho' principle compels communities to support those in need out of moral obligation (Rankopo et al., 2007). Mati (2011) outlines how in many African countries the dominant model is actually that of people from Southern countries volunteering in other countries in the Global South, whereby the socio-economic profile of volunteers is the same of that of the people they work with. But we tend to be so focused on the dominant model of North to South sending and the 'White Saviour' complex, that we do not pay attention to what we might learn from these models. Or indeed how we could support them if we were truly interested in meaningful development cooperation. There are many different ways we could rethink teaching and learning approaches, if more equitable partnerships were modelled. Rankopo et al. (2007) argue that through education links, Southern teaching colleagues can co-create teaching and curricular materials for use in Northern schools as ways of mitigating traditional dominant models. Overall, there is a real lack of Southern voices contributing to the discourse around sending programmes. Martin and Griffiths (2012) acknowledge that while the need for Southern voices is recognised, their inclusion is a rare occurrence in typical North–South partnerships. It bears repeating that sending programmes are set up merely for 'sending' purposes, and as a consequence, do not typically lend themselves to the principles of exchange.

Pedagogical playgrounds

Bryan and Bracken (2011) state that engagement with DE in an Irish context can sometimes take on the reductive form of the 'three Fs – fasting, fundraising and fun' (p. 19). To borrow the idea of 'fun' and join it with Said's (1978) idea of the 'oriental space' reveals something disturbing about how Africa is often perceived among Irish teachers. Post-colonial writers use the idea of the 'imaginary' (Taylor in Martin & Pirbhai-Illich, 2015) to illustrate how people and cultures are often represented more through symbolism than reality. In this sense, the colonial imaginary represents the people and places of Africa as "simplistic rather than multidimensional, exotic rather than everyday" (Martin & Pirbhai-Illich, 2015, p. 137). We have seen previously how stereotypical messaging and positioning can sometimes represent Africa as something to be 'saved'. But in a seemingly contradictory way, Africa also exists as an exotic 'Other' in which to have 'fun'; a playground if you will, where 'adventure', reminiscent of the colonial mindset of exploring and using, can be combined with personal and professional learning opportunities.

From a Southern perspective, host organisations are often all too aware of the allure of the 'playground'. In a Ugandan context, college principals overwhelmingly identified 'adventure' as one of the motivating factors for Northern student teachers participating in a sending programme (Mbaguta, 2013). In Tanzania, stakeholders recognised that while international volunteers were often motivated by a genuine commitment to help others and promote change, they reported that some demonstrated a greater interest in tourism and social activities, and lack of commitment to the overall aims of their project (Perold et al., 2011).

It is interesting to note that in the literature affirming sending programmes, the majority focus on the additive value to Northern participants. Sending programmes offer experiences that are emotionally and professionally elevating for rich White Northerners, arguably at the expense of resource-poor black communities. This idea of "holidays for humanity" (Bamber & Hankin, 2011, p. 192) paints a paradox whereby Northern teachers can be perceived as selfless, while simultaneously being self-serving.

The deficit ideology behind sending programmes can reinforce the 'Othering' process. According to Martin and Griffiths (2012), Africa as the 'Other' is framed as 'child-like' (p. 910), unable to help themselves without the benevolent Northern actor. In an education context, this paternalism becomes even more pronounced, where whole communities become infantilised in order for inexperienced teachers to practise and hone their emerging pedagogical skills. Martin and Griffiths (2012) believe that the othering process can ultimately "dehumanize" (p. 910) people as a result. This bears out in the playground analogy, whereby we exoticise the land and people, and use Black children as accessories in photo opportunities, or as classroom anecdotes upon return. Using young African pupils in this way, not least in the context of short-term placements and with resulting attachment issues for children, raises significant questions about the ethics of sending programmes and how Northern teachers view the South as an additional site of learning.

Time spent in Africa is viewed as a stopgap or glorified holiday, a break from reality before we return to our 'regular' jobs as teachers and our 'normal' pupils. It is conceptualised as leisure in that it is separate to our usual focus and our usual way of teaching. The lived experiences of resource-poor communities become interesting asides in job interviews or footnotes on curriculum vitae. While poverty and inequality are daily realities for many in the South, for Northern teachers they are temporary challenges, but ones that our privilege affords us the freedom to escape at any time.

Teacher as un-learner

In pursuit of praxis?

Straubhaar (2015) argues that from a Freirean perspective, a great deal of personal reflection and transformation must be undertaken by privileged individuals who wish to demonstrate solidarity with marginalised groups in the Global South. He further argues that Freire's concept of 'critical consciousness' can be a useful framework for problematising this privileged mindset (Straubhaar, 2015). Becoming aware of yourself, your privilege, and your cultural identity is an essential process for teachers. Freire (1970) argues that critical consciousness will support privileged teachers to give up their perceived 'expert' status as part of the process of continual self-evaluation. Theory and critical reflection inform our actions and vice versa. "Praxis is the constant reciprocity of our theory and our practice" (Wink, 2011, p. 73).

Kumar (2008) suggests that global education is a form of emancipatory and dialogical learning based on critical humanist pedagogy. Such dialogical education, he suggests, is where learners collaboratively pose problems, enquire, and seek solutions. This approach builds on Freire's notions of teachers and students being co-investigators in an open and ongoing enquiry, and can therefore be considered a 'pedagogy of global justice', as its questioning and critically reflective nature inevitably raises a desire amongst learners to bring about positive and progressive social change (Skinner, Blum, & Bourn, 2014, p. 11). Teachers in this sense need to be both teachers and learners of global education, through a continuous process of thought, action, and reflection in the context of parity and partnership.

As we have seen, the mechanisms of sending programmes are value-laden, and as a result intentionality around values should form part of the reflective process. Centring praxis will support participants in realising that issues of global inequality are inevitably multifaceted and there are no simple 'right' or 'wrong' answers. Instead, we should strive to name and articulate our values in such a way that they guide our thoughts and actions. Intentionality towards values can shift pity to compassion, charity to human rights, service to solidarity, and disconnect to congruence. Once we discern the values we hold and the concepts we value, we can embed them in our interactions with the 'Other'. Intrinsic values are closely linked with how global justice educators should go about their work on a daily basis. As teacher educators we should not strive to 'teach' specific values in relation to equality, human rights, or solidarity, but rather devise a process through which a broad values dialogue could take place (Bowden, 2013).

Concluding thoughts

Levels of interest in sending programmes as vehicles for global learning have increased in recent years, but whether this represents a similar growth in our understanding of the impact of sending programmes remains to be seen. Kiely (2004) argues that many studies that emphasise the positive changes arising from sending programmes (intercultural competence, perspective transformation, etc.) all focus on the short-term. Meaningful longitudinal research in this area is required. In an Irish context, there is a critical need for long-term empirical research on the impact of return volunteers' commitment to social justice, further conceptualising about teachers' motivations in the context of power and privilege, and a need to hear the voices of our Southern partners in future iterations of sending programmes. Stronger foundations are needed for this work in the future.

> A teacher who is not a global citizen and global learner cannot teach global citizenship effectively. In other words, a teacher who has not experienced global learning ... will find it very difficult to practice global education grounded in an ethics of solidarity.
>
> Andreotti (2012, p. 2)

Teachers and teacher educators alike have a responsibility to model the values of global justice education for their students. Many teachers strive for ways to encourage students to take action for a more just and caring world. Teaching in the Global South in a voluntary capacity is often presented unproblematically as one such form of taking action. But there are many complexities involved, and good intentions often lead to bad practice. Exposure to different cultures does not automatically make you culturally competent. A global experience does not automatically make you a global teacher. Intention to act does not always result in action.

Teachers need to reflect deeply on these paradoxes before signing up to sending programmes. Reflection should focus on understandings of power, resistance to name whiteness and unpack privilege, and a commitment to un-learning. But many of these concepts can be intimidating, personally confronting and often inaccessible for the White teacher. The theoretical connotations, the ever-shifting parameters, and the fear of doing the 'wrong' thing can mean that sometimes teachers are paralysed into inaction. But in the long run, we want teachers to summon the courage to act. Feelings of hopelessness or impotence resulting in inaction would be ultimately detrimental to the overall goals of global justice education and the broader `ethics of solidarity' we hope to enact.

The aim of this chapter was to support prospective visitors to the Global South in becoming more 'intentional' about their involvement. As counter-intuitive as it may seem, while always being careful not to centre the white experience, it is nonetheless important to engage with the experience of the privileged when it comes to the notion of taking action. Privileged teachers have social, cultural, and economic capital and have the potential to be allies for global justice and agents of social change. Continued problematising of sending programmes should have as their goal a "wide-awakeness that might make injustice unendurable" (Greene, 1998, p. xxix).

Notes

1 Irish Aid is the Irish government's programme for overseas development and is managed by the Development Cooperation Division at the Department of Foreign Affairs and Trade.

2 The Réalt Teaching and Learning Programme offers student primary teachers in Dublin City University the opportunity to participate in an eight-week teaching and learning placement in several African countries.

References

Andreotti, V. (2006). Theory without practice is idle, practice without theory is blind: The potential contributions of post-colonial theory to development education. *The Development Education Journal*, 12(3), 7–10.

Andreotti, V. (2012). Global citizenship education. In L. Jääskeläinen, T. Kaivola, E. O'Laughlin, & L. Wegimont (Eds.), *Becoming a global citizen. Proceedings of the international symposium on competencies of global citizens*. Espoo, Finland: The Finnish National Board of Education.

Baily, F., Regan, C., & Lyons, C.W. (2010). *The impacts of student teaching placements in a developing context*. Limerick: Mary Immaculate College, Curriculum Development Unit.

Bamber, P., & Hankin, L. (2011). Transformative learning through service-learning: No passport required. *Education and Training*, 53(2/3), 190–206.

Bamber, P., & Pike, M. (2013). Towards an ethical ecology of international service learning. *Journal of Curriculum Studies*, 45(4), 535–555.

Bamber, P. (2016). *Transformative education through international service-learning realising an ethical ecology of learning*. Oxon: Routledge.

Birdwell, J. (2011). *This is the Big Society without borders: Service International*. London: Demos.

Blasco, M. (2012). On reflection: Is reflexivity necessarily beneficial in intercultural education? *Journal of Intercultural Education*, 23(6), 475–489.

Bourn, D. (2012). Development education: from the margins to the mainstream. *The International Journal of Development Education and Global Learning*, 1, 25–40.

Bourn, D. (2016). Teachers as agents of social change. *International Journal of Development Education and Global Learning*, 7(3), 63–77.

Bowden, R. (2013). *Motivating the core: A values-led approach to owning a common future: A discussion paper*. London: Think Global.

Bringle, R.G., & Hatcher, J.A. (2011). International service learning. In R.G. Bringle, J.A. Hatcher, & S.G. Jones (Eds.), *International service learning: Conceptual frameworks and research* (pp. 3–28). Sterling, VA: Stylus.

Bryan, A. (2013). 'The impulse to help': (Post) humanitarianism in an era of the 'new' development advocacy. *International Journal of Development Education and Global Learning*, 5(2), 5–29.

Bryan, A., & Bracken, M. (2011). *Learning to read the world? Teaching and learning about global citizenship and international development in post-primary schools*. Dublin: Irish Aid.

Crabtree, R. (2008). Theoretical foundations for international service-learning. *Michigan Journal of Community Service Learning*, 15(1), 18–36.

Darling-Hammond, L. (2013). *Powerful teacher education*. San Francisco, CA: Jossey-Bass.

DICE Project. (2010). *Volunteering charter*. Dublin: DICE Project.

Fiedler, M. (2007). Postcolonial learning spaces for global citizenship. *Critical Literacy: Theories and Practices*, 1(2), 50–57.

Freire, P. (1970). *Pedagogy of the oppressed*. New York: Continuum

Greene, M. (1998). Teaching for social justice – Introduction. In W. Ayers, J. Hunt, & T. Quinn (Eds.), *Teaching for social justice: A democracy and education reader*. New York: New Press.

Hall, S. (1997). *Representation: Cultural representations and signifying practices*. London: Sage.

Honan, A. (2005). Opportunities for development education within formal education in the Republic of Ireland. *Policy and Practice: A Development Education Review*, 1(Autumn), 20–30.

Keane, E., & Heinz, M. (2016). Excavating an injustice?: Nationality/ies, ethnicity/ies and experiences with diversity of initial teacher education applicants and entrants in Ireland in 2014. *European Journal of Teacher Education*, 39(4), 507–527.

Kiely, R. (2004). A Chameleon with a complex: Searching for transformation in international service-learning. *Michigan Journal of Community Service-Learning*, 10(Spring), 5–20.

Kothari, U. (1996). *Development studies and post-colonial theory*. Manchester: Institute for Development Policy and Management, University of Manchester.

Kumar, A. (2008). Development education and dialogical learning in the 21st century. *International Journal of Development Education and Global Learning*, 1(1), 37–48.

Ladson-Billings, G. (2001). *Crossing over to Canaan: The journey of new teachers in diverse classrooms*. San Francisco, CA: Jossey-Bass.

Leavy, A. (2005). 'When I meet them, I talk to them': The challenges of diversity for pre-service teacher education. *Irish Educational Studies*, 24(2), 159–177.

Lentin, R., & McVeigh, R. (2002). *Racism and anti-racism in Ireland*. Belfast: Beyond the Pale.

Loughran, J. (2007). *Developing a pedagogy of teacher education: Understanding teaching and learning about teaching*. New York: Routledge.

Martin, F., & Griffiths, H. (2012). Power and representation: A postcolonial reading of global partnerships and teacher development through North-South study visits. *British Educational Research Journal*, 38(6), 907–927.

Martin, F., & Pirbhai-Illich, F. (2015). Service learning as post-colonial discourse: Active citizenship. In R. Reynolds, D. Bradbery, & J. Brown (Eds.), *Contesting and constructing international perspectives in global education*. Rotterdam: Sense.

Mati, J. (2011). *Youth volunteer exchange programmes in southern and eastern Africa: Models and effects*. Johannesburg: University of the Witwatersrand; VOSESA.

Mbaguta, A. (2013). *Report on research carried out on Réalt teaching and learning programme in Uganda*. Dublin: Réalt Project.

McCloskey, S. (2014). Transformative learning in the age of neoliberalism. In S. McCloskey (Ed.), *Development education in policy and practice*. London: Palgrave Macmillan.

McCormack, O., & O'Flaherty, J. 2010. An examination of pre-service teachers' attitudes towards the inclusion of development education into Irish post-primary schools. *Teaching and Teacher Education*, 26: 13329.

McIntosh, P. (1989). White privilege: Unpacking the invisible knapsack. *Peace and Freedom Magazine*, July/August 1989, pp. 10–12.

Mezirow, J. (1978). Perspective transformation. *Adult Education*, 28, 100–110.

Niehaus, E., & Crain, L. (2013). Act local or global?: Comparing student experiences in domestic and international service-learning programs. *Michigan Journal of Community Service Learning*, 20(1):31–40.

Nussbaum, M. (2010). *Not for profit: Why democracy needs the humanities*. Princeton, NJ: Princeton University Press.

Oxfam. (2019). *Public good or private wealth?* Oxford: Oxfam.

Perold, H., Mavungu, E., Cronin, K., Graham, L., Muchemwa, L., & Lough, B. (2011). *International Voluntary Service in SADC: Host organisation perspectives from Mozambique and Tanzania*. Trust Africa: VOSESA.

Picower, B. (2009). The unexamined whiteness of teaching: How White teachers maintain and enact dominant racial ideologies. *Race, Ethnicity and Education*, 12(2), 197–215.

Rankopo, M., Osei-Hwedie, K. & Moroka, T. (2007). *Issues in service and volunteerism in Botswana*. Special Issue on Civic Service in the Southern African Development Community. Johannesburg: Volunteer and Service Enquiry Southern Africa.

Réalt Project. (2012). *Handbook for participants*. Dublin: Réalt Project.

Ryan, A. (2012). Integrating experiential and academic learning in teacher preparation for development education. *Irish Educational Studies*, 31(1), 35–50.

Said, E. (1978). *Orientalism*. New York: Pantheon Books.

Sharpe, E., & Dear, S. (2013). Points of discomfort: Reflections on power and partnerships in International Service-Learning. *Michigan Journal of Community Service Learning*, 19(2), 49–57.

Simpson, J. (2016). *A study to investigate, explore and identify successful 'interventions' to support teachers in a transformative move from a charity mentality to a social justice mentality*. Global Learning Programme Innovation Fund Research Series: Paper 2. London: GLP.

Skinner, A., Blum, N., & Bourn, D. (2014). *Development education and education in international development policy: Raising quality through critical pedagogy and global skills*. Paper 2. Brussels: DEEEP.

Sleeter, C. (2008). Preparing White teachers for diverse students. In M. Cochran-Smith, S. Feiman-Nemser, & J. McIntyre (Eds.), *Handbook of research in teacher education: Enduring issues in changing contexts* (3rd ed., pp. 559–582). New York: Routledge.

Solomon, R., Portelli, J. Daniel, B.J., & Campbell, A. (2006). The discourse of denial: How White teacher candidates construct race, racism and 'white privilege'. *Race Ethnicity and Education*, 8(2), 147–169.

Spivak, G. (1988). Can the subaltern speak? In C. Nelson & L. Grossberg (Eds.), *Marxism and the interpretation of culture*. Basingstoke: Macmillan Education.

Stein, S., & Andreotti, V. (2015). Higher education and the modern/colonial global imaginary. *Cultural Studies and Critical Methodologies*, 17(3), 1–9.

Straubhaar, R. (2015). The stark reality of the 'White Saviour' complex and the need for critical consciousness: A document analysis of the early journals of a Freirean educator. *A Journal of Comparative and International Education*, 45(3), 381–400.

Whitaker, M., & Valtierra, K. (2018). The dispositions for culturally responsive pedagogy scale. *Journal for Multicultural Education*, 12(1), 10–24.

Whitley, M. (2014). A draft conceptual framework of relevant theories to inform future rigorous research on student service-learning outcomes. *Michigan Journal of Community Service Learning*, 19–40.

Wink, J. (2011). *Critical pedagogy: Notes from the real world.* New York: Pearson.

5 Teachers' experiences of global justice education through the lens of trade

Elaine Haverty, Paula Murphy, Laura O'Shaughnessy, Lisa-Maria Whiston, and Barbara O'Toole

Introduction

This chapter examines research data that emerged from the study carried out by four teachers who piloted *Just Trade* in 2016; it details our experiences and insights, and our impressions of the impact of the lessons in our classrooms. As the material in the chapter was generated by us in our school settings, we are anonymised here for the purposes of shielding the identity of our schools. All of us are White Irish, settled, and English-speaking, and as such, we reflect the demographics of the teaching profession in Ireland (Keane & Heinz, 2015), whereas the student groups involved in the project were ethnically diverse. This juxtaposition of a white teaching profession and an ethnically diverse student population, and the implications of this 'diversity gap' (Heinz & Keane, 2018), is of increasing concern in Ireland and forms a backdrop to the study findings outlined here.

The chapter includes extracts from observation records kept by two teachers (T-3 and T-4) as we taught a selection of lessons from *Just Trade*; these comprised our reflections on children's responses during activities, along with our impressions of children's overall engagement with the material. The chapter also draws from original work done by pupils during the intervention. Throughout the data analysis phase (January to June 2017), two of the teachers (T-R1 and T-R2) and Barbara O'Toole met on a weekly basis, and as we analysed the data, we also engaged in an ongoing reflective process; extracts from those reflections are included here. The data analysis brought to light certain strengths and weaknesses of *Just Trade*, so the chapter includes recommendations for revising lessons to make them more robust. These recommendations were incorporated into a new edition produced in 2018, re-titled *Just Connections, Just Trade* (Larkin et al., 2018) (www.mie.ie/justtrade).

The chapter begins with an outline of how the study was initiated and the series of phases it went through from start to finish, before going on to thematically detail insights about the study findings; and finally, signposting key learning from the intervention along with empirical lacunae in the field.

The research study

Just Trade 1.0

The principle guiding the research was that of collaborative inquiry (Ntelioglu, Fannin, Montanera, & Cummins, 2014; Ravitch, 2014): four primary school teachers took on the role of practitioner researchers working in partnership with a lecturer in a college of education (Barbara O'Toole). Cochran-Smith and Donnell (2006, p. 508) state that "having the practitioner take on the role of researcher contrasts with conventional research on teaching and teacher education where practitioners are the subject of study". This inquiry involved the teachers working as co-researchers: piloting teaching materials in classrooms, gathering data, keeping observation notes, and finally, two of us analysing those data (with Barbara O'Toole) over the course of several months.

Gathering data in classrooms

In order to gather data before and after the implementation of *Just Trade*, six 'auditing' activities were adapted from Reading International Solidarity Centre (Allum et al.), specifically from '*How do we know it's working?*' (2015). These comprised a combination of visual and text-based methodologies:

- Activity 1: 'What would you see in a country in Africa?' On a blank map of Africa, pupils were asked to draw and/or write their responses.
- Activity 2: 'What causes global poverty?' Children recorded their ideas on flip chart pages, using different colour pens for both stages (e.g. red for baseline; blue for endline).
- Activity 3: 'Why are some people hungry?' This was a 'diamond ranking' or 'card sort' (Hopkins, 2010) exercise whereby pupils ranked nine statements from 'most significant' to 'least significant' (Bucknall, 2007; Clark, 2012; Niemi, Kumpulainen, & Lipponen, 2015) (Appendix 3).
- Activity 4: 'How can I make the world a better place?' The children recorded their ideas on flip chart pages.
- Activity 5: Photo elicitation – pupils wrote what they thought was happening in two photographs (provided by the NGO Proudly Made in Africa) which were situated in two community enterprises such as those featured as case studies in the pack.

Along with these pre- and post-activities, the teachers completed standardised observation schedules as soon as possible after lessons were taught (Appendix 2). Two teachers (T-3 and T-4) completed these. Two (T-R1 and T-3) also returned folders of children's work, comprising 16 country-focused studies which had been completed during the intervention.

Ethnicities across the schools were mixed[1]: the majority of pupils were White, either Irish, or 'any other White background', which mainly comprised Eastern

European countries (Appendix 1). However, one school had a significant African-identified population of 30%, another 15%, while the other two had 6% and 5% respectively. Notwithstanding the ethnic diversity of the schools and the number of African-identified children involved, there was no discernible difference in overall findings from the study: baseline data indicated that stereotypical views about Africa were prevalent across all settings, including the school with a relatively high African-identified population at 30%.

The study began with the hypothesis that, in Ireland, primary schoolchildren's views about Africa would be strongly influenced by stereotyping and deficit thinking (Suas, 2012; Tallon, 2012; Oberman, 2013; Tallon & McGregor, 2014). As explained in Chapters 1 and 3, this supposition proved to be correct: when baseline data were analysed, findings confirmed the initial hypothesis and this was the case across all four schools, regardless of ethnicity. When endline data were analysed on completion of the project, some changes had occurred in children's perceptions and knowledge; however, these changes were not uniform across the four schools or reflected in all activities. This chapter details these findings: it analyses and discusses the study's results and points the way towards further empirical research in global justice education.

Perceptions of African countries: using stories as a methodology for change

Many activities in *Just Trade* were based upon stories; these included extracts from *Olanna's Big Day* (Mac a'Bhaird, 2009), *Ikenna goes to Nigeria* (Onyefulu, 2007), along with seven case studies which focused on stories of small businesses in a number of African countries: Kenya, South Sudan, Ethiopia, and Malawi. Dolan (2014) highlights the role that story can take in teaching about global issues, focusing on picture books in particular, while De Sisto (2014) states that stories can be powerful vehicles of communication that enable links to be made across cultures, as well as to challenge assumptions and counteract stereotyping. Similarly, Bourn (2015, p. 106) comments on the importance of stories about "people and communities in the Global South that challenge the mindset, stories that are positive and show evidence of change".

Ikenna goes to Nigeria (Onyefulu, 2007) features a boy who leaves his London home to visit Nigeria for the first time, where his family originally comes from and where he has relatives. All four teachers had misgivings about using this picture book, with a fairly uncomplicated storyline, with 11-to-12-year-old pupils, and were initially concerned that it might be overly simplistic. On the contrary, it was received very positively, with one teacher recording:

> The children really enjoyed the story and as it developed, began to discuss expectations and misconceptions. Despite being in groups, Nigerian children called across to each other making reference to the book; correcting mistakes and mispronunciations. At times they were really silent, for information they were not aware of. All other children in the class were very

> interested in hearing about Africa, discussing similarities and differences. Children with no connections to Africa were much quieter and listened attentively to their peers. Some children were seeking more complex information than is available in this story.

This was the school with an African population of 30%, and in this setting the story provided the Nigerian children and those with connections to other African countries, an opportunity to be involved in the lesson as "primary knowers" (Thwaite & Rivalland, 2008, p. 49); to be the 'experts' on the topic under discussion and to be the 'holders' of knowledge (Martin, Pirbhai-Illich, & Pete, 2017). The story could thus be interpreted as a vehicle through which African children's 'subjugated knowledges' (Kitching, 2014) and 'funds of knowledge' (Gonzalez, Moll, & Amanti, 2005) in the context of a Eurocentric curriculum could be given expression. However, what counts as 'knowledge' is also a consideration. The storybook has a chapter on the Osun Festival in Western Nigeria, in which Ikenna participates during his visit. In endline data for the audit activity 'What would you see in a country in Africa?', a new theme of "cultural activity" emerged across all schools, with drawings or commentary related to 'dancing', 'festivals', and 'music', material that was largely absent from baseline responses. As researchers, we speculated that this emerging theme could have been linked to new knowledge gained through the storybook. Although this represents an improvement from the overwhelming emphasis on poverty and deprivation in baseline data (Chapter 3), teachers need also to be mindful of the drawbacks of exchanging stereotypes of poverty and charity with those of music and dance. As Simpson (2016, p. 3) states:

> the tokenistic attempts at promoting the 'Other' through dance, art and music, along with the image of poverty-stricken countries and peoples, have unintentionally undermined educators' attempts to engage their pupils with the real issues, and possibly reinforced stereotypes and prejudices.

Stories can be a starting point for examining issues to do with global justice. As noted, they can be a vehicle for bringing 'funds of knowledge' into the classroom, but it is important that stories are not used as a means of avoiding more complex questions, or as Kitching (2014, p. 182) describes: "hiding the historical inscription of injuries and producing objects of pleasure and amusement" and "giving value via the white imaginary of popular blackness" (ibid., p. 156).

Imaging the world differently?

Just Trade was not based purely upon story; it included activities to investigate links between Ireland and the African continent, followed by independent research on specific countries. Children engaged with maps and examined different representations of the world in Mercator vs Peters charts; they looked at the comparative sizes of countries and continents, including the size of Ireland compared to the continent of Africa.

We noted pupils' fascination with this exercise, with T-4 stating: "The comparative size of Ireland and Africa were discussed at great length". It would seem that as children began to realise how many times Ireland would fit into the landmass of Africa, many of them were "pulled up short" (Kerdeman, 2003, p. 293) and started to question their assumptions about the world. Gannon (2002, p. 27) points out that the smaller representation of Southern countries on Mercator world maps "supports the perception that they are not as important as the richer Northern countries". This mapping activity represented a challenge to Eurocentric worldviews and countered assumptions about the planet communicated via Western cartography, which as Mignolo and Walsh (2018) remind us, was in itself a means of epistemic control.

One of the map-based activities focused on 'interdependence' and involved tracking trading and other relationships between Ireland and African countries, using pieces of string to represent these links on the map.[2] T-4 wrote: "children were extremely shocked as to how many lines of interdependence they drew between Ireland and African countries"; recorded comments included: "Wooow I never realised Ireland and Africa had so much to do with each other"/"look at all the lines, I didn't think there would be this many". Again, it would seem that pupils were 'pulled up short' by this exercise. There was no record in the observation notes about *why* the pupils were so surprised, but as this work had been done quite soon after the audit activity: 'What would you see in a country in Africa?', the existence of these reciprocal relationships may have been new information for many children. As such, the activity may have challenged their assumptions about Western dominance and superiority, along with perceptions that North/South relationships are predicated upon aid.

Pupils carried out group research projects into a selection of African countries. Oberman et al. (2012) and Lawson (2018) point to the limitations of increased knowledge about a country leading to changed perceptions of that country. Oberman et al. (2012, p. 47) state that a focus on geography "remains in safe territory as against the introduction of more justice-related concerns". However, the idea of including this kind of work in *Just Trade* was two-fold. First, it aimed to broaden pupils' knowledge about African countries in order to move them beyond the stereotypical depictions that were recorded in the audit activity: 'What would you see in a country in Africa?' Second, it aimed to ensure that knowledge was grounded in facts; baseline data indicated that pupils across all schools had very imprecise information about the continent and countries of Africa.[3]

On examination of completed projects however, it was clear that the quality of learning was contingent on the sources the children had used for research. Chapter 3 identified the overwhelmingly deficit depictions of African countries in school textbooks in Ireland, generally rooted in Eurocentric perspectives and reflecting modernisation thinking. This places clear limitations on the value of many available texts which children might use when carrying out research. On the positive side, project work revealed learning about languages spoken across the continent, population, land area, exports, and elements of popular culture. However, it also revealed the influence of at least one source of information was rooted in coloniality; whether this was a written text or an internet source was unclear. Among the colourfully presented 'facts' about Zimbabwe which one group displayed, they explained that Victoria Falls waterfall was 'discovered' in 1855; that it was 'named' after Queen Victoria; and that the capital Harare was "originally called Salisbury in 1880 in honour of the British Prime Minister, Lord Salisbury". The power of colonial 'naming' is immense, whereby the "history, plurality, social, cultural, economic, spiritual, territorial, and existential foundation" of conquered lands became "seen and defined from the European gaze" (Walsh, 2018, p. 22), in the process annihilating all that had come before. A powerful learning from this research therefore, was the need for teachers to be made aware of the limitations of certain source material and to guide children away from Eurocentric texts/sources informed by neocolonial perspectives which "take European superiority for granted" (Scheunpflug, 2011, p. 104). This can be particularly challenging when many available textbooks and internet sources are rooted in such worldviews. It also relies on teachers having the awareness to recognise that reference sources are embedded in such perspectives in the first place, a self-reflexivity that in itself can be elusive, as it necessitates awareness of and reflection on the "collective social, cultural and historical narratives that unequally position individuals and groups" (Kerr & Andreotti, 2017, p. 15).

Teaching about trade – a methodology to challenge perceptions?

The idea of researching African countries was to provide children with a knowledge base about the continent as well as to scaffold subsequent lessons which introduced more complex material related to trade. As explained in Chapter 2, the aim was to challenge pupils' worldviews using *trade* as a lens through which to examine global power structures, specifically looking at supply chains and value chains in the production of commodities such as chocolate and coffee. Children learned that when products are fully manufactured within an African country, the 'value added' to the local community is significantly higher than when raw materials are exported. This point was further illustrated through a series of case studies focusing on local businesses in Malawi, Kenya, South Sudan, and Ethiopia. Bourn (2015, p. 108) is critical of the tendency in development education for global power imbalances to be located in "predominantly economic terms", citing 'trading game' simulations which are often used in classrooms. He points to the danger of a reductionist approach through these kinds of activities, in which capitalism is stereotyped and more complex social and cultural factors are overlooked, leading to an unhelpful 'binary' between North and South.

Nonetheless, the authors of *Just Trade*, and of this current volume, believed trade to be a crucial lens through which to examine global issues and to highlight, in age-appropriate ways, how 'economic colonialism' and global structural inequalities can perpetuate poverty. Moreover, Scheunpflug (2011, p. 37) highlights research carried out amongst student teachers in Germany which showed a lack of awareness of how economic and trade factors can impact on the incidence of famine in African countries; she concludes: "mass media played a greater role in the construction of their knowledge about these issues than validated information or informed theories".

We were largely positive in our assessment of how the trade lessons were received by pupils and how their 'economic literacy' (Taylor, 2003) had improved as a result. However, we also emphasised the 'newness' of this material and noted that we needed to frontload (i.e. pre-teach) certain terminology and concepts before lesson activities could be carried out. Terms such as ***manufacturing, infrastructure, import and export, living wage, livelihood,*** and ***consumerism***, which were at the heart of some lessons, were very new to pupils, many of whom were hearing these words for the first time. T-R2 noted a particular challenge for minority language pupils, and that vocabulary related to trade had to be specifically taught. T-4 also stated: "I didn't expect the children's knowledge of the content-specific language to be so weak: import, export, agriculture, natural, raw, manufactured etc." However, when vocabulary teaching had been specifically taught at the start of the lesson, pupils became more involved. In a session on 'interdependence' T-4 noted: "a huge amount of time was spent on the introduction: teaching children the vocabulary around imports and exports, natural resources, agricultural goods, manufactured goods, technological goods". This time seemed to have paid off, as children were "very enthusiastic and very engaged" in the activity. It was still not without its challenges. For example, regarding the 'value chain': "children spent a long time discussing the difference between manufacturer and supplier; also supplier and retailer. This was quite confusing". T-3 asked the children themselves to find out the meanings of the terms through their own research: "They learned new terms such as living wage, consumer, consumerism, sustainable and sustainability: they enjoyed the research – looking up these words and learning about them".

One of the first trade-related concepts to which children were introduced was the difference between 'cooperation' and 'competition', and how to engage in a transaction that benefited both parties. This was done through a trade simulation entitled 'Riceland/Beanland', adapted from Taylor (2003) for a primary school age group, and which featured two fictional countries (Appendix 4). Initially, teachers were nervous about this activity as it seemed quite complex; however, all acknowledged that children enjoyed the simulation, with T-3 recording that they: "looked at the negotiations as a challenge" and "some were very business-minded and really looked for the best deal they could get". Two groups in this school created 'Briceland'; a cooperative group across both 'countries', explaining: "it was easier to do 50/50 rather than to argue" and that they decided that "cooperation would lead to more profit". In another case, one group tried to outsmart the opposition by trading four bags of rice for three bags of beans but the plan "backfired" and they ended up giving more of their product than they intended. The teacher recorded: "I didn't know if the children would be as interested in this lesson given they had to negotiate but they loved it and saw it as a challenge to get the best deal". In another school, T-4 noted the time required to explain the idea of 'negotiating' before children could usefully engage in the simulation: "it took some time as children are used to debating in class and felt they needed to win. Some pupils found it challenging to use the language of agreement and disagreement".

Further lessons built on learning about 'negotiating' and 'cooperating' as essential to trading relationships. A later lesson explored the impact of external factors on trade; these included environmental or global issues such as currency changes, coffee wilt disease, rising oil prices, increased taxes, and so on, and children had to think about how these factors would affect coffee or chocolate production in a local community. Perhaps not surprisingly given the age of the pupils, their main concerns were around the impact on themselves:

> At first, children were concerned that this would impact on their own ability to buy coffee or chocolate locally, but with further probing and discussion the children began to see the cyclical impact of these situations: at first the majority of children were fixated on the fact that Ireland might have no chocolate or coffee. But one pupil in the class intervened to point out: "the people in Africa would lose their jobs", leading to another pupil saying: "and this would have a negative effect on their country". (T-4)

The teacher recorded that it was after these two interventions that opinions started to shift and children began to empathise with African communities which were impacted by the external factors listed in the activity. However, she noted her surprise that pupils were so focused on how Ireland would be affected in the different scenarios, and wrote that she "wasn't expecting to have to wait for so long for children to talk about African people and African countries when discussing scenarios that may affect interdependence". One pupil said: "If their economy had problems it could in turn have negative effects on ours, they may be unable to import some of the goods we export". This focus on their own lives wasn't unique to this school. T-3 recorded that while the topic of chocolate was of interest to children and drew them into lessons on the supply chain and value chain, "the children said they love chocolate so much they would just purchase the cheapest bar available regardless of it being Fairtrade or not". And in the same school: "Some children said it would be dishonest not to admit they still wouldn't choose what others and famous people are wearing. One child said that despite having learned so much about Africa, it made her realise how important it is to buy Irish. This was evident in all groups as nearly all the children agreed this was very important".

Children's focus on the availability of their favourite products is perhaps unsurprising given their age and interests; their responses also reveal the honesty and openness with which they approached discussions rather than giving answers they thought might be desired. At the end of the project, all four teachers felt the trade lessons had been useful to varying degrees. T-4 noted how pupils, after investigating the origins of food products in cupboards at home, independently came to the conclusion that some goods might be made in one country and packaged elsewhere, suggesting a growing awareness about the complex routes by which some products make their way to supermarket shelves. T-R1 felt the lessons represented a first step in paving the way for children in her class to embark on a process of investigating power structures that underpin and reproduce inequalities. She said: "awareness of this previously unseen global economy allowed children in my class to acknowledge, discuss and come to an understanding of the role of the Global North in global inequality and poverty". There was also an unexpected outcome in another school, in that T-3 reported that the lessons on 'livelihoods' prompted an "animated discussion on what quality of life means" and that it also led to connections being made to their own life experience: some children talked about their own families' migration from countries in eastern Europe "and what they had had to sacrifice in the process". In this classroom, the lesson on 'livelihoods' opened the door for links to be made to children's own lives, and helped to heighten their awareness of similarities between groups of people.

Endline data revealed that children's knowledge around trade (economic literacy) had increased in that they now had a range of vocabulary to accurately describe and discuss aspects of global economic activity. This process of 'demystifying the economy' was highlighted by Taylor (2003) as a crucial part of political education. For example, in the audit activity, 'What would you see in a country in Africa?', a new theme of 'economic activity' emerged at endline, one that was largely absent at the start. The children's comments suggested greater understanding of product manufacturing and trade relationships, including the concept of 'value added'; for example: "It is more profitable for Africa to make their own chocolate/Africa's own chocolate brand is called Madecasse[4]/Africa mostly exports cocoa beans, coffee beans, tobacco, textiles, tea, coffee etc/Farmers being payed (sic) poorly for their work when its (sic) manufactured in other countries/Farmers are payed (sic) more when there (sic) working for manufacturers in there (sic) country".

Endline data also indicated that lessons had impacted on the children's perceptions of the African continent. The baseline results demonstrated a narrowness of views, predominantly rooted in the 'natural world' of exotic animals and birds, and with a uniform climate of heat and sun. At endline, comments about the natural environment were more than halved (from 196 to 74). Perceptions of poverty and hardship, reflected at baseline in 48 comments such as: 'starvation', 'poverty', 'drought', 'Ebola', 'many diseases there', 'girls not being educated', 'most places in Africa are poor', 'not proper roads', 'more hungry people', had been halved at endline, from 48 to 24 such comments.

In terms of references to the built environment, this broadened on completion of the project. Instead of references to 'mud huts' and 'houses made of straw' which were predominant at the start, children wrote/drew factories, airports, shops, cities, and 'chocolate farms', thus suggesting a more balanced and rounded knowledge of the diversity of the African continent.

Images of Africa

Findings at endline were not uniformly positive. As previously noted, one of the activities involved photo elicitation (Prosser & Loxley, 2008) in which children were asked to respond to two images which had been sourced from cooperative businesses in Africa, through the NGO Proudly Made in Africa (PMIA[5]):

> Photo A: depicted two outdoor workers picking tea leaves on a cooperative farm in Kenya
>
> Photo B: depicted a staff member of an independent coffee company in Ethiopia who was weighing ground coffee (indoors)

Both photos were deliberately chosen to depict people at work and to counter the more stereotypical images of African people often utilised in fundraising campaigns. Unlike other audit activities that demonstrated changes in children's perceptions, we found a persistence of negative perceptions from baseline to endline in children's interpretation of these images, particularly of Photo A.

Baseline findings indicated that, overwhelmingly, children across all four schools interpreted Photo A through a lens of poverty and hardship, with many making assumptions about the living conditions of the two people pictured: "they live in mud huts/they can't afford real baskets/forced to work/gets paid only around €1.50 per day/does not get many days off/they look poor/they have big baskets on their backs". Photo B elicited more factual comments such as: "a man working in a coffee shop/he is working with coffee beans and powder/there are coffee beans in the background". Interpretations of this image were generally more neutral, with a small number of observations along the lines of: "he might be working in a kitchen for very little/he makes minimum wage".

Findings at endline indicated that children *continued* to interpret Photo A from a deficit perspective, even following work that had been carried out on countering stereotypes and teaching about trade. Endline responses included: "they probably live in a dilapidated house/they're poor/they are falling from carrying the baskets/it looks like they'll be doing this until they're old". There was evidence of change in relation to Photo B, where comments now incorporated knowledge about trading relationships and structures, such as: "he works for a coffee company, the company is worldwide/he may sell the coffee powder after in a shop/I think the coffee is going to be exported to another country to be sold/I think he sells coffee and chocolate to people".

Evidence of negative perceptions remained however, with responses such as: "he is probably thinking about how poor his family is/he probably gets paid extremely little for his hard work/he looks like he's poor so he really needs this money".

Why did children's perceptions, particularly of workers in the tea cooperative (Photo A), remain so entrenched in stereotypes even after a module that focused on challenging those perspectives and on teaching about reciprocal relationships through trade? Downes (2016, p. 21) describes how images can be 'polysemic' in that they can have "multiple possible readings depending on the experiences, knowledge and perceptions of the viewer", the implication being that the particular lens through which an image is viewed is just as important as the image itself. It is not simply a matter of a teacher presenting a photograph depicting a person at work, it is also about children's 'ways of seeing' a photograph like this in a context of such a proliferation of negative imagery of the Global South (Goldfinger, 2006; Manzo, 2006; Young, 2012; Downes, 2016). The saturation of images of African poverty may have exerted a powerful influence on these children's 'ways of seeing', so much so that negative perceptions remained in place for many of them despite participating in a module that focused on challenging those perceptions. The entrenchment of these negative perceptions is especially apparent in the case of Photo A, perhaps because this image is more typical of those that children are accustomed to seeing, in that it depicts a rural, outdoor setting, characteristic of the kinds of images used by aid and charity organisations. The data would suggest that many children had screened out the possibility of reciprocity and parity of esteem with people in the photograph, and instead, continued to 'see' deprivation even in its absence.

This finding emerged even in the schools with 30% and 15% of children from an African background, echoing concerns raised by Young (2012) about the impact of negative imagery of Africa on the African diaspora. She states that images of Africans as helpless, needy, dependent, and suffering "feed into a negative self-image of Africans living elsewhere" and produces a distancing and alienation from the region on the part of those who have left: "creating a need for Africans and those of African descent ... to distance themselves from the Africa/Africans as they are represented in these images" (2012, p. 26). Similarly, Downes (2016) emphasises that the proliferation of imagery of starving and needy Africans has consequences for African diaspora communities who may feel stigmatised and stereotyped as a result. Thus the 'single story' of Africa, put forward in the media and compounded by many textbooks, encourages all learners to see Africa and its people in a derogatory light, and has the added consequence of potentially impacting on how African people feel about their own ethnicity and cultural heritage (Manzo, 2006). This issue is taken up again later in this chapter.

Meanwhile, the following section looks at the potential for impacting on children's perceptions through teaching about trade, before explaining how the resource was strengthened in the light of the research findings.

Moving on from Just Trade

"Too little too late"

T-R2 was despondent about the potential of a module introduced so late in pupils' primary school experience to leave any long-term impression. Indeed, she summed up the intervention as "too little, too late". This was echoed in observation records from T-3, which included several references to children being "distracted" by end-of-year events. Pupils who participated in *Just Trade* were in the final term of the school year and most were in their final year of primary school, with the attendant distractions associated with that time period. T-R2 remarked that children "had one foot out the door" and this had impacted on the desire they had to participate in many activities, especially those that were deeper and more complex. The overwhelming conclusion of all four teachers was that an intervention such as this needs to take place at an earlier stage in the year, and in the penultimate year of primary school if possible, so that it can be revisited, built upon, and consolidated during the remaining time.

At present, the Irish primary school curriculum introduces 'Trade and Development' as part of the Social Environmental and Science Education (SESE) Geography curriculum, for 5th and 6th classes. However, there is scope to introduce global justice education in earlier years: in the 'People and other lands' strand in SESE Geography and in the 'Developing citizenship' strand of Social, Personal and Health Education (SPHE) (Government of Ireland, 1999), both of which begin in 3rd class (8–10 years).

Indeed, Oberman et al. (2012) have demonstrated how children as young as three-to-six-years-old can be introduced to critical perspectives on global justice through the medium of story. Their study showed how teachers integrated this work into *Aistear: The Early Childhood Education Framework* (National Council for Curriculum and Assessment, 2009). These authors emphasised the importance of including global citizenship education in early childhood education, stating that it can be seen as "integral to building an understanding of the wider world" (ibid., p. 53), and as necessary to "complexify the messages children receive from outside the classroom" (ibid.).

The scope for carrying out this work and embedding it into the curriculum is clearly present in the primary school; the question seems to be about teachers' openness to possibilities for integration, as well as their knowledge of and confidence with material. A very strong recommendation that arose from *Just Trade* was that global justice education needs to be introduced at an early stage in the primary school "if it is to combat the pervasiveness of negative stereotypes in relation to Global South embedded in our thinking and reinforced by the media and the wider society" (T-R1). The teacher went on to reflect:

> If children's development education in the Irish primary school context solely consists of a couple of lessons ... where charity-based actions are proposed as solutions to global poverty, then the possibility of coming to an understanding of the causes of global poverty is lost.

Just Connections, Just Trade

It was clear from research findings that elements of the pack needed to be strengthened and developed. As Bourn (2015, p. 186) states, "good quality materials should be based on evidence, should include engagement with teachers, and should emerge from the practice of teachers". This section summarises changes made to the materials based on evidence that emerged from the research.

Images and perceptions

The revised edition of the pack was named *Just Connections, Just Trade*, reflecting the need for increased emphasis on countering stereotypes and negative perceptions, particularly following evidence from the photo elicitation activity which demonstrated the intractability of deficit perspectives of African people regardless of the context of the image shown.

For example, a photo activity in the pack presents an image depicting two women working in a forest in Uganda[6]; pupils are asked to examine this photo from a variety of perspectives and 'interests', such as that of the women themselves, a logging company, the women's families, a local utility company, an NGO, and so on. Although this activity featured in the original pack it was developed to include the Compass Rose (TIDE, 1998) so that pupils would begin to identify environmental, economic, social, and political questions that could be used as a lens of enquiry:

N – Natural – questions about the environment: climate, landscape, vegetation, wildlife, and so on.

S – Social – questions about who people live with and how they relate to other people in their society, including family members.

E – Economy – questions about how people in this community provide for themselves and their families.

W – Who decides? – questions about who makes decisions that affect people's lives and the lives of their families.

The Compass Rose thus facilitates a deeper and more complex investigation into social justice issues which impact on people's lives. The idea is that these kinds of questions could subsequently be used to interrogate any photograph or story of a situation in the Global South, encouraging pupils to maintain a critical interrogatory stance in the face of images and messages.

Trade

Although findings showed progression from baseline to endline, with more balanced and accurate knowledge about African countries and definite learning about trade, closer examination of children's responses at endline demonstrated that this learning was uneven. One example concerned the 'value chain' in trading relationships. The outcome of Activity 1, 'What would you see in a country in Africa?' evidenced a new theme of 'economic activity' at endline, which was not present at the start. However, pupils in only two of the four schools demonstrated understanding of one of the key teaching and learning points of the pack; namely, the ***added value*** to local communities when products are manufactured locally as opposed to when raw products are exported (Chapter 2). Given that the 'value added' of local production comprised a central teaching and learning point of *Just Trade*, the fact that evidence of this emerged in only two of the four schools at endline was a concern.

Moreover, Activity 2 required pupils to record their views at baseline and endline about: 'What causes global poverty?' 'Trade' emerged as a theme at endline, not having featured at all at baseline, with comments including: "manufacturers get most of the money/unequal trade/Fairtrade/some brands should partner with Fair Trade". While these comments indicate partial knowledge about trading relationships including the value chain, as researchers we also noted a certain confusion and vagueness in pupils' responses, including their understanding of the FairTrade movement. The value-added dimension of products manufactured locally exceeds the impact of FairTrade for local communities and constitutes a different model of trading (see Chapter 2). It was clear that this element of the pack required strengthening to make this distinction clearer and to stress the changes to the value chain when products are manufactured locally. In the revised pack, this was emphasised and made more explicit through more detailed and extended activities in which comparisons between the 'standard bar' of chocolate and the 'chocolate bar made in Africa' were clearly shown (see below). Teachers' Notes were further developed to support understanding of the value-added process and updated to include recent statistics on imports and exports between Ireland and African countries. The FairTrade movement was explained so that teachers could see how it differed to initiatives described in the case studies in which the value of the production was retained locally.

	Standard bar manufactured outside Africa *% received*	*Chocolate bar made in Africa* *% received*
Farmers	**5**	**9**
Manufacturers	50	**31** (African-based manufacturing)
Suppliers/distributers	9	24
Wholesalers/retailers (shopkeepers)	17	17
Government tax	19	19

Numbers in bold indicate profits in the country where the cocoa is grown

These revisions aimed to strengthen the political aspects of *Just Trade*, so that pupils could look beneath the surface and understand that there are geopolitical and structural factors at play such as trade practices and unequal pay. This kind of work, particularly in relation to the value chain, aims to draw attention to the kinds of structural injustices in the global economic order that contribute to poverty in African countries. It introduces primary school pupils to the notion of Northern complicity in maintaining unjust systems of trade whereby value added is removed to Northern countries. As Dobson (2006, p. 172) states, "causal responsibility produces a thicker connection between people ... and it also takes us more obviously out of the territory of beneficence and into the realm of justice".

Concluding comments

Bourn (2015) notes that in global learning "there may be no right or wrong answers or simple solutions" (p. 173). When engaging children and young people in learning about complex situations such as global trade, no one can guarantee that the results will be what one was hoping or wanting or expecting. The results of the *Just Trade* study were mixed. It was a short-term intervention, with endline findings elicited as soon as the module was completed: the medium-to-long-term impact of such a module would need to be investigated, requiring follow-on study at intervals after the completion of lessons.

Furthermore, the study raised a number of crucial questions. Findings in relation to images of Africa were of particular concern, especially as many negative views persisted to endline. The fact that this outcome was present in all schools, including the school with an African-identified population of 30%, is a matter of specific disquiet and raises challenging questions for educators. For example, how can the education system address these problems when the system itself helps to maintain and reinforce the 'single story' which has resulted in the distancing from and stripping away of African self-image (Young, 2012), as well as perpetuating the deficit perceptions of White students towards Africa and its people? Andrews (2018) states that diversifying the curriculum or offering courses in black studies does not in itself change the nature of the system. Merely striving for 'balance' in curricula through a trade justice module does not constitute the radical shift that is required in order to address systemic injustices. Transformation requires a deeper, more root-and-branch approach. It necessitates an examination of what counts as 'knowledge' in the education system and on who constitutes 'holders of knowledge' (Martin et al., 2017). It involves undoing the "epistemic abyss that keeps on drawing worlds apart along the colonial difference" (Icaza & Vazquez, 2018, p. 123). It requires moving beyond the "assumed normalcy of whiteness and white culture" (Martin et al., 2017, p. 236), a change which, by definition, includes the diversification of the teaching profession at all levels: primary, secondary, and tertiary. Real transformation can only take place through the "laborious work of structural change" (Gebrial, 2018, p. 29). Until then, initiatives such as the trade project described in this chapter, although valuable and necessary, will only meet short-term goals. Long-term change requires Black and White allies working together towards systemic reform and towards lasting goals of social justice and equity.

Notes

1 School statistics are presented here according to the Central Statistics Office Census categories: White Irish; Irish Traveller; any other white background; African; any other black background; Chinese; any other Asian background.
2 Some of the Africa–Ireland links which were discussed in *Just Trade* included musical and sports connections, two-way migration links, human rights activists, and well-known African-Irish personalities.
3 Knowledge at baseline mainly centred on Egypt and Nigeria. Pupils in only one of the schools referred to Africa as a continent at baseline, and their estimates about the number of countries ranged from 20 to 51.
4 At the time of designing the pilot trade resource, Madecasse chocolate was produced from bean to bar in Madagascar; since then, production has moved to Italy.
5 See Chapter 2 for further information on PMIA.
6 The photo was taken in Mount Elgon National Park and was reprinted in *Just Trade* with permission from IRIN News https://www.irinnews.org/content/about-us

References

Allum, L., Dral, P., Galanská, N., Lowe, B., Navojsky, A. Pelimanni, P., …, Zemanová, B. (2015). *How do we know it's working?. Book 2, Tracking changes in pupils' attitudes.* Reading, UK: Reading International Solidarity Centre (RISC).

Andrews, K. (2018). The challenge for Black Studies in the neoliberal university. In G.K. Bhambra, D. Gebrial, & K. Nisancioglu (Eds.), *Decolonising the university.* London: Pluto Press.

Bourn, D. (2015). *The theory and practice of development education.* Oxon and New York: Routledge.

Bucknall, S. (2007, September 5). Researching young researchers in primary schools: Responding to children's evaluations of a participatory technique. *British Educational Research Association New Researchers/Student Conference*, Institute of Education, University of London, London.

Clark, J. (2012). Using diamond ranking as visual cues to engage young people in the research process. *Qualitative Research Journal*, 12(2), 222–237.

Cochran-Smith, M., & Donnell, K. (2006). Practitioner inquiry: Blurring the boundaries of research and practice. In J.L. Green, G. Camilli, & P. Elmore (Eds.), *Handbook of complementary methods in education research.* Mahwah, NJ: Lawrence Erlbaum for AERA.

De Sisto, F. (2014). From conflict escalation to conflict transformation: Actual and potential role of stories and storytelling among marginalised occupational minorities in Southern Ethiopia. *International Journal of African Development*, 1(2), 83–92.

Dobson, A. (2006). Thick cosmopolitanism. *Political Studies*, 54, 165–184.

Dolan, A.M. (2014). *You, me and diversity: Picturebooks for teaching development and intercultural education.* London: Institute of Education.

Downes, L. (2016). *Imaging global perspectives: Representations of the global south in a higher education environment.* Retrieved from http://www.diceproject.ie/research/papers-reports/

Gannon, M. (2002). *Changing perspectives.* Dublin: CDVEC. Retrieved from https://developmenteducation.ie/resource/changing-perspectives-cultural-values-diversity-and-equality-in-ireland-and-the-wider-world/

Gebrial, D. (2018). Rhodes must fall: Oxford and movements for change. In G.K. Bhambra, D. Gebrial, & K. Nisancioglu (Eds.), *Decolonising the university.* London: Pluto Press.

Goldfinger, D. (2006). *Development pornography: Images of the global south*. The Democracy and Governance Network. Retrieved, 5 May 2017, from http://www.comminit.com/democracy-governance/content/development-pornography-images-global-south

Government of Ireland (1999). *Primary school curriculum*. Dublin: Stationery Office.

Gonzalez, N., Moll, L.C., & Amanti, C. (2005). *Funds of knowledge: Theorizing practices in households, communities and classrooms*. Mahwah, NJ: Lawrence Erlbaum.

Heinz, M., & Keane, E. (2018). Socio-demographic composition of primary initial teacher education entrants in Ireland. *Irish Educational Studies*, 37(4), 523–543.

Hopkins, E. (2010). Classroom conditions for effective learning: hearing the voice of key Stage 3 pupils. *Improving Schools*, 13(1), 39–53.

Icaza, R., & Vazquez, R. (2018). Diversity or decolonisation? Researching diversity at the University of Amsterdam. In G.K. Bhambra, D. Gebrial, & K. Nisancioglu (Eds.), *Decolonising the university*. London: Pluto Press.

Keane, E., & Heinz, M. (2015). Diversity in initial teacher education in Ireland: The socio-demographic backgrounds of entrants in 2013 and 2014. *Irish Educational Studies*, 34(3), 281–301.

Kerdeman, D. (2003). Pulled up short: Challenging self-understanding as a focus of teaching and learning. *Journal of Philosophy of Education*, 37(2), 293–308.

Kerr, J., & Andreotti, V. (2017). Crossing borders in initial teacher education: Mapping dispositions to diversity and inequity. *Race, Ethnicity and Education*, 22(5), 647–665.

Kitching, K. (2014). *The politics of compulsive education*. Oxon: Routledge.

Larkin, T., Morris, L., O'Caoimh, C., Muzanenhamo, P., Wilson, B., & O'Toole, B. (2018). *Just Connections, Just Trade: A teaching resource about Africa*. Dublin: Marino Institute of Education & Proudly Made in Africa.

Lawson, H. (2018). *Primary pupils' attitudes towards and understandings of poverty* (Research Paper No. 19). London: Development Education Research Centre, Institute of Education.

Mac a'Bhaird, N. (2009). *Olanna's big day*. Dublin: The O'Brien Press.

Manzo, K. (2006). An extension of colonialism? Development education, images and the media. *The Development Education Journal*, 12(2), 9–12.

Martin, F., Pirbhai-Illich, F., & Pete, S. (2017). Beyond culturally responsive pedagogy: Decolonising teacher education. In F. Pirbhai-Illich, S. Pete, & F. Martin (Eds.), *Culturally responsive pedagogy: Working towards decolonisation, indigeneity and interculturalism* (pp. 235–256). Palgrave Macmillan.

Mignolo, W., & Walsh, C. (2018). *On decoloniality: Concepts, analytics, praxis*. Durham: Duke University Press.

National Council for Curriculum and Assessment. (2009). *Aistear: The early childhood education framework*. Dublin: NCCA.

Niemi, R., Kumpulainen, K., & Lipponen, L. (2015). Pupils as active participants: diamond ranking as a tool to investigate pupils' experiences of classroom practices. *European Educational Research Journal*, 14(2), 138–150.

Ntelioglu, B.Y., Fannin, J., Montanera, M., & Cummins, J. (2014). A multilingual and multimodal approach to literacy teaching and learning in urban education: A collaborative inquiry project in an inner city elementary school. *Frontiers in Psychology*, 5, 533.

Oberman, R., Waldron, F., & Dillon, S. (2012). Developing a global citizenship education programme for three to six year olds. *International Journal of Development Education and Global Learning*, 4(1), 37–60.

Oberman, R. (2013). From research to resource: Critical literacy and global citizenship education in middle primary school. *Proceedings of the Irish Association for Social, Scientific and Environmental Education (IASSEE) Annual Conference 2013*, pp. 29–39.

Onyefulu, I. (2007). *Ikenna goes to Nigeria.* London: Frances Lincoln Books.

Prosser, J., & Loxley, A. (2008). *Introducing visual methods.* ESRC National Centre for Research Methods Review Paper.

Ravitch, S.M. (2014). The transformative power of taking and inquiry stance on practice: Practitioner research as narrative and counter-narrative. *Perspectives on Urban Education*, 11(1), 5–10.

Scheunpflug, A. (2011). Global education and cross-cultural learning: A challenge for a research based approach to international teacher education. *International Journal of Development Education and Global Learning*, 3(3), 29–44.

Simpson, J. (2016). *A study to investigate, explore and identify successful 'interventions' to support teachers in a transformative move from a charity mentality to a social justice mentality.* Global Learning Programme Innovation Fund Research Series: Paper 2. London: Development Education Research Centre.

Suas. (2012). *National Survey of third level students on global development report.* Dublin. Retrieved from http://www.suas.ie/sites/default/files/documents/Suas_National_Survey_2013.pdf

Tallon, R. (2012). The impressions left behind by NGO messages concerning the developing world. *Policy & Practice: A Development Education Review*, 15(Autumn), 8-26.

Tallon, R., & McGregor, A. (2014). Pitying the Third World: Towards more progressive emotional responses to development education in schools. *Third World Quarterly*, 35(8), 1406–1422.

Taylor, M. (2003). *Looking at the economy through women's eyes: A facilitator's guide for economic literacy.* Dublin: Banúlacht.

Thwaite, A., & Rivalland, J. (2008). How can analysis of classroom talk help teachers reflect on their practices? *Australian Journal of Language and Literacy*, 32(1), 38–54.

TIDE. (1998). *Fat felts and sugar paper: Activities for speaking and listening about issues.* Birmingham: TIDE/DEC.

Walsh, C. (2018). Decoloniality in/as praxis. In W. Mignolo & C. Walsh (Eds.), *On decoloniality.* Duke University: Duke University Press.

Young, O. (2012). *African images and their impact on public perception: What are the Human Rights implications?* Northern Ireland: African and Caribbean Support Organisation.

Appendix 1

Ethnic representation in participating schools (in line with census categories)

1 **School A**: 10% White Irish, 46% any other white background, 15% African, 1% any other black background, 1.6% Chinese, 25% any other Asian background (24 in class)
2 **School B**: 16% White Irish, 36% any other white background, 30% African, 1% any other black background, 2.5% Chinese, 9% any other Asian background, 5% multiple ethnic background (20 in class)
3 **School C**: 33% White Irish; 27% any other white background; 6% African; 19% Chinese; 15% any other Asian background (23 in class)
4 **School D**: 75.5% White Irish, 13% any other white background, 5% African, 0.5% Chinese, 6% any other Asian background (16 in class)

Appendix 2

Classroom Observation Framework

Physical setting:
What is the physical environment like? (You might want to draw a classroom map)
How is space allocated? What objects, resources, technologies are in the setting?

Participants:
Describe who is in the scene, how many people and their roles.

Activities and interactions:
What is going on? (Which activity are you working on?)
How do the children interact with the activity and with one another?
What norms or rules structure the activities and interactions?
When did the activity begin?
How long did it last?
Is it a typical activity or unusual?

Conversation:
What is the content of conversations?
Who speaks to whom?
Who listens?
Quote directly, paraphrase, and summarise conversations.
Note silences and non-verbal behaviours that add meaning to the exchanges.

Subtle factors:
Informal and unplanned activities
What does not happen (especially if you were expecting it to happen?)

Appendix 3

Diamond ranking statements
Reason 1: There are too many people
Reason 2: People can't grow enough food because of wars
Reason 3: People in rich countries don't give enough in aid or charity
Reason 4: Poor farmers are not allowed to sell their food to rich countries
Reason 5: The best land is used to grow food for other countries
Reason 6: There is not enough food to go around
Reason 7: Farmers don't use new ways of growing more food
Reason 8: People are too poor to buy enough food
Reason 9: People in poor countries are not paid enough for what they grow

Appendix 4

Riceland and Beanland (adapted from Taylor, 2003)

> The people of the neighbouring island countries, Riceland and Beanland, both need rice and beans as part of their staple diet.

Both countries can grow both crops. However, Riceland is better suited to growing rice than beans. One worker in Riceland can grow twice as much rice as beans in a year. Beanland is better suited to growing beans than rice. One worker in Beanland can grow twice as many beans as rice in a year.

At the moment with no trade between the countries, in one year:

- Riceland produces two crops of Rice and one crop of Beans
- Beanland produces two crops of Beans and one crop of Rice

You need equal amounts of both beans and rice for a balanced diet. So what are you going to do about it?

6 Representations of Africa

Irish NGOs, media, and educational resources

Oluromade (Rom) Olusa and Cecelia Gavigan

Introduction

Oluromade (Rom) Olusa: I am a female person of African descent. I migrated to Ireland in the early 2000s. In the course of engaging in postgraduate education to achieve a Postgraduate Diploma in Social Policy and a Master's in Social Work, and subsequently practising as a professionally qualified social work practitioner and educator, I have witnessed first-hand how persons from the black community are perceived and how such perceptions in turn impact on their sense of belonging, integration into the community, and their health and well-being. My interests in issues relating to the black diaspora emerged from experiences of first-hand and indirect forms of individual and institutional discrimination of black and minority ethnic communities in Ireland. My firm belief in social justice and decolonisation of old and new Eurocentric ideologies culminated in enrolment in PhD studies in social work. I am involved in practice education and lecture occasionally on anti-discriminatory and anti-oppressive social work practice with a specific focus on racism.

Cecelia Gavigan: I am a White, cisgender, bi/queer, non-disabled, female primary school teacher, and educational activist. I was raised in rural Ireland as part of a small farming family and attended local Catholic primary and secondary schools. I became especially interested in issues of equality while in teacher education and have since completed a Master's degree in Equality Studies. Since qualifying as a teacher, I have taught in an Educate Together school in a diverse community in north Dublin. My philosophies are grounded in anti-racism, social justice, and radical egalitarianism.

Globalisation and migration are realities of the Northern and Southern hemispheres. The resulting profound effect of migration and globalisation in Ireland is the significant diversity of ethnicities and cultures found in all spheres of society. In this chapter, we draw on a postcolonial lens along with Critical Race Theory (CRT) as a race-conscious approach with which to examine and challenge the reinforcement of negative perceptions of Africa and the Global South within the Irish primary school system. We critically examine how the Global North perceives the South in relation to projected images of the African continent as portrayed in fundraising campaigns from non-governmental organisations (NGOs) and in educational materials used in Irish primary schools. We conclude with recommendations for approaches to tackle and address stereotyping and deficit portrayals of children and peoples of Africa.

The social and political construct of being Black

European colonisation and enslavement of people in countries in the Global South impacted and still impacts on the lives of the formerly colonised peoples. This is linked to the myth of European superiority which continues to manifest in Western literary and philosophical discourse which depicts the Global South as 'primitive other'. Scholarship from the 1960s (Fanon, 1967) up till present (Day, 2013; Ingrao, 2015; Rasheem and Brunson, 2018; Williams & Bernard, 2018) has highlighted the dehumanising impacts of slavery and colonisation on the black race. Alasuutari and Andreotti (2015) opine that a dominant global imaginary, underpinned by a single story of development and superiority of knowledge, has negative implications for the Global South. They argue that a typical African child, irrespective of their geographical location, becomes alienated from their African context the moment they come in contact with formal education, mainly because of the Eurocentric curriculum which negates and oftentimes portrays negative imagery of Africa. According to Martin and Griffiths (2012), children in the Global North form stereotypes based upon the images they see, messages they hear and prejudices transmitted from adults around them. Sarti, Schalkers, and Dedding's (2015) title, based on their study of children aged eight to fourteen years, 'I am not poor. Poor children live in Africa' succinctly captures how children in the Global North perceive their counterparts in Africa whom they identify as homeless, poor, and dying of starvation (Downes, 2016). According to Chimamanda Adichie, a prominent and contemporary Nigerian author,

> If I had not grown up in Nigeria and if all I knew of Africa were from popular images, I too would think that Africa was a place of beautiful landscapes, beautiful animals, and incomprehensible people fighting senseless wars, dying of poverty and AIDS; unable to speak for themselves and waiting to be saved.
>
> Adichie (2009)

Bias and prejudice, underpinned by the disparaging images of African children as being constantly afflicted by war, poverty, and AIDS is exacerbated by the media's continuous representation of Africa as a disease-afflicted continent bereft of development and populated with corrupt recipients of charity and aid monies. According to Sankore (2005) and as alluded to by Young (2012), the issue of 'development pornography' whereby images of unclothed starving children are used by development agencies to raise funds from the public in the Global North contributes towards deeper prejudice against children and adults. While the poverty is real, the subliminal message that development 'pornography' conveys is unreal (Manzo, 2006). The causes of poverty transcend and are more complicated than pictures can ever convey. In Africa, previous undemocratic rule, facilitated or conveniently accepted by many Western governments, continues to this day to ensure institutional imbalances in the development of the political and democratic process. The continent has endured four hundred years of slavery which, directly or indirectly, killed and displaced over a hundred million Africans and, in the process, inhibited sustainable social, political, and economic progress for four centuries. Additionally, subsequent colonial repression, which in some places lasted over a hundred years, has meant that most of Africa has only been independent for between twenty and eighty years (with the exception of South Africa and Egypt that became independent in 1910 and 1922 respectively). Ethiopia gained independence in 1942 and was followed a few years later by Libya in 1951. Other African countries like Ghana, Morocco, Guinea, Nigeria, Kenya, Togo, Niger, Rwanda, and Uganda gained independence in the 1950s and 1960s. Moreover, for most of this period, the leaders of many of these countries were ruling under the influence of Cold War enemies who were jostling for strategic influence in the region. It is therefore no wonder that following enslavement, colonial repression, unequal trade relations, and iniquitous interests on loans which have existed for over 500 years, the continent presents as bruised and battered. It is the only continent known so far to have undergone such exploitative treatment. The images used by NGOs or charities do not adequately capture and explain this; what development 'pornography' shows is the result of five centuries of aggressive exploitation of a continent but does not address the root causes.

It is important to question the guiding philosophies and ultimate motives of some of the NGOs operating in the region. While presumably set up to fight injustice, in reality some of these perpetuate colonialism by misrepresenting the Global South which, in fact, makes up the majority of the world's population. This effectively acts as a barrier to African children's access to a socially just global community. African children in diaspora are also denied the opportunity to be proud of their cultural heritage as they experience stigmatisation and are perceived as the helpless colonial African children for whom money is being collected in churches, schools, and in public spaces. Hilary (2014) identified such NGOs as 'Merchants of Misery'. He enjoined them to act in solidarity by challenging colonial forces that oppressed, and are still oppressing Africa. He argued that continuing to engage in the portrayal of colonial images of helpless African children awaiting salvation from their 'White Saviours' has no place in the twenty-first century so we must be ready to challenge such depictions wherever they appear. David Lammy, a Black British politician and Member of Parliament (MP), declined invitations to partake in filming for annual Comic Relief in 2019, and accused Stacey Dooley, a White British media personality of reinforcing "tired and unhelpful" pervasive stereotypes by "white saviours" (Badshah, 2019). Dooley had visited Uganda for Comic Relief and posted a picture on social media that she took with a Black child while filming on location. By his action, Lammy could be seen challenging perpetuation of the colonialist legacy through the use of misleading images of African people. Another example is the ubiquitous images of children 'who need our help' portrayed on fundraising boxes year after year with profound reliance on images of children from the Global South as a tool for eliciting donations. The educational materials produced to accompany these drives have, in recent years, shown a somewhat more nuanced portrayal of the issues, but the fact that the same people sometimes feature in both the fundraising and educational materials underpins the whole endeavour with a message of perceived deficit.

These images may meet the short-term needs of NGO fundraising campaigns but they inadvertently reinforce the perception of the powerful North extending charity and 'help' to the 'needy' South. The challenge of decolonising foreign missionary and development endeavours in Africa led Olivia Alaso and Kelsey Nielsen, two social workers, to establish 'No White Saviors' (sic). Alaso is of African heritage and Nielsen is a White development worker; however both work together, through their co-owned organisation, to challenge white privilege or as they term it, 'White Saviour Complex', as exemplified in the above case of Stacey Dooley. Following their observations of white privilege, Alaso and Nielsen aimed to challenge how 'development' and evangelism is carried out in Africa, following first-hand observations of unwarranted privilege accorded to White people (Akumu, 2019). They argue that white privilege, an outcome of the legacy of discriminatory and unequal power imbalance between White and Black people, has led to the emergence of white saviourism. They maintain that white saviourism assumes Black people are helpless. While accepting that significant levels of poverty exist in Africa, they highlight that aid given to African countries is often not what they have asked for but what the white saviour charities and evangelical organisations assume is needed. These aids, according to these activists, also come with strings attached.

Unidimensional portrayals such as those mentioned above create an uneven playing field. They depict a single dominant story of progressive and superior development on one side of the world while another part of the world is 'lagging behind' in time and development. Such differentiated portrayal of cultures as 'ahead' and 'backward' (Mahadeo & McKinney, 2007) does not seem to take into account that it ascribes supremacy to the North and validates the violent dissemination of a global perception that discounts continents in the Global South, particularly Africa. Telling one-sided or single stories (Adichie, 2009), which the West has systematically done for centuries, has resulted in stereotyping and generalisations of Africa and its indigenes irrespective of their geographical location, socio-economic or political status (Adegoke, 2017). The dearth of significant knowledge about this second largest continent means that there are few other sources to help mitigate the harmful messages about Africa and the Global South. As the majority of people from the West will never visit Africa, they will continue to carry and transmit these images that they hold to be 'fact'. This is as true of teachers as of the rest of the population, which poses particular challenges with regard to the transmission of these stereotypes as fact to young children within the school system.

Portrayal of the African continent in primary school materials

In order to evaluate how this phenomenon is impacting upon the Irish primary education system, it is necessary to examine how the African continent and Black children more generally are portrayed in this setting. 'Black children' as referenced in this chapter refers to children of African descent and of black skin colour (University of Scotland, 2013). Media "produces and reproduces, constitutes and re-inscribes ideas about how the world is racially organised, and about how race and racism are to be understood and acted upon, particularly in the arenas of education and schooling" (Vilenas & Angeles, 2016, p. 36). This is especially true for children, as children's vision of themselves, the world, and their place in the world are greatly influenced by the literature and images they see (Dedeoğlu, Ulusoy, & Lamme, 2011). One of the most common sources of images that pupils are exposed to every day is textbooks developed by educational publishers. It has already been established that materials developed by NGOs with a fundraising agenda can be extremely problematic in terms of the negative imaging of the African continent. However, textbooks developed exclusively for educational purposes should be unbiased and accurate sources of information. Chapter 3 examined the 'pedagogic authority' of the textbook and explored how textbooks can often operate as unquestioned sources of truth and definitive sources of knowledge in the classroom; in the following section we take this investigation further and focus specifically on the portrayal of Africa in school texts.

Portrayal of the African continent in primary school textbooks

Given the powerful position that textbooks play in classrooms, it is necessary to ensure that the messages pupils are receiving from them are truthful, inclusive, and accurate. In order to ascertain what kinds of images pupils are being exposed to through textbooks, we conducted a systematic review of those currently available from Irish educational publishers for use in Irish primary schools. To ensure a fair and impartial assessment, a number of criteria were created before selecting texts. The full set from Junior Infants to Sixth Class were examined in order to get a complete picture of the series as designed by the publishers and to avoid any omission of items that may be only be present at certain class levels. Textbook series older than ten years were excluded from the review so as to ensure that books examined were representing the most recent offerings from publishers. Textbooks designed for Social, Environmental and Scientific Education (SESE) were prioritised as these are the most likely source of content related to the African continent. Where a SESE textbook was not available, Geography and History were examined, as again these are the curricular areas that contain objectives most explicitly related to the African continent. Only pupil textbooks were considered; teacher photocopiable books and resource manuals were excluded on the basis that there is far less certainty that pupils would be exposed to all elements of these types of book.

The products of the main education publishers providing textbooks to primary schools were examined for eligibility and two of these had books that fulfilled the selection criteria. These were *Unlocking SESE* from Folens and *Small World* from CJFallon. The early level books in the *Window on the World* series from The Education Company (EdCo) fell just outside the ten-year limit and so was excluded. The eligible textbooks from both series were examined from Junior Infants up to Sixth Class. The formats of both differ slightly from the junior to senior school. *Small World* is a combined SESE textbook until Second Class and from Third Class onwards is separated into *Small World History* and *Small World Geography and Science*. Both options at the senior level were examined so as to cover both Geography and History. *Unlocking SESE* is a combined SESE textbook until Second Class and from Third Class onwards is offered as either a combined SESE textbook or a separate *Unlocking History, Unlocking Geography*, and *Unlocking Science*. To ensure as much consistency as possible, we examined the combined SESE book, *Unlocking SESE*, from Junior Infants up to Sixth Class. Textbooks were examined for references to the African continent in either images or text. These were then noted in tabular form and examined to see what themes emerged. The findings are summarised in the following sections.

The continent of Africa presented as a single homogenous entity

The entire continent is frequently referred to as 'Africa' with little cognisance of the richness and diversity that exists between different countries therein. In *Small World Senior Infants,* children are asked to imagine "If you go on a safari in the Serengeti in Africa ..." (p. 54). In the First Class book of the same series, an item on the Sahara desert uses a world map which has the labels 'Ireland' and 'Africa', despite similar items on Mexico and Australia being labelled with country names. When looking at cold and hot places, pupils are asked to "Colour Africa red on the globe. ... The temperature in Africa is very very hot" (p. 95). In *Small World Second Class*, the item on bird migration uses a map labelled 'Ireland' and 'Africa'. The birds are repeatedly described as flying to Africa without any mention of the different countries they may fly to (p. 16). Later in the same book pupils are told "Wildebeest live in [Africa]" (p. 73) despite wildebeest only in fact being found in quite a small region of southern and east Africa. This page also has two separate maps both showing Africa as one entity. In one map the word Africa is inserted over the top of the map, even though the map itself shows the political borders of countries. This important trend of the African continent being labelled as one homogenous place despite other countries being labelled individually is further seen in the *Small World: History Third Class* (p. 76) and *Small World: History Fifth Class* (p. 28). *Small World Second Class* has an item on Zambia but the follow-up questions refer to Africa – "John was in Africa in 1968. ... Write a list of ways that John could contact his home in Ireland if he was living in Africa today" (p. 92). *Unlocking SESE Sixth Class* includes some reference to the diversity of countries and languages across the continent but pupils are asked to "Find Africa and Ireland on a map of the world. How are they different?" and "Would you expect Ireland and Africa to have similar myths and legends or different ones?" (p. 94) again conflating all African countries as one homogenous entity.

Egypt depicted as unrelated to Africa

Ancient Egypt is a common theme in primary school textbooks. Despite the fact that Egypt is located on the continent of Africa, this linkage is rarely present in materials presented. In an item on Egyptian hieroglyphs in *Small World First Class* (pp. 92 and 93), there is no mention of it being located on the African continent. In *Small World: History Third Class*, the map used is labelled with Egypt and Africa but there is no explicit link mentioned in the text (p. 46). Further instances of information on Egypt being presented as divorced from Africa are found in *Small World: Geography and Science Fourth Class* (pp. 89 and 97), *Small World: Geography and Science Fifth Class* (p. 16), *Unlocking SESE Third Class* (p. 80), *Unlocking SESE Fourth Class* (p. 128), and *Unlocking SESE Fifth Class* (p. 104). None of these states that Egypt is located in Africa and so the wonders associated with that civilisation remain unconnected to Africa in the minds of pupils. The one small exception to this pattern is found in the unit on Egypt in *Small World: Geography and Science Third Class* (pp. 68–72). The first character, Jamila, introduces herself as living in Egypt, Africa. The rest of the chapter, which includes profiles of characters living in Cairo, living in Bedouin tribes, and information about the Nile makes no further mention of being on the African continent. The multifaceted portrayal of life in Egypt (albeit still relying on certain tropes) is in stark contrast to the homogenous ways in which other African countries are portrayed.

Portrayal of African countries as lacking technology, backward, and poor

With the exception of historical Egypt, countries from the African continent are portrayed as lacking technology, backward, and poor. In *Unlocking SESE First Class*, Kenya appears as one of the countries featured in the context of 'national costumes' using an image of traditional Maasai-like clothing (p. 66). It does not state that these would be traditional dress rather than something that all Kenyans would wear for everyday purposes. Nor does it distinguish which Kenyan culture this dress would be associated with, thus leading to the conflation of all Kenyans as sharing the same culture and also as wearing traditional dress every day. In *Small World Second Class*, Kenya and South Africa are both featured within fact files for homes around the world. Pupils are asked to choose an appropriate word from a given word bank to complete the sentences. For Kenya, the text exercise reads "Some African people [build] their homes with mud" with an accompanying image of a mud hut (p. 28). For the fact file on South Africa, the focus is exclusively on townships and the text exercise reads "Houses are usually small and [overcrowded]" (p. 29). Within the same book the method of keeping cool in Chad is described as "We like to rest under the shade of the mango [tree]". In contrast, the method of keeping cool in Croatia is by using a ceiling fan and in Crete by painting their houses white (p. 65). Similarly, in the story of Muna from Ethiopia, her family of seven live in a two-room mud hut and Muna talks about fetching water after school (p. 77). *Small World: Geography and Science Fifth Class* includes the story of Leonta from Somalia (p. 96) which focuses on the famine in 2010 and 2011 and the story of Aaeesha from Darfur which focuses on the lack of rainfall and the violence of the Janjaweed (p. 97). *Small World: Geography and Science Sixth Class* tells the story of Numbi, an 11-year-old Sierra Leonean who has worked 18 hours a day in a gem mine since he was nine years old (p. 117) and an item looking at unfair trade uses a photograph captioned "A poor cotton farmer in Ghana" (p. 118).

Unlocking SESE Sixth Class includes a chapter on Malawi. The objectives are to learn about the African country of Malawi, the lives of people living in Malawi, poverty in Malawi, and Irish aid in Malawi (p. 88). This is in stark contrast to the previous chapter on Brazil wherein the objectives are to learn how to locate South America and Brazil on a map, some interesting facts about Brazil, about biodiversity in the Amazon rainforest, what life is like for a child living in Rio de Janeiro, and about Brazil's beef industry and how it affects Ireland (p. 82). The chapter on Malawi begins with a blog from an Irish aid worker and immediately portrays Malawi in a negative light – "Roads, hospitals, clean running water and proper schools ... are not available to a large section of the population in Malawi" (p. 88). The chapter then includes some more factual geographical-type information before a specific section on poverty in Malawi. This discusses the fact that more than 70% of the population of Malawi live on less than €1 per day, that problems in Malawi "include poor nutrition, poor access to medical treatment, insufficient school education and difficult climatic conditions" and "Famine in this century has meant that the population has suffered from starvation and has relied on international organisations to supply food" (p. 91). This item is accompanied by an image of a sad-looking child being held by their mother and a young boy whose ribs are showing. The items in the visual summary for Malawi again focus on poverty, malnutrition, drought, famine, and receiving aid. One of the final activities in the chapter asks pupils to identify four other developing countries and to write down anything they notice about their locations. Children will likely find them to be located on the African continent, thus expanding the story of poverty in Malawi to become the story of the entire African continent. It raises a question on intent: given that children using this series have not studied any other African country in depth (aside perhaps from Egypt in a historical sense), why choose the country which paints the most negative image?

There are some rare exceptions to this preponderance of negative imagery. There is some neutral factual information on Ethiopia before the story of Muna and her family in *Small World Second Class* (p. 76). In *Small World: Geography and Science Third Class*, it mentions that houses are built from sun-dried clay bricks in Morocco (p. 106). In *Small World: Geography and Science Fourth Class* Tanzania is mentioned as the area where the first tools were found (p. 64) and South Africa is mentioned as the location of the first human heart transplant (p. 76). In *Small Word: Geography and Science Fifth Class*, it mentions Tunisia as the birthplace of Hannibal (p. 75). These however are passing references and are not the main focus of lessons. The combination of Africa being portrayed as a singular entity, paired with the predominantly negative imagery of African countries when they do feature in textbooks, is extremely problematic with regard to the influence this has upon the perceptions pupils develop about the African continent.

Irish people portrayed as 'Helpers' either through aid or volunteering

Where Irish people are portrayed as connected to countries in Africa, this is predominantly in terms of being 'helpers' who are making a positive difference to the African countries they are in. The chapter on Famine in *Small World Geography and Science Fifth Class* lists possible solutions to the situations of famine outlined. These include:

> Sharing money: An Irish pop star named Bob Geldof has helped to raise millions for countries affected by famine. He began helping charities in 1985 when he persuaded a number of other pop stars to perform at fundraising concerts called "Live Aid" (p. 97)

and

> Sharing time and skills: Many Irish volunteers travel to developing countries, where they help to build houses and wells. They use skills they have learned on building sites or farms to help provide electricity and food to those in need. Other volunteers teach in schools and work in clinics and hospitals (p. 97).

It concludes with three final items on 'helping'. The first, 'Prevention is Better than Cure' focuses on an organisation called *Self Help Africa* and states that their work "may involve helping [local people] to find land on which to grow crops, and a source of fresh water to keep their crops alive. It may also involve teaching them the skills needed to become successful farmers, and other skills such as reading and writing" (p. 98). This item is accompanied by an image of White teacher and Black student captioned "A volunteer teacher in South Africa". The second piece is about an Irish organisation working in Malawi called *Wells for Zoe* and states "The country has high rates of annual rainfall, but farmers do not always have the skills or resources to store water" (p. 98). The final item is on Relief Agencies and states "The Irish Government sends food, tents, blankets and money to people in need. Many Irish people work for relief agencies that distribute food and medicine and provide advice and education to people in developing countries" (p. 98).

As mentioned above, in *Unlocking SESE Sixth Class*, the chapter on Malawi begins with a blog from an Irish aid worker who states "There is so much work to be done here, but the feeling when you help a village to help itself, knowing the positive impact it will have, is fantastic" (p. 88). The chapter then goes on to focus on 'Irish Aid for Malawi' and states that

> [w]ith the help of donations from the Irish people, Irish-based charities such as Concern, Trócaire and GOAL have been tackling the needs of Malawi in a number of different ways. As there are so many problems in Malawi, different organisations focus on different areas that need help. (p. 92)

It then outlines what the three NGOs have been doing. The activity for pupils based on this is to imagine that they are a farmer from a village in Malawi and to write "a letter to an aid organisation describing how you have benefitted from their work" (p. 92). This page is accompanied by a White woman (presumably an aid worker) holding two small Black girls.

Even when the Irish person is not specifically an aid worker, the relationship is one of providing services the country needs. In *Small World Second Class*, pupils are invited to examine a letter sent home by an Irish engineer who had moved to Zambia in the 1960s (p. 92). He describes Lusaka as "a new city, with building sites everywhere" and says "It's no wonder they need engineers" (p. 92). He goes on to say that he will be working for Lusaka Water Supply Scheme as the city "needs a good supply of clean drinking water" (p. 92). This is in contrast to the references to African people coming to Ireland. These are portrayed as either neutral relationships or ones where the migrants to Ireland benefit. In *Unlocking SESE Third Class*, Joshua was born in Nigeria but is now an Irish citizen (p. 16). Similarly, in *Unlocking SESE Sixth Class*, it references Ottah, a Security Officer on the LUAS who moved from Nigeria to Ireland in 2004 (p. 113). *Unlocking SESE Fifth Class* mentions that

> [t]housands of people came to Ireland from Poland and other eastern European countries, and from African countries such as Nigeria … looking for work and a better life for their families. Some of these people sent the money they earned in Ireland back to their families at home (p. 147).

While the next chapter includes a section asking pupils to identify benefits that migrant workers can bring to a country, this section does not make any explicit link to Africa (p. 151).

Lack of criticality of colonialism and transatlantic slave trade

The lack of criticality portrayed in relationships between Ireland and African countries is mirrored in the discussion on the impact of Europeans in Africa. While colonialism is never mentioned or explored in detail, there are some references to the transatlantic slave trade. *Small World: History Fifth Class* explores the consequence of the voyages of discovery. It lists "The transatlantic slave trade began, as Africans were shipped to colonies of the New World" on the same level as "New types of food such as sugar, cocoa, tomato, potato, turkey, peanuts, tea and coffee, as well as tobacco, were imported to Europe" (p. 32). There is no further discussion or reference to the impact this may have had on the African continent, either within the text or the follow-on questions. In a subsequent piece on the Industrial Revolution, the text states that "Colonies in the New World could supply cotton, tea, coffee, sugar cane and many other products" without any reference to the enslavement of people it took to produce them (p. 86).

Inaccurate mapping of Africa

We also observed an inaccurate mapping of Africa from our examination of textbooks. In the case of the *Small World* series, it includes a world map in the Geography and Science textbook from Third Class upwards. However, despite the series having been published in 2013 and 2014, the map does not include the country of South Sudan. This is also true of the map used in *Unlocking SESE Sixth Class* published in 2013. In *Small World Second Class*, a map shows Zambia coloured red but it is labelled as Lusaka. An additional issue is that the Third and Fourth Class books in the *Small World* series use maps which do not convey the true size of the African continent. This is however rectified in the Fifth and Sixth Class books.

Portrayal of Black characters in primary school textbooks

It is interesting to note that in contrast to the almost ubiquitously negative portrayals of the African continent in textbooks, publishers have evidently made greater effort to ensure that Black people living in Ireland are portrayed in more positive ways, especially in Irish language textbooks. As these books are used to support conversational language, they tend to focus on situations that are familiar to pupils. Consequently they are usually based on everyday life within schools and communities. The Census figures from 2016 indicate that 64,639 of the 4,689,021 population identified as black, black Irish, or any other black background (1.38%) (Central Statistics Office, 2017). For primary school-aged children (0–14 years), these figures rise to 25,202 out of 1,002,337 representing 2.52% (Central Statistics Office, 2017). To be an accurate representation from a statistical perspective, textbook characters should be at least 2.52% black. Two series of Irish textbooks were examined to determine what percentage of the character illustrations showed Black children. This was determined by counting the incidence of illustrations of Black characters and determining this as a percentage of the total number of images shown. There were some challenges in terms of determining ethnicity based on cartoon illustrations but if a character could possibly have been intended to portray a Black character, the illustration was credited as such in order to prevent possible underestimation. The table below summarises the findings.

	Bua na Cainte/Béal Beo (EdCo)		*Abair Liom (Folens)*	
Class Level	*Number of Appearances*	*Percentage*	*Number of Appearances*	*Percentage*
Junior Infants	0 out of 37	0%	7 out of 244	2.9%
Senior Infants	0 out of 53	0%	48 out of 440	10.9%
First Class	67 out of 305	21.7%	12 out of 490	2.5%
Second Class	21 out of 981	2.1%	30 out of 891	3.4%
Third Class	55 out of 495	11.1%	40 out of 818	4.9%
Fourth Class	15 out of 399	3.8%	40 out of 871	4.6%
Fifth Class	28 out of 529	5.3%	50 out of 704	7.1%
Sixth Class	99 out of 699	14.2%	32 out of 771	4.2%

While these figures may be promising at first glance, there are some important caveats. Firstly, the Black characters were always secondary or background characters. Secondly, the way in which Black children were portrayed is sometimes problematic. In *Bua na Cainte 1,* one of the main characters, Liam, is Black (and accounts for the very high percentage of appearances of Black children at this level). However this is marred by the fact that both stories which focus mainly on his character result in negative experiences. In the first story (p. 15) he puts/spills paint on the wall (the text says "Chuir sé ..." which means 'He put' but the illustration suggests it was an accident) and laughs about it. This results in the teacher becoming cross. He is then disciplined and warned not to do it again. In the second story (p. 24), he spills milk and again the teacher becomes angry with him. This is in contrast to stories that focus solely on White characters. Oisín (the White boy character) is shown in a story wherein he wakes up, gets out of bed, and it's a lovely day (p. 46) and in another wherein he is going to sleep, takes off his clothes, puts on his pyjamas and gets into bed (p. 52). The story that focuses solely on Niamh (the White girl character) talks about her going to the toy shop, buying a doll and being happy (p. 81). Liam is no longer a featured character in *Bua na Cainte 2* but makes one of his few appearances as the winner of a race (p. 52). This could be argued to be in line with stereotypes of Black male athleticism. In *Béal Beo 4*, the majority of the representation is in the context of a trip to Tanzania wherein the White characters go on a safari and visit a Maasai family wearing traditional dress and living in mud huts (pp. 191–192). Additionally, despite the positive representations of Black children and children of other ethnicities in illustrations in the *Abair Liom* series, the content of the actual lessons has not diversified in the same way. For example, in a chapter focused on hair in *Abair Liom D*, the children learn how to say they have blond hair, brown hair, black hair, short hair, long hair, straight hair, and curly hair (pp. 112–117). Yet, they do not learn how to say 'I have braids'. This absence of vocabulary required for Black children to describe themselves is replicated at all levels and indicates that while illustrations may have improved in terms of representation, the actual content of the language being taught has not been examined to ensure that multiple perspectives are portrayed. The text operates from a narrow understanding of what it means to be a child in an Irish primary school classroom and those outside the 'assumed Irish' i.e. those that are not White, settled, Catholic, and English-speaking (Gavigan, 2013) are not facilitated in developing the language they would need to authentically engage in conversation.

Consequences of negative imagery

As argued elsewhere in this volume, the proliferation of negative imagery regarding the African continent has consequences for diaspora African communities. It also impacts upon children who are not part of the African diaspora as they develop understandings that are incomplete, inaccurate, and based upon negative stereotypes. Ruane et al. (2010) found that children as young as three had pre-existing 'knowledge' which connected Africa with the concept of food shortage. One child, Helen, whose family were participating in a child sponsorship scheme in Africa stated "In Africa, nobody can get no food, they have no sheep, no cows ... we have to help the people in Africa" (ibid., p. 93). Teachers of children who participated in the research identified the media as a source of information, reporting that many children had mentioned seeing images of Africa on the television. Ruane et al. (2010) noted that the experiences of children, through child sponsorship schemes and media, may instil an essentialist view that Africa is poor and that Irish society has the means and responsibility to provide solutions. They also noted that there was significant evidence that although the children were very young (between three and six years old), they had already begun to form stereotypical ideas of Africa related to poverty and these preconceptions dominated their ideas of Africa and African people even when they were shown positive images through the research process.

Similarly, in research with seven-to-nine-year-old children, Oberman and Waldron (2017) found that poverty was assumed to be synonymous with developing countries and they perceived the relationship between Ireland and developing countries to be primarily a charitable one. One element of the research involved children examining images, including an image of a Kenyan family eating their main meal of the day. In the follow-up discussion, one child stated "I think it's not fair because, they have a house and they have lots of things. They have things to eat, to sit on and they have things to do they they're not happy. They should be grateful to God" (ibid., p. 10). This perspective was not exceptional among children in the research and indicates that they were operating with the expectation that people living in African countries would only have the materials required for basic survival.

Children's conceptions of Africa were largely essentialised and dominated by images of a place that was ubiquitously poor, arid and where people had to travel far to get water. One child stated that he did not expect people in Africa to have homes while others referenced people in Africa not having food, clothes, bowls, chairs, tables, or radios. The presence of basic facilities in the photo in Kenya led some children to suggest that the image was not taken in Africa, and others to claim that the people in the photo were 'lucky' or must have been helped or have borrowed money to have the provisions shown. Stereotypes such as these impact upon how children interact with Black and African people they encounter in their daily lives. A Black social worker in Ireland in the late 1990s, Zubeda Flaherty during a home visit to a family availing of social services support, was asked by a young member of the family if she was "one of the people we collect the money for in school" (Moroney, 1998). Stereotypes of the African continent, and by association Black people in Ireland, as being somehow deficit have huge implications for the kinds of relationships that develop between people of different ethnicities. It is imperative that these stereotypes are challenged and dismantled as a matter of urgency in order to ensure the building of a cohesive Irish society into the future.

Implications for critical global citizenship education

Teaching young children about their global world helps them to develop a sense of global citizenship. However, as shown throughout this chapter, the choice of information presented and how children are encouraged to think about and interact with the issues, are fundamentally important to this endeavour. Educational materials developed for this purpose should be child-friendly and should portray positive images and perceptions in order to help pupils develop awareness and understanding of both simple and complex global issues. Information relating to the African continent as it relates to global trade and global justice needs to be disseminated in non-violent creative ways that will foster positive perceptions for young children.

Lee and Ryu (2013) found that participants who were exposed to positive information about a region prior to negative information, were more likely to develop a balanced view of that region than those who were exposed to negative information before positive information, even in the context of just one lesson. The exposure to positive messages first allowed pupils to interpret the later negative details in a more nuanced and balanced manner. They recommend that teachers should avoid strengthening students' overly negative regional perceptions, even when studying negative aspects of these regions. This has profound implications for educational textbook publishers and any organisation developing materials that may be used by children. A balanced attitude towards other regions and cultures is essential for true global citizenship. As such, any material claiming to be developed for global citizenship purposes must lay heavy emphasis on the positive aspects of life in the country or region long before addressing any challenges (Young, 2010). Given the fact that Ruane et al. (2010) found that children as young as three already hold negative stereotypes about Africa from family and media, it would be better practice if materials for younger children focused on solely positive messages in an effort to try to balance out the latent negativity already present in their perceptions. This is not to create a rose-tinted ideal of 'developing' countries but rather to ensure a balanced view replaces the solely negative stereotypes that dominate presently.

This also has important implications for the types of media messages to which children are exposed. Given the damaging impact of negative messages on the development of balanced perspectives, advertisements that portray African countries through a deficit lens, such as in NGO fundraising campaigns, cannot be regarded as suitable for young children. The national broadcaster in Ireland, RTÉ, operates a 'watershed' policy i.e. that all programming prior to 9 pm should be suitable for a family audience (RTÉ, 2008). Any advertisement that portrays a solely negative image of a developing country should only be broadcast after the watershed with ethical codes in place to prevent such advertising straying into the arena of 'development pornography'. Similar standards could also be developed for online media. All images of developing countries, especially those that hurt and damage marginalised groups, require strict editorial oversight, and NGOs appealing for donations should advise of how debt, poverty, and unfair trade laws have positioned Africa where it is today (Dóchas, 2014).

Given the damaging effect that these negative messages have, particularly on Black children within Irish primary schools, teacher education programmes should include specific content on this matter in order to tackle stereotypes and negative perceptions held by student teachers themselves. Failure to allow for self-reflection and challenging of their own stereotypes at this stage may result in lack of criticality in choosing educational materials for use in classrooms and consequently negative stereotypes being transmitted to pupils they teach. Similarly, the Department of Education and Skills (DES) and the National Council for Curriculum and Assessment (NCCA) should ensure that in-service teachers are also educated with regard to the unconscious bias they may hold and on how to critically evaluate educational resources before using them in their classrooms.

Conclusion

Short-term gains achieved through the projection of negative images of the African child in war-torn or famine-stricken countries by NGOs continue to perpetuate lifetime discrimination, stigma, inequality, and racism. New ways must be found to reach the public and to more clearly explain the real reasons behind poverty in Africa. Discomforting stereotypical images of Africa as found on fundraising materials, portrayed by the media and used in educational resources for children, should be replaced with balanced and positive representations of the diverse cultural knowledge, skills, and abilities that this continent and its people possess. Educational resources need to explore diversity and the range of perspectives within countries and continents, so that children are encouraged to identify plurality, diversity, and their attendant complexities (Weldon, 2010; Picton, 2008). Actions such as these will help to address notions of Western superiority and systems of racial inequality, thus contributing to the development of a cohesive Irish society imbued with a strong sense of community into the future.

References

Adegoke, D. (2017). Africa and the media. In O. Aknale, & J. Adésina (Eds.), *The development of Africa: Issues, diagnoses and prognoses* (pp. 173–189). London: Springer.

Adichie, C.N. (2009). *The Danger of a Single Story* [Video file]. Retrieved, 13 January 2019, from https://www.ted.com/talks/chimamanda_adichie_the_danger_of_a_single_story.

Akumu, P. (2019, March 3). Charity at heart of 'white saviour' row speaks out. *The Guardian*. Retrieved from www.theguardian.com.

Alasuutari, H., & Andreotti, V. (2015). Framing and contesting the dominant global imaginary of north-south relations: Identifying and challenging socio-cultural hierarchies. *Policy and Practice: A Development Education Review*, 20, 64–92.

Badshah, N. (2019, February 28). 'White saviour' row: David Lammy denies snubbing Comic Relief. *The Guardian*. Retrieved from www.theguardian.com.

Central Statistics Office. (2017). *E7015: Population Usually Resident and Present in the State 2011 to 2016 by Ethnic or Cultural Background, Nationality and Census Year.* Retrieved, 13 January 2019, from https://www.cso.ie/px/pxeirestat/Statire/SelectVarVal/Define.asp?maintable=E7015&PLanguage=0.

Day, P.J. (2013). *A new history in social welfare policy* (7th ed.). Upper Saddle River, NJ: Pearson Education.

Dedeoğlu, H., Ulusoy, M., & Lamme, L.L. (2011). A content analysis of international children's picture books: Representation of poverty. *Eurasian Journal of Educational Research*, 43, 37–52. Retrieved from http://ejer.com.tr.

Dóchas. (2014). *The illustrative guide to the Dóchas code of conduct on images and messages.* Retrieved from https://dochas.ie/sites/default/files/Illustrative_Guide_to_the_Dochas_Code_of_Conduct_on_Images_and_Messages.pdf.

Downes, L. (2016). *Imaging global perspectives: Representations of the Global South in a higher education environment.* Retrieved from http://www.diceproject.ie/research/papers-reports/.

Fanon, F. (1967). *Black skin, White masks* (C. L. Markmann, Trans.). New York: Grove Press.

Gavigan, C. (2013). *Invisible, Inequitable and Intersectional: The Privilege of 'Assumed Irish' Identity in Ireland.* (Unpublished master's thesis). UCD, Dublin.

Hilary, J. (2014). The unwelcome return of development pornography. *New Internationalist.* Retrieved, 5 May 2017, from https://newint.org/features/2014/12/01/development-pornography.

Ingrao, C. (2015). Celebrating our heroes: African-American social service pioneers. Retrieved 13 December 2018, from https://socialwork.simmons.edu/celebrating-heroes-african-american-social-service-pioneers/.

Lee, D.M., & Ryu, J. (2013). How to design and present texts to cultivate balanced regional images in geography education. *The Journal of Geography*, 112(4), 143–155.

Mahadeo, M., & McKinney, J. (2007). Media representations of Africa: Still the same old story? *Policy & Practice: A Development Education Review*, 4, 14–20.

Manzo, K. (2006). An extension of colonialism? Development education, images and the media. *The Development Education Journal*, 12(2), 9–12.

Martin, F., & Griffiths, H. (2012). Power and representation: A postcolonial reading of global partnerships and teacher development through North–South study visits. *British Educational Research Journal*, 38(6), 907–927.

Moroney, A. (1998). Negotiating an island culture: Zubeda Flaherty in conversation with Ann Moroney. *Irish Social Worker*, 16(3), 5–6.

Oberman, R., & Waldron, F. (2017). "They should be grateful to God": Challenging children's pre-conceptions of the Global South through human rights education. *Policy & Practice: A Development Education Review*, 25(Autumn), 9–33.

Picton, O.J. (2008). Teaching and learning about distant places: Conceptualising diversity. *International Research in Geographical and Environmental Education*, 17(3), 227–249.

Rasheem, S., & Brunson, J. (2018). She persisted: The pursuit, persistence, & power of African American women in social work graduate programs at Historically Black Institutions (HBI). *Social Work Education*, 37(3), 378–395.

RTÉ. (2008). *RTÉ programme standards and guidelines*. Dublin, Ireland: RTÉ.

Ruane, B., Kavanagh, A., Waldron, F., Dillon, S., Casey, M., Maunsell, C., & Prunty, A. (2010). How young children engage with issues of global justice. *Trócaire Development Review*, 22, 85–100. Retrieved from https://www.trocaire.org.

Sankore, R. (2005) Behind the image: Poverty and 'development pornography'. Retrieved, 5 January 2019, from https://www.pambazuka.org/governance/behind-image-poverty-and-development-pornography

Sarti, A., Schalkers, I., & Dedding, C. (2015). 'I am not poor. Poor children live in Africa': Social identity and children's perspectives on growing up in contexts of poverty and deprivation in the Netherlands. *Children and Society*, 29(6), 535–545.

Universities Scotland (2013). *Race Equality Toolkit*. Retrieved from https://www.universities-scotland.ac.uk/raceequalitytoolkit/.

Vilenas, S.A., & Angeles, S.L. (2016). Race talk and school equity in local print media: the discursive flexibility of whiteness and the promise of race-conscious talk. In K. Gulson, Z. Leonardo, & D. Gillborn (Eds.), *The edge of race: Critical examinations of education and race/racism* (pp. 36–56). Oxfordshire: Routledge.

Weldon, M. (2010) The wider world. In S. Scoffham (Ed.), *Primary geography handbook* (pp. 205–227). Sheffield: Geographical Association

Williams, C., & Bernard, C. (2018). Black History Month: A provocation and a timeline. *Critical and Radical Social Work* 10(30), 1–30.

Young, H. (2010). Naming the world: Coming to terms with complexity. *Policy and Practice: A Development Education Review*, 10(Spring), 99–104.

Young, H. (2012). African Images and their Impact on Public Perception: What are the Human Rights Implications? Retrieved from https://www.acsoni.org/app/uploads/

Appendix

SESE Textbooks

- Griffin, A., & Sheehy, L. (2015). *Small World. Junior Infants*. Dublin: CJ Fallon
- Griffin, A., & Sheehy, L. (2015). *Small World. Senior Infants*. Dublin: CJ Fallon

- Daly, L., Finn, D., Fletcher, A., & McCarthy, S. (2015). *Small World. First Class.* Dublin: CJ Fallon
- Connolly, C., Fletcher, A., & McCarthy, S. (2015). *Small World. Second Class.* Dublin: CJ Fallon
- Kirwan, D., & O'Hara, M. (2013). *Small World History. Third Class.* Dublin: CJ Fallon
- Boyle, M., Fanning, K., & Hurley, M. (2013). *Small World Geography and Science. Third Class.* Dublin: CJ Fallon
- Dundon, A. (2015). *Small World History. Fourth Class.* Dublin: CJ Fallon
- Boyle, M., Fanning, K., & Hurley, M. (2013). *Small World Geography and Science. Fourth Class.* Dublin: CJ Fallon
- Ó Súilleabháin, A. (2014). *Small World History. Fifth Class.* Dublin: CJ Fallon
- Boyle, M., Fanning, K., & Hurley, M. (2014). *Small World Geography and Science. Fifth Class.* Dublin: CJ Fallon
- Brennan, E. (2014). *Small World History. Sixth Class.* Dublin: CJ Fallon
- Boyle, M., Fanning, K., & Hurley, M. (2014). *Small World Geography and Science. Sixth Class.* Dublin: CJ Fallon
- Lewis, S., & Lewis, R. (2013). *Unlocking SESE. Junior Infants.* Dublin: Folens
- Lewis, S., & Lewis, R. (2013). *Unlocking SESE. Senior Infants.* Dublin: Folens
- Lewis, S., & Lewis, R. (2013). *Unlocking SESE. First Class.* Dublin: Folens
- Lewis, S., & Lewis, R. (2013). *Unlocking SESE. Second Class.* Dublin: Folens
- Lewis, S., & Lewis, R. (2013). *Unlocking SESE. Third Class.* Dublin: Folens
- Lewis, S., & Lewis, R. (2013). *Unlocking SESE. Fourth Class.* Dublin: Folens
- Lewis, S., & Lewis, R. (2013). *Unlocking SESE. Fifth Class.* Dublin: Folens
- Lewis, S., & Lewis, R. (2013). *Unlocking SESE. Sixth Class.* Dublin: Folens

Gaeilge Textbooks

- Ní Fhátharta, M., & de Brún, S. (2016). *Bua na Cainte A.* Dublin: An Comhlacht Oideachais
- de Brún, S., & Ní Fhátharta, M. (2016). *Bua na Cainte B.* Dublin: An Comhlacht Oideachais
- Ní Fhátharta, M., & de Brún, S. (2016). *Bua na Cainte 1.* Dublin: An Comhlacht Oideachais
- de Brún, S., & Ní Fhátharta, M. (2016). *Bua na Cainte 2.* Dublin: An Comhlacht Oideachais
- de Bhaldraithe, B., Ní Dhóibhlin, S., Ní Mhacdha, Ó., & Ní Thiarnaigh, Á. (2015). *Béal Beo 3.* Dublin: An Comhlacht Oideachais
- de Bhaldraithe, B., Ní Dhóibhlin, S., Ní Mhacdha, Ó., & Ní Thiarnaigh, Á. (2015). *Béal Beo 4.* Dublin: An Comhlacht Oideachais
- de Bhaldraithe, B., Ní Dhóibhlin, S., Ní Mhacdha, Ó., & Ní Thiarnaigh, Á. (2015). *Béal Beo 5.* Dublin: An Comhlacht Oideachais
- de Bhaldraithe, B., Ní Dhóibhlin, S., Ní Mhacdha, Ó., & Ní Thiarnaigh, Á. (2015). *Béal Beo 6.* Dublin: An Comhlacht Oideachais

- Ní Dhúill, A. (2015). *Abair Liom A*. Dublin: Folens
- Ní hAnnáin, M. (2015). *Abair Liom B*. Dublin: Folens
- Mhic Craith, A. (2015). *Abair Liom C*. Dublin: Folens
- Ó Conghaile, F., & Pertl, L. (2015). *Abair Liom D*. Dublin: Folens
- MacMathúna, U. (2016). *Abair Liom E*. Dublin: Folens
- MacMathúna, U. (2016). *Abair Liom F*. Dublin: Folens
- Mac Pháidín, D., MacMathúna, U., Mac Giolla Seanáin, P., Ní Choinne, M., Ugán, K., Bhreathnach, C., & Nic Giolla Phádraig, L. (2017). *Abair Liom G*. Dublin: Folens
- Mac Pháidín, D., MacMathúna, U., Mac Giolla Seanáin, P., Ní Choinne, M., Ugán, K., Bhreathnach, C., & Nic Giolla Phádraig, L. (2017). *Abair Liom H*. Dublin: Folens

7 Translating critical thinking into meaningful action

Sandra Austin

Introduction

The issues encountered in global justice education are often not easily defined; the processes involved may be difficult to untangle, and there may not be practicable solutions available. Some educators take trade justice as their focus; they demonstrate the impact of trading rules and trading relationships on livelihoods in African communities, and they argue for sustainable and just solutions to global poverty. Other educators are preoccupied by the persistence of negative stereotyping of the Global South in Northern classrooms and highlight how such views can become reinforced through fundraising campaigns and representations in school textbooks. In 1973, Horst Rittel and Melvin Webber identified what they termed as 'wicked problems' of social policy (Rittel & Webber, 1973). These are problems with no definite formulation, where each problem is essentially unique, and each can be considered to be a symptom of another problem. This notion of 'wicked problems' may be a useful one when considering the concerns under discussion in this book: issues such as trade justice or North/South relations have a factual and historical dimension, but they also have affective and ethical dimensions in that they involve perceptions, attitudes, and deep understandings. Learners need skills and competencies to navigate all of these. Students should have the opportunity to develop and practise the skills that will enable them to discuss and critically reflect upon matters they engage with in classrooms, and ultimately to take ethical action as informed global citizens.

Young people are increasingly showing interest in issues that will have an impact on their own lives and on the future of the planet. Trade justice may be one of these concerns, and we have seen the growth of the FairTrade movement in recent times. We have also witnessed the effectiveness and global reach of Greta Thunberg's school strike initiative on climate change. Many young people learn about the Sustainable Development Goals (SDGs), with other programmes such as BBC's Blue Planet bringing the impact of plastic pollution of the marine environment to the fore in public consciousness in the UK and Ireland. Education has a part to play and it must empower students to think more clearly about such matters and give them the skills to address them when they encounter such situations now and in the future.

This chapter will argue that the ability to think and engage critically with global justice issues is greatly enhanced when a ***culture of inquiry*** exists in a classroom, and where ***participatory pedagogies*** are the norm. I will further argue that critical thinking is merely the first step, and that true critical engagement includes meaningful action informed by understanding, which flows naturally from a process of inquiry.

A geographical view

Although the issues at stake within global justice education encompass a wide range of topics and curricular areas, throughout this chapter much of the focus will be through the lens of geography education, for a number of reasons. First, my own perspective is that of primary geography education, since that is what I do. My views are also coloured by my background in science, and as a White European female who has lived and worked in the USA and UK, I recognise a need to mediate larger global concerns in classrooms and learning spaces of the North. For example, an issue such as plastic pollution cannot be understood purely as a technological or environmental one, but also as one that encapsulates deeper questions about consumerism, inequality, and exploitation.

Second, it is often within the geography curriculum that learners encounter global justice issues, particularly at primary level. 'Trade and development issues' is a strand unit for fifth and sixth classes in the Human Environments strand of the Irish Primary Geography curriculum (DES/NCCA, 1999) in which children explore a wide variety of issues, including FairTrade, issues of inequality between the 'developed' and 'developing' world, and the work of multinational aid organisations. A strand unit on 'Living in the local community' for junior classes provides a platform for the investigation of diversity and inclusion, social responsibility, and citizenship. Geographical skills, knowledge, and understanding can have lifelong influence on learners, particularly when critical thought and active involvement are nurtured in the classroom (Norman, 2017). Geography prepares young people to "make sense of their world, and to face the challenges that will shape our societies and environments at the local, national and global scales" (Geographical Association, 2009, p. 13).

Furthermore, geographical inquiry skills – questioning, observing, predicting, investigating and experimenting, estimating and measuring, analysing, evaluating, recording and communicating – all of these are uniquely positioned to be of particular use in untangling the complex issues of global justice. As Roberts makes clear, while inquiry skills may be developed within many subject contexts,

> geography can make a major contribution to their development because of the range of questions it addresses, its varied sources of information presented in different formats, sometimes from different viewpoints, and its use of different analytical and interpretive techniques.
>
> Roberts (2017, p. 8)

The point of learning about distant and different places – for example, students in Northern classrooms learning about African countries or learning more generally about the Global South – must be more than just knowing something about somewhere else. First and foremost it must involve an ethical and equitable 'knowing'. We see the world "from here rather than there"; our knowledge of the world is always from a certain standpoint (Allen & Massey, 1995, p. 2), and when this concerns the Global South, those views are often situated in deficit thinking. Therefore when students engage in global justice education, it must also involve learning something more about themselves and expanding their ways of knowing, perceiving, and understanding. Students can become aware that their worldview is just one among many (England, 2015), and that no knowledge is neutral. Geography learning can empower children and young people – making possible their agency, participation, and action.

From powerful knowledge to transformative learning: Curriculum and pedagogy in global justice education

Over a decade ago, Michael Young coined the term 'powerful knowledge', describing it as knowledge that empowers learners to think beyond the limitations of their own experience, and arguing that the main purpose of schools is to teach such knowledge (Young, 2008, 2009). Young differentiates between academic and everyday knowledge, where academic knowledge is characterised by structure, coherence, rationality, and systematic organisation, and is therefore authoritative. Everyday knowledge is personal, unformed, and unsystematic, and is therefore naïve. This concept is hotly debated, particularly with regard to what kinds of knowledge are powerful.

Catling and Martin (2011), for instance, make the case that children bring to the classroom their own powerful geographical knowledge (naïve and partial, perhaps, but based on their experience of the world) and this should be recognised and valued in dialogue with "authoritative" (or academic) subject knowledge, not as subservient to it. It is the dialogue that is critical to learning and understanding.

Learners, no matter how young, each bring their life experiences, their ideas, their understandings of the world, and how it works to the classroom. It is well-recognised that children's understandings of the world are also strongly influenced by their lives beyond the classroom, by their family and home life, by the media, both traditional and social, to which they are exposed (Borowski, 2011; Oberman, Waldron, & Dillon, 2012). All of these shape children's perceptions of the world beyond their immediate experience.

These understandings may be problematic, in that they may be rooted in thinking which privileges a white, Eurocentric worldview. Equally, it is important to note here the extent to which we as educators reflect upon the academic knowledge we present to learners, and how much we question our own assumptions and worldviews when planning content for teaching and learning. It is through challenging these perceptions, through a dialogue that acknowledges both academic and everyday knowledge, and holds both up to the light of interrogation, that we help learners to develop the intellectual tools to critically assess both, and it is in the interplay between the two that learners' understandings of the world may be challenged and reshaped.

It is essential to give learners the chance to challenge, articulate, reflect upon, and test their own ideas so that they can evaluate their truth and utility in the world. This calls to mind Barnes' argument that learners often operate as if there are two boxes of knowledge in their head, one for the action knowledge they use in their everyday lives, and one for the knowledge they learn in school (Barnes, 1976). The question is how to integrate the two boxes, so that their 'knowledges' are grounded in an authoritative geographical foundation that incorporates an understanding of political, economic, and historical processes, and so that learners are using their (now ethical and informed) action knowledge both inside and outside school.

Maude (2016, 2018) encourages us to identify powerful knowledge not by what it is like, or how it is produced, but by ***what it can do*** for those who have it. Knowledge is powerful if:

> it enables young people to discover new ways of thinking; to better explain and understand the natural and social worlds; to think about alternative futures and what they could do to influence them; to have some power over their own knowledge; to be able to engage in current debates of significance; to go beyond the limits of their own experience.
>
> Maude (2018, pp. 180–181)

Knowledge is no longer merely information, an accumulation of facts, but is reconceptualised as understanding, and as the basis for informed action. By giving learners the opportunity to articulate, justify, and test their ideas, and to collect and analyse data, they are then supported to revise their ideas and formulate a new hypothesis, to change their understanding of the world, and to act accordingly. It is only in this way, through testing and evaluation of ideas and concepts through a lens of global justice that knowledge can lead to transformation. Transformative learning, in which the learner's ideas and actions undergo a fundamental and enduring change, is powerful learning, and powerful learning requires a powerful pedagogy. It may be about "identifying opportunities in the curriculum to engage students with concepts in ways they might not previously have considered" (Maude, 2016, p. 70).

Why inquiry?

Engaging with global justice issues requires certain skills and dispositions – the ability to 'unlearn'; to engage in deep reflection and self-questioning. The focus of this chapter is on the kind of pedagogical approach(es) that might embody such deep practices as self-reflexivity and self-questioning, ultimately with a view to being an empowered and engaged (active) global citizen.

Margaret Roberts argues that education must move beyond critical thinking, which is underpinned by "a commitment to reasoned rationality", in order to engage in critical pedagogy, which is "concerned with the potential emancipatory power of reasoned thinking and is underpinned by a commitment to equality and social justice" (Roberts, 2015, p. 56). Critical pedagogy encourages debate, dialogue, and critical literacy. It requires students to probe underlying assumptions, to subject all evidence, no matter how widely accepted, to critical scrutiny. These are key skills indeed, particularly in the context of effective global justice education.

If they are to understand global issues, learners must explore, navigate, and untangle a complex web of cultural and material processes (Andreotti, 2006). So, educators must provide learners both with the skills and the learning environment that will empower them to do this. Students are more likely to become critical thinkers if educators have established a culture of critical enquiry in which they are constantly expected to ask questions, scrutinise data, and consider the extent to which evidence supports claims and conclusions (Roberts, 2015). Roberts' view of learning, influenced by Vygotsky, is that students need to be actively involved in the construction of knowledge, and that this can be achieved through incorporating dialogue and an inquiry approach into one's pedagogy. Inquiry skills are powerful because they enable students to interrogate, analyse, and interpret information (Roberts, 2017).

If global justice education is to move beyond curricular subjects, if it is to permeate a teacher's practice across the curriculum and into the whole school, the use of an inquiry approach to explore, break down, and address complex issues, whether scientific, geographic, social or historical, is essential. Inquiry-based learning encourages – in fact, demands – deep, critical thinking; the deconstruction of currently held assumptions and preconceptions; the gathering and analysis of information/data; formulation of new understanding, which, I would argue, moves us to action.

Inquiry as a stance for approaching critical pedagogies in classrooms

Inquiry requires more than "simply answering questions and getting the right answers. It engages, interests, and challenges students to connect their world with the curriculum" (Kuhlthau, Maniotes, & Caspari, 2015, p. 4). Through inquiry, students are motivated to question, explore, and formulate new ideas about issues that they find personally relevant.

Inquiry, real inquiry, is not just a process or methodology. Kath Murdoch describes it as a way of being (Murdoch, 2015); Kathy Short describes inquiry as a stance on curriculum, which is as much about *how* we live as learners as it is about *what* we learn (Short, 2009).

A stance of inquiry invites us as educators to change our thinking about learning, and about our role in the classroom. When working through inquiry, teachers and learners are collaborating in a process of 'curriculum-making', defined by the UK Geographical Association as a "creative act of interpreting a curriculum specification and turning it into a coherent, challenging, engaging and enjoyable sequence of teaching and learning" (Geographical Association, 2019, para. 1). Thus the shift to an inquiry culture in the classroom is not subtle; it may in fact be seismic.

Inquiry recognises the co-learning that takes place between teachers and students as they engage in their investigations. It is, by its nature, a participatory process. If teachers remain the ones who pose the problems then students never fully experience inquiry. Teachers often fear handing over control to their students, but students need to know how to determine what is significant and worth pursuing – they need to be able to 'question the questions', to find which problems matter and are worth solving. Thus we must support teachers, both during initial teacher education and continuing professional development, to embrace the inquiry approach. At Marino Institute of Education we have recently developed a Master of Education Studies in Inquiry-based Learning (MES-IBL) to help address this issue and I will return to this later in the chapter.

Inquiry is a collaborative process "of connecting to and reaching beyond current understandings" (Short, 2009, p. 12). As we reach beyond, we need collaborators to challenge us to outgrow ourselves. "Inquiry takes place in participation, not in individual minds. It is a way of being *in* the social world, not just coming to know *about* that world" (Short, 2009, p. 18). Thus, inquiry is enhanced by involvement with a community of learners, each learning from the other in social interaction.

A stance of inquiry encourages us to wonder and question. It is a conceptually based approach to curriculum, where knowledge and information are tools to explore conceptual understanding rather than ends in themselves. To even begin to identify and address the critical issues of our time, such as sustainability, climate change, racism, discrimination, and global interdependence, both children and adults need to be able to think conceptually, combining creativity and analysis. In the section below, I will outline a framework for inquiry through which these skills can be developed.

The inquiry cycle

There are many different descriptions of what constitutes a cycle of inquiry (see, for example Murdoch (2015) or Roberts (2013)), but I find Kathy Short's framework particularly useful in the context of social justice. It is both comprehensive and flexible, and each stage of the process highlights competencies and understandings relevant to social justice issues/thinking/conceptualisation. Short uses her inquiry cycle framework for planning and implementing curriculum. She terms it an 'authoring' process, as the learners author or construct meaning for themselves as they move through the cycle (Short, 2009).

There are nine stages to the inquiry cycle as outlined by Short (2009) – connection, invitation, tension, investigation, demonstration, revision, representation, valuation, and action – and movement between each of these phases is fluid and multidirectional. Above it all is a requirement for the teacher or educator to keep in their vision the particular concept or 'problem' which will underlie the inquiry – for example, human rights, interdependence, power, fairness/unfairness. I will now outline how global justice issues might be investigated through the framework of Short's inquiry cycle.

Earlier in this chapter I highlighted the importance of integrating the academic and the everyday worlds of the learner. Thus, each inquiry begins with a point of **Connection**, linking the concept under inquiry with the life experiences and understanding of the learners. Short (2009), for example, describes the beginning of a human rights inquiry. Children might struggle conceptually with understanding the concept of *rights* as the *needs* we have as human beings in order to live in a society (Amnesty International, 2003). Thus to begin, children might explore fairness and unfairness as they experience these in their lives (e.g. at lunchtime, in the playground, in their housing situations, etc.). Students might create a 'fair map' and an 'unfair map' of their school, marking the places where they have experienced 'fairness' or 'unfairness'; these could then be discussed, providing a conceptual understanding of human rights as something relevant to their own lives and communities, rather than something that is distant and abstract.

When beginning a workshop on trade justice with my own students in initial teacher education, we often start by counting the number of coffees on classroom tables, then discussing the students' experience of the campus coffee shop as a place to relax and meet friends, and how that differs from the coffee shop as a workplace, before moving on to an exploration of coffee as a commodity and its trade journey. Similarly, a class survey on favourite chocolate bars may serve as a prelude to a chocolate Bean-to-Bar inquiry, such as the one in the Just Connections, Just Trade module (Larkin et al., 2018). Thus, an inquiry into value chains and profit share is personalised to the learner's own life and experience.

This moves naturally into an **Invitation** to learners to go beyond their current understandings by immersing themselves in a number of engagements or provocations to expand their knowledge, experiences, and perspectives. The learners are tuning in to the inquiry, exploring a range of materials relevant to the issue to be explored. The purpose of this is manifold. Primarily it is to enable learners to pose meaningful inquiry questions (it is hard to question something you know little about), and also to expose them to a range of information, ideas, concepts, and views about the topic or concept they are going to investigate. For instance, with the coffee inquiry, students were provided with reference texts about the *Coffea* plant, its life cycle and ecology; a globe; several adverts about coffee (TV, print); images of coffee plantations, harvesting, transport, processing; texts, video, and web links related to the history of coffee and coffee production from different perspectives (e.g. Coffee Association, FairTrade). Whenever they encountered something that puzzled or intrigued them, or that they wanted to find out more about, students were encouraged to post questions on a shared "Wonder Wall", which was used to decide what lines of inquiry to pursue.

At this point, the inquiry is guided by the teacher, who provides access to resources and experiences that are related to the inquiry focus. This brings a responsibility not only to select resources wisely and but also to present these in ways that encourage the learners to engage critically with them. It is preferable to set aside the textbooks, and instead engage with a variety of sources beyond the norm, that challenge stereotypes that can arise when working from a single source (see Table 7.1). Be creative in providing photos, newspaper articles, storybooks, audio and video interviews. However, this requires learners to question the narratives behind the images and stories presented (*Who is telling this story? What is their viewpoint?*), and learners may need to practise

Table 7.1 Some useful online resources to provoke inquiry

Newspapermap *Newspapermap.com*	Local and national newspapers from across the globe presented on a map for easy searching. Enables learners to compare local and international perspectives, to access local viewpoints, to hear the 'voice on the street'. Articles are automatically translated to English via Google Translate.
Worldmapper *Worldmapper.org*	A collection of world maps, called cartograms, where the spatial geometry of the map is distorted to reflect a theme, such as wealth, rainfall, or oceanic conditions. A useful introduction to issues of cartographic representation. Developed by Benjamin Hennig at University of Oxford (Hennig, 2011).
Follow the things *Followthethings.com*	An open access research output designed to resemble an online store. Few of us know who makes the things we buy. Occasionally there's a news story, a documentary film, or an artwork showing the hidden ingredients in our coffee, T-shirts, or iPads. This site brings these works together and allows you to access them.
Global Dimension *Globaldimension.org.uk*	This platform brings together resources, case studies, and background information to help teachers and other educators bring a global dimension to their work.
DevelopmentEducation.ie *www.developmenteducation.ie*	Online resources to stimulate debate and discussion about global justice issues.
Centre for Global Education *www.centreforglobaleducation.com*	A comprehensive collection of teaching and research resources on global issues for all sectors of education.
Proudly Made in Africa *www.proudlymadeinafrica.org/education/*	Ireland-based and other general exercises for learning about African countries. The education section has a range of resources for secondary/tertiary levels for exploring African countries and trade and global links.
Irish Aid Teaching and Learning Resources *www.irishaid.ie/teaching-and-learning/*	A wide variety of global education resources for all levels.

'putting themselves in the picture' to develop these skills. Learners must also learn to distinguish between observation and inference (*What does the picture actually show,* and *What assumptions am I making about it?*). Stories and narrative are powerful tools in enabling young children to engage with abstract or complex issues, to put themselves in someone else's shoes, to begin to consider an issue from multiple perspectives. When choosing resources, it is useful to bear in mind best practice with regard to the use of images and messages, as advised by Dóchas and others (Fiedler, Gill, O'Neill, & Pérez-Pinán, 2008; Dóchas, 2019). Choose resources that challenge stereotypes, that focus on what people have in common as well as celebrating diversity. Seek out resources that incorporate young people's voices, that link actions to consequences, that elicit positive responses rather than provoking pity or disempowerment. Provide students with information about the resources you select – who produced them, when and why. Encourage them to question the perspectives and motives behind the resources they examine, so that they can begin to identify bias, inaccuracy, or omission.

As students expand their understanding of the inquiry focus, they begin to identify **Tensions** – wonderings or issues – that are significant and compelling for them and that they want to investigate further. This signals the shift from teacher-guided to student-driven inquiry. Working with Master of Education in Inquiry-based Learning students recently, an inquiry into 'place affordance' (as in, the opportunities for learning afforded by a particular environment) was centred on a field trip to the National Gallery of Ireland. Before the visit, I provided students with access to the gallery's website and visitor documentation, invited them to watch videos and read research articles about children's learning in cultural spaces, and I provided them with Abigail Hackett's framework for thinking about experience of place (Hackett, Procter, & Kummerfeld, 2018). From this invitation, several students identified tensions they were keen to explore which I could not have fully anticipated – questions about disability and access, about audience demographics and exclusion, about the intended versus actual use of public space, about who makes the decisions regarding what art is displayed. While I had hoped to encourage thinking about the social dimensions of the gallery, through the range and variety of the resources I had provided, I found that by giving the students the freedom to identify their own tensions the quality and diversity of the questions was far richer than had I chosen the direction of the inquiry myself. By relinquishing control, by allowing students to find the problems that mattered to them, I as a teacher was enabled to step outside the narrow frame of my own understanding, to be impacted by alternative views and diverse perspectives. Furthermore, the students felt more ownership of the inquiry because they identified, and could pursue, the questions that mattered to them.

These wonderings were then used as the foundation for a number of different **Investigations** undertaken by the students. In the investigation phase, learners may work collaboratively, in partnership or in small groups, to investigate in-depth a particular issue or question. The focus is on unpacking complexity.

These investigations will look different in every classroom, and are difficult to determine in advance, because they arise from what is significant to students themselves. For example, in the National Gallery investigations mentioned above, students interviewed the gallery's curator, visitor guides, and members of the education team; they requested the gallery's policy documents on access and disability, they designed and delivered a visitor survey, as well as recording their own observations of the gallery space. This reflects the characteristics of critical pedagogy identified by Roberts (2015): students did not accept policy documents or corporate views at face value, but subjected them to critical scrutiny and rigorous questioning. Once again this highlights the value of inquiry-based learning in empowering learners to challenge the accepted view, to weigh the evidence and make critically informed decisions. These inquiry skills, developed here in a local context, can be used similarly to analyse more complex and sensitive issues in future investigations.

The key role of the teacher is to provide support for students to structure/organise their investigations, to make sure that learners do not get sidetracked, or lose sight of the research question they are investigating. There is a balance to be struck between giving students the freedom to follow their own investigations, and providing gentle guidance, through discussion and dialogue, to ensure those investigations are meaningful. There are fundamental critical-thinking skills that learners need to practise and develop if they are to avoid uncritically accepting bias and stereotype. It is important for the teacher, particularly in school settings, to monitor sources of information, drawing attention to potential bias. For example, certain vulnerable groups, including travellers, minority ethnic groups, migrants, and asylum seekers and refugees, may be depicted in a pejorative light in some newspaper articles. During an investigation, the teacher might **demonstrate** research strategies, such as note-taking or internet searching, to support students to develop a critical lens in their investigations. This could be something as simple as deciding upon the reliability of an information resource. For example, when researching a newspaper article on world chocolate shortages (Martin, 2018) for Bean-to-Bar activities, learners could grapple with the following key questions:

- What is the story here? *Rising temperatures are affecting growth of cacao trees. Demand for cocoa already outstrips supply. Chocolate supplies could run out.*
- Whose perspective am I seeing? *The expert quoted is an agribusiness consultant (maybe for companies such as Mars, Hershey, Nestlé) How might that perspective differ from a farmer's perspective? From a local cooperative member? From a local manufacturer?*
- Who has something to gain from this story? *Chocolate manufacturers will be able to demand higher prices from consumers if product is in short supply. Who will benefit from this? Depends on where the chocolate is manufactured; if the chocolate is manufactured in Europe, then the value is stripped from the growers and the farmers/communities don't gain anything.*

- What are the facts? *Most cacao is produced in West African countries such as Ghana and Côte d'Ivoire, and rising temperatures could reduce the amount of land suitable for its production. However, African and Northern scientists are working to develop varieties with increased disease resistance* (Schmitz & Shapiro, 2012; Andres et al., 2017). *Cacao is also grown in several other places around the world, including the Caribbean, India, and Australia.*
- What questions do I have? What do I need to understand? *Is there a link between climate change and disease? What do the farmers of Ghana and Côte d'Ivoire have to say? What is being done to alleviate the problem?*

Throughout the process of inquiry, it is vital that students have opportunities to pull back and reflect on their learning. This **re-visioning** helps them to make sense of what they are learning, to connect new ideas with their thinking, to create new understanding that will guide them in their inquiry. For instance, during the Bean-to-Bar inquiry, students working on particular investigation questions may have an opportunity to present the data they have gathered to date and to open it up for questioning, which may lead them to shift the direction of their research. This re-visioning may also prompt them to probe more deeply, to ask more substantial questions, to look beyond the superficial. When looking into chocolate production, they may decide to visit websites from local producers, or to invite speakers from non-governmental organisations such as Proudly Made in Africa.

Public **representation** of the fruits of their investigation enables learners to recognise how much they have learned as well as what they still need to know. These representations can take many forms, from drama to petitions to posters or reports. Presenting what they have learned to an audience allows learners to reflect on what is of value from their learning for themselves and for the world. This **valuation** gives them the opportunity to reposition themselves in the world. This in itself may be sufficient **action** arising from the inquiry, or it may drive further inquiry or wider action. For instance, children from the International School, Bologna, wrote an article detailing their inquiry into how they could apply the UN Global Goals for Sustainable Development (SDGs) and saw it published in Primary Geography (Whittle & ISB Grade 3 pupils, 2016). At Balbriggan Educate Together School, an inquiry into human rights and the nine grounds for discrimination in Irish law, as outlined in the Equal Status Act (Government of Ireland, 2000) led to children holding a referendum on whether they thought the school could be better at preventing unfairness or discrimination against any of the groups affected (Pike, 2016, p. 165). Recently, students at two Irish schools petitioned the Minister for Justice not to deport their classmates (Clarke & Pollak, 2018; McMahon, 2018). In both cases, the petitions led to the deportation orders being revoked, and in one case the school went on to receive a humanitarian award from the Irish Red Cross (Red Cross Award for Tullamore College, 2018).

From critical thinking to informed action

Thus far, I have argued that action must be informed by understanding, and that this understanding must be grounded in ethical inquiry. I have demonstrated that at times, this inquiry needs to be subtly guided by the teacher so that the sources used for research and investigation are situated in justice perspectives. I have also highlighted how sources/resources can be critiqued and evaluated as part of the inquiry process itself. In this section I will now outline some of the reasons why I believe action is a necessary element of global justice education.

Firstly, as outlined above, thoughts and ideas become understanding *through* action; real learning transforms not only our thinking but also our behaviour. Simpson highlights that a social justice mentality also encompasses outward action, defining it as "a commitment to equality – a developed critical or independent thinking that results in ethical action" (Simpson, 2017, p. 91).

Action is empowering; it shows how we as individuals can make a difference. Taking climate change as an example, The Cambridge Primary Review (Alexander & Hargreaves, 2007) stated:

> Pessimism turned to hope when witnesses felt they had the power to act. The children who were most confident that climate change would not overwhelm them were those whose schools had replaced unfocused fear by factual information and practical strategies for sustainability.
>
> (p. 44)

Everything depends too on our view of children, of their capabilities and competence. The UN's Convention on the Rights of the Child (UN General Assembly, 1989) recognises the right of children to participate in decision-making about issues that involve them. Anne Smith makes the point that if children are viewed as citizens, "they are respected, treated as capable and responsible people, and thus encouraged to participate in and make contributions to community life" (Smith, 2010, p. 103). This comes with acknowledgement of their strengths and capabilities/competencies.

Recognising young children's capabilities

Grappling with complex issues at primary school level is a challenge. Fran Martin (2007) points out that teachers may fear that the global dimension will be beyond children's grasp. Teachers may fear that global education may bring matters of unfairness and injustice, which are beyond children's control, to their awareness and attention, and that this may give them a sense of powerlessness and helplessness in the face of large problems. We must be conscious against, as David Sobel warned, prematurely asking children "to deal with problems beyond their understanding and control … [recruiting them] to solve the mammoth problems of an adult world" by teaching them too abstractly, too early (Sobel, 1996, p. 5). Abstract and complex problems may also evoke simplistic responses to world issues.

Gaynor (2016), for example, cautions against equating activism with consumerism ("shopping to save the world", ibid., p. 78).

Yet, Grunsell makes clear that children deserve to know that their fate is inextricably linked to and affected by the lives and decisions of others around the world. They have a right to understand the crucial issues facing the planet and to know they can personally play a part in helping shape the future (Grunsell, 2007).

Where does a teacher begin when faced with a question like "How can I make a difference to such a problem?" This is an even bigger question when that 'problem' might concern unjust trade relationships, misrepresentation of people through media images, racism, stereotyping, or misuse of the environment, or climate change. The challenge is how to equip young people to grapple with these questions for themselves in such a way that they also develop an understanding of the entitlement they and others have to social justice. Defining what social justice means at a global scale is not a simple matter. So, we must recognise and build on children's capabilities in ways that are appropriate to their age and experience. We must begin to nurture inquiry skills by choosing issues with which children can identify, that have relevance and meaning in their lives and worlds.

Bruner's view was that "any subject can be taught effectively in some intellectually honest form to any child at any stage of development" (Bruner, 1977, p. 33). In other words, even complex ideas can be made accessible. Indeed, Oberman, Waldron, and Dillon (2012) developed a global citizenship education programme for 3 to 6 year olds, which identified suitable strategies for, and challenges to, engaging young children with global citizenship education. Using specially developed materials such as a stimulus storybook, character puppets, and a variety of photographic images the programme addressed stereotypes about Kenya and the everyday lives of Kenyan people.

Similarly, numerous examples of how young children are able to propose ways in which places can be improved and sustained can be found in Pike (2016) and Catling & Martin (2011). Whether it is displaying the school communities' rights and responsibilities, improving their local environment, or considering how to make their school more inclusive, children can see problems, offer solutions, and are keen to get involved in making the changes themselves. At the time of writing this chapter for example, the student council at a primary school in Greystones, Co., Wicklow, prompted the school management board and parents to adopt a gender-neutral uniform policy at the school (O'Brien, 2019). Therefore, it is perhaps by first exploring concerns at home that students are better positioned to begin to tackle the complexity of issues on a wider scale/further afield.

Think global, act local?

Pike (2016) demonstrates the meaningful contribution children can make in their schools and communities through inquiry-driven action, and details the ways children value and use their local area, and develop deep connections with their local environment. Children in fifth and sixth classes (10–12 years old) at an urban school in Dublin carried out an investigation into their local area, which included a shopping centre, busy road, and underpass. They came up with their own inquiry questions (including 'What do people think of this area?' and 'Which places should change?'), and they collected data through surveys, interviews, taking photographs, and recording their own and each other's thoughts on the area. They invited members of their local community, and local and national representatives, to a presentation of their findings, including their suggestions on what might be done with the underpass and surrounding area (which was identified as neglected and a no-go area by the children). They were invited to present at local council meetings, leading to a redevelopment of the area around the underpass as a skate park (Pike, 2016). According to Pike, children learn "far more through carrying out an inquiry about an issue that is important to them, and acting on it to facilitate change, than they will from trying to solve all the problems of the world" (p. 179). Pike reminds us that as teachers we can take the idea of children's citizenship into the curriculum "encouraging and harnessing children's thinking so that not only do they learn but they can also take action about things they would like to change" (p. 167). Through this inquiry, the children realised that they had power to affect the decisions that influenced their lives and locality. They grappled with issues of antisocial behaviour, citizenship, and local government.

More recently, teachers participating in the Master of Education Studies in Inquiry-based Learning (MES-IBL) at Marino Institute of Education undertook a variety of local inquiries with the children in their classes. At one school, an inquiry which began with an exploration of the local beach developed into an investigation of marine pollution, littering, and domestic plastic consumption, driven by the research interests of the children. The class organised a local beach clean-up, contributed to a global social media campaign highlighting the issues (#trashtag, #2minutecleanup); they consulted with local businesses to reduce packaging waste and wrote to local politicians to lobby for additional litter and recycling bins on the beach (A. Nolan, personal communication). Thus, what begins as a local inquiry can be a springboard to more global concerns, underpinned by real and authentic understanding because of the local connection. This is an example of an environmental issue, but the same fundamental inquiry process could be used in a social justice context.

Conclusion

In this chapter I have argued that global justice education demands that we not only re-examine the content of what we teach, but more radically, that we also change the manner in which we approach our teaching, our classrooms, and our learners. We can view the learners in our classrooms, however young, as potential change agents, as young citizens, with competencies and capabilities that enable them to evaluate issues, make decisions, and act upon them to bring about a different future for themselves and society.

Inquiry requires us to reframe our thinking about knowledge(s), moving away from knowledge as information, and recognising knowledge as understanding. Inquiry is inherently participatory, critical, and reflective. Inquiry develops all of the skills which have been identified as essential for engaging in global justice education. Inquiry is, however, more than a process or pedagogy; it is a way of being, a stance; a culture within the classroom. Inquiry leads to the development of a community of inquiry, a collaborative community in which multiple viewpoints are recognised and valued.

Indeed, inquiry provides a holistic approach to learning; it is multidimensional, encompassing the self, the local, and the global. It empowers learners to explore the affective and moral dimensions of social justice. David Hicks argues for a "holistic criticality in global education" – meaning that education is about changing both self and society, and that this is what should underpin the global dimension of the curriculum (Hicks & Holden, 2007, p. 30).

Returning to Maude's (2016) definition of powerful knowledge, we can see that the inquiry process supports learners to better explain the world, to think about alternative futures, and, importantly, how they might influence them. Through inquiry, as outlined above, learners may experience new ways of thinking, are given power over their own knowledge, and are empowered to go beyond the limits of their own experience. Thus inquiry learning can be truly transformative, characterised by agency, participation, and action.

Finally, inquiry meets the requirements for teaching *through* social justice (Grunsell, 2007). By planning and taking action for change in their own local community, students are experiencing social justice in action in their own lives. Inquiry leads naturally to action, and that action is meaningful – relevant to the learner, and informed by understanding. Even through small actions we can make a difference, both to ourselves and to world in which we live.

References

Alexander, R.J., & Hargreaves, L. (2007). Community soundings: The primary review regional witness sessions. Primary Review, University of Cambridge Faculty of Education.

Allen, J., & Massey, D.B. (1995). *Geographical worlds*. Milton Keynes/Oxford/New York: Open University/Oxford University Press.

Amnesty International. (2003). *Lift off*. Amnesty International. Retrieved from https://www.amnesty.ie/wp-content/uploads/2016/08/LIFT-OFF-Resource.pdf

Andreotti, V. (2006). Soft versus critical global citizenship education. *Policy and Practice: A Development Education Review*, 3, 40–51.

Andres, C., Gattinger, A., Dzahini-Obiatey, H.K., Blaser, W.J., Offei, S.K., & Six, J. (2017). Combatting cocoa swollen shoot virus disease: What do we know?. doi:https://doi-org.dcu.idm.oclc.org/10.1016/j.cropro.2017.03.010

Barnes, D. (1976). *From communication to curriculum*. Harmondsworth: Penguin Education.

Borowski, R. (2011). The hidden cost of a red nose. *Primary Geography*, 75(Summer), 18–20.

Bruner, J.S. (1977). *The process of education*. Cambridge: Harvard University Press.

Catling, S., & Martin, F. (2011). Contesting powerful knowledge: The primary geography curriculum as an articulation between academic and children's (ethno-) geographies. *Curriculum Journal*, 22(3), 317–335.

Clarke, V., & Pollak, S. (2018, October 11). Offaly student 'overwhelmed' after deportation order revoked. *The Irish Times*. Retrieved from www.irishtimes.com

DES/NCCA. (1999). In Department of Education and Science/National Council for Curriculum and Assessment (Ed.), *Primary school curriculum - geography*. Dublin, Ireland: The Stationery Office.

Dóchas. (2019). The Dóchas code of conduct on images and messages. Retrieved from https://dochas.ie/images-and-messages

England, R. (2015). Countering stereotypes through global learning. *Teaching Geography*, 40(2), 64–66.

Fiedler, M., Gill, B., O'Neill, C., & Pérez-Pinán, A. (2008). *Global dimensions: A guide to good practice in development education and intercultural education for teacher educators*. Dublin, Ireland: DICE Project.

Gaynor, N. (2016). Shopping to save the world? Reclaiming global citizenship within Irish universities. *Irish Journal of Sociology*, 24(1), 78–101.

Geographical Association. (2009). *A different view: A manifesto from the Geographical Association*. Sheffield: Geographical Association.

Geographical Association. (2019). Curriculum-making. Retrieved 25 June 2019, from https://www.geography.org.uk/Curriculum-making

Equal Status Act. (2000). Government of Ireland. Retrieved from https://www.lawreform.ie/_fileupload/RevisedActs/WithAnnotations/HTML/EN_ACT_2000_0008.HTM

Grunsell, A. (2007). Social justice. In C. Holden & D. Hicks (Eds.), *Teaching the global dimension: Key principles and effective practice* (1st ed.) (pp. 82–91). London: Routledge

Hackett, A., Procter, L., & Kummerfeld, R. (2018). Exploring abstract, physical, social and embodied space: Developing an approach for analysing museum spaces for young children. *Children's Geographies*, 16(5), 489–502.

Hennig, B.D. (2011). Rediscovering the world: Map transformations of human and physical space. Retrieved from https://www.springer.com/gp/book/9783642348471

Hicks, D., & Holden, C. (2007). *Teaching the global dimension: Key principles and effective practice*. London: Routledge.

Kuhlthau, C.C., Maniotes, L.K., & Caspari, A.K. (2015). *Guided inquiry: Learning in the 21st century* (2nd ed.). USA: Libraries Unlimited.

Larkin, T., Morris, L., O'Caoimh, C., Muzanenhamo, P., Wilson, B., & O'Toole, B. (2018). *Just connections: Just trade: A teaching resource about Africa*. Dublin, Ireland: Marino Institute of Education, Proudly Made in Africa. Retrieved from https://www.mie.ie/en/Research/Just_Connections_Just_Trade_A_Teaching_Resource_about_Africa/

Martin, F. (2007). The wider world in the primary school. In C. Holden & D. Hicks (Eds.), *Teaching the global dimension: Key principles and effective practice* (1st ed.) (pp. 164–175). London: Routledge.

Martin, S. (2018, January 2). Chocolate warning: Crisis as scientists reveal cocoa bean extinction is on the horizon. *Daily Express*. Retrieved from https://www.express.co.uk/news/science/899114/chocolate-shortage-cocoa-bean-cacao-tree-climate-change-global-warming-extinction

Maude, A. (2016). What might powerful geographical knowledge look like? *Geography*, 101(2), 70.

Maude, A. (2018). Geography and powerful knowledge: A contribution to the debate. *International Research in Geographical and Environmental Education*, 27(2), 179–190.

McMahon, A. (2018, October 26). Eric Zhi Ying faces 'no imminent threat of deportation', says Simon Harris. *The Irish Times*. Retrieved from www.irishtimes.com

Murdoch, K. (2015). *The power of inquiry: Teaching and learning with curiosity, creativity and purpose in the contemporary classroom*. Northcote, Australia: Seastar Education.

Norman, M. (2017). Editorial: Powerful geography. *Teaching Geography*, 42(1), 5.

Oberman, R., Waldron, F., & Dillon, S. (2012). Developing a global citizenship education programme for three to six year olds. *International Journal of Development Education and Global Learning*, 4(1), 37–60.

O'Brien, C. (2019, June 19). Primary school to introduce gender neutral school uniform policy. *The Irish Times*. Retrieved from www.irishtimes.com

Pike, S. (2016). *Learning primary geography: Ideas and inspiration from classrooms*. Oxford: Routledge.

Red Cross Award for Tullamore College. (2018, November 29). *Offaly Independent*. Retrieved from www.offalyindependent.ie

Rittel, H.W.J., & Webber, M.M. (1973). Dilemmas in a general theory of planning. *Policy Sciences*, 4(2), 155–169.

Roberts, M. (2013). *Geography through enquiry: Approaches to teaching and learning in the secondary school*. Sheffield: Geographical Association.

Roberts, M. (2015). Critical thinking and global learning. *Teaching Geography*, 40(2), 55–59.

Roberts, M. (2017). Geographical education is powerful if. *Teaching Geography*, 42(1), 6–9.

Schmitz, H., & Shapiro, H. (2012). The future of chocolate. *Scientific American*, 306(2), 60–65.

Short, K. (2009). Inquiry as a stance on curriculum. In S. Davidson & S. Carber (Eds.), *Taking the PYP forward: The future of the IB primary years programme* (pp. 9–26). Woodbridge: John Catt Educational.

Simpson, J. (2017). 'Learning to unlearn' the charity mentality within schools. *Policy and Practice: A Development Education Review*, 25, 88–108.

Smith, A.B. (2010). Children as citizens and partners in strengthening communities. *American Journal of Orthopsychiatry*, 80(1), 103–108.

Sobel, D. (1996). *Beyond ecophobia: Reclaiming the heart in nature education*. Great Barrington, MA: The Orion Society.

UN General Assembly, Convention on the Rights of the Child. (1989, November 20). United Nations, Treaty Series, vol. 1577, p. 3. Available at https://www.refworld.org/docid/3ae6b38f0.html (accessed 24 June 2019).

Whittle, J., & ISB Grade 3 Pupils. (2016). World changers report. *Primary Geography*, 91(Autumn), 10–11.

Young, M. (2008). From constructivism to realism in the sociology of the curriculum. *Review of Research in Education*, 32(1), 1–28.

Young, M. (2009). Education, globalisation and the 'voice of knowledge'. *Journal of Education and Work*, 22(3), 193–204.

Part 3

Intersectionalities

Knowledge justice, race, and education

8 Knowledge justice as global justice

Epistemicide, decolonising the university, and the struggle for planetary survival

Alice Feldman

Introduction

> If the "colour line" was indeed the major problem of the 20th century as articulated by William E B DuBois (1903), then that of the 21st century is the "epistemic line". The "epistemic line" cascades from the "colour line" because denial of humanity automatically disqualified one from epistemic virtue. The epistemic line is sustained by … an imperial reason that reduced some human beings to a sub-human category with no knowledge.
>
> Ndlovu-Gatsheni (2018a, p. 16)

> In our view, to think of social struggles as epistemic struggles is an invitation not so much to study them as objects, but rather to recognize the questions that they pose to our forms of understanding. With this, we aim to instigate an engagement with social struggles that includes not only their relation to economic and political forms of domination … but also their capacity to generate knowledges and reveal the limits of our academic frameworks.
>
> Icaza and Vasquez (2013, p. 684)

What if we considered *knowledge justice* as being a matter of *global justice*? How might principles like "epistemic freedom", "cognitive justice", and "intellectual sovereignty" – along with the international literatures from which they arise – provide new resources for responding to the current crises that threaten planetary survival?[1]

The current moment of far-reaching, impossibly complex and deeply interconnected planetary cataclysms places in stark relief the bankruptcy of Western-centric values, traditions, and interests. Ndlovu-Gatsheni observes that "What the world is facing is a broad 'civilizational crisis' which loudly proclaims that modernity has produced many modern problems for which it has no modern solutions" (2018b, p. 256). He conceives of this as a "double crisis", in which systemic crises, such as the global financial crash for example, are intertwined with epistemic ones. Epistemic crises refer to a critical deficit of knowledge, and in particular, a lack of a *diversity* of knowledges.

They therefore constitute both the *causes* of these emergencies as well as the *obstacles* to their resolution. But how is such a "deficit" possible? How do knowledges disappear?

This question speaks to Adichie's (2009) warnings about "the danger of a single story", but on a planetary scale. As Ndlovu-Gatsheni has identified, the "story" in this case is the story of modernity. The epistemic crisis surrounding it is, itself, a systemic one. The "singularity" of this story arises in the wider global histories and legacies of Anglo-European colonialism, modernity, and Eurocentrism. These phenomena evolved to form a knowledge architecture that Grosfoguel (2013) argues is delimited by only 6% of the world population (i.e., by White men from just a few Anglo-European countries, as he is fond of saying). It exemplifies the ways in which the story *particular* to the white, Western, Anglo-European worldview has been imposed as "the" story of how the world should be understood, judged, and inhabited.

How, then, is this a matter of injustice? Throughout the past five centuries, the epistemic violence from the *universalisation* of this worldview has operated to displace, usurp, and render unviable knowledges of those subjugated by Anglo-European conquest, colonisation and imperialism. The single story of Eurocentrism became a hegemonic knowledge system that wielded such power that scholars are increasingly using the term "epistemicide" to capture the magnitude of this phenomenon (Lebakeng, Phalane & Dalindjebo, 2006; Grosfoguel, 2013; Fataar & Subreenduth, 2015; Ndlovu-Gatsheni, 2017, 2018a, 2018b). Within the colonial enterprise, epistemicide operated through genocides that would eliminate the *sources and practices* of diverse knowledges. And through the forced assimilation exacted under colonial rule that exterminated the *ways of life*, *being*, and *knowing* from which they arose.

That Eurocentrism continues to hold sway today, deeply implicates Westernised education institutions in the perpetuation of epistemicide. The "epistemic racism" (Maldonado-Torres, 2004) and "cognitive injustice" (Santos, 2007) woven into the research, teaching, and institutional structures of Westernised universities have robustly and purposefully generated a "manufactured absence" of world knowledges that continues today (Fataar & Subreenduth, 2015). The architecture of Eurocentrism has maintained such a "deathgrip" (Darder, 2016, p. x) that epistemicide is reproduced even within educational institutions in the Global South, in countries long having achieved their independence from Western European colonial rule. Centuries of epistemic imperialism have not only contributed to the global injustices that now define the present moment, but also the lack of access to sufficient knowledge resources necessary to transform them.

What, then, is the link between the work of knowledge justice and social justice? There is, of course another side to this story. While the histories of Western modern/colonial epistemicide are long and far-reaching, those of survival, resistance and transformation tell different stories. They not only draw attention to the continued "presents" of coloniality, but they embody the transformative and decolonising potentials of knowledge renascence and mobilisation in the recuperation of personhood and the remaking of worlds. Such knowledge interventions turn on "moving the centre" (Ngũgĩ, 1993). As Ngũgĩ observes,

> "there could never be only one centre from which to view the world but that different people in the world had their culture and environment at the centre. The relevant question [is] therefore how one centre relate[s] to other centres ..." (1993, p. 9).

Re/cultivating and indigenising silenced knowledges through embodied experiences and histories function to "pluriversalise" (Mignolo, 2011) the knowledge landscape and thus *de-centre* Eurocentrism. This process is a cornerstone of epistemic justice. Walking through the corridors of the average university, however, it seems to be "business as usual", as if these stories do not exist. It appears that no such epistemic crises exist in the academy.

As a White cis-woman from New York whose postgraduate studies in the 1990s at Arizona State University involved indigenous peoples' religious freedom and sovereignty movements, I took for granted the diversity of the academic staff and the curricula there. Moving to Europe with the expectation that I was relocating to the "belly of the beast" in terms of it being the origin of global coloniality, I was shocked to find such an endemic level of colonial amnesia. Moving to Ireland, I was shocked to find myself in such a white society, that was also underpinned by a profound colonial amnesia, and working in such a white university. I found that, despite its own experience of British colonialism, the country had enthusiastically embraced Europeanisation and, in contrast to other post-decolonialisation nations and other peoples who have sought to reclaim their indigenous traditions. The very longstanding history of the participation of Irish people in British colonialism and in religious colonisation, particularly in Africa, is a story largely un-known (see Feldman, 2018). As such, my scholarship here has largely focused on the question posed to most migrants, but particularly in relation to African and black Irish living on the island, *Why are you here?*

In 2015 at the height of the "boat migration crisis", I saw a call for papers for a law conference entitled *Europe's Shared Burden: Collective Responsibility for Migrants at Sea*, that sought to explore the debates concerning the "willingness" and potential "collective responsibility" of European states "to share in the burden of saving lives at sea". I inquired about the title, but it seems that the reference made to Kipling's book, *The White Man's Burden* was not a "conscious" one. That, and coming across one course reading list too many that consisted of all White men moved me to initiate a Decolonising the Curriculum (DtC) Platform in association with a new MA Race, Migration and Decolonial Studies at University College Dublin (UCD). The invitation to contribute to this volume gave me an opportunity to reflect more deeply on the #RhodesMustFall movement (#RMF) engaged in 2015 by students at the University of Cape Town, and which galvanised DtC and Decolonising the University movements across Britain.

Much of my research and teaching over the past many years has been influenced by indigenous, race critical, and decolonial scholarship originating in the Americas.

The present inquiry led me to a cohort of African scholars who are advancing decolonial analyses of African and South African universities and higher education. The concentration of work on the subject of epistemicide that the African literature imparts inspired and coalesced my thinking around my own decolonial knowledge work and its link to the focus of this book. In the face of the current planetary epistemic crisis, and the ongoing "work" of Western colonial Eurocentric epistemicide to eradicate the very knowledges –and peoples and ways of life – desperately needed in this struggle, I am moved to ask the question, What happens if we conceive of epistemicide as a crime against humanity and the planet?

This chapter presents a necessarily brief engagement with the ideas, histories, contexts, and issues provoking and arising in these propositions. It sketches a cartography of three overlapping knowledge-political histories and landscapes that I critically explored in order to develop a more dynamic frame for engaging with and in contemporary mobilisations for epistemic justice within the university. The first section considers key dynamics that underpin the epistemicidal architecture of Eurocentrism and how Western scholarship functioned in the contexts of Anglo-European conquest and colonial rule, particularly in relation to Africa. The second overviews some of the indicative African scholarship that critically analyses the ongoing influence of colonial rule and Eurocentrism in the reproduction of epistemicide in contemporary African and South African universities. And the third charts the ways that projects of Africanisation – of knowledges, disciplines, and universities – have intertwined with anti-colonial, anti-apartheid, and post-independence movements, creating the ground for #RMF. The chapter closes with some reflections on the idea of knowledge justice as a matter of global justice, and the implications of #RMF for the Irish context.

I am extremely conscious of the impossibility of engaging these infinitely vast, complex, and contradictory landscapes with any kind of degree of adequacy -- and the perceived arrogance, ignorance, and/or overambition of taking on such a task. What I hope to accomplish here is to map a conceptual journey that has begun, for me, to illuminate, contextualise, and analyse the critical coordinates of knowledge-political mobilisations as they inform decolonial possibilities and practices. The narrative that follows only gestures towards how this work may proceed, and, hopefully, provides gateways for readers to explore, through the authors and scholarship cited herein.

Eurocentrism and the "Invention of Africa": An idea becomes a science

> Man is a story-making animal. He rarely passes up an opportunity to accompany his works and his experiences with matching stories. The heavy task of dispossessing others calls for such a story and, of course, its makers … Let us imagine that someone has come along to take my land from me. We would not expect him to say he is doing it because of his greed or because he is stronger than I. Such a confession would brand him as a scoundrel and a bully. So he hires a story-teller with a lot of imagination to make up a more

> appropriate story which might say, for example, that the land in question could not be mine because I had shown no aptitude to cultivate it properly for maximum productivity and profitability. It might go on to say that the reason for my inefficiency is my very low I.Q. and explain that my brain had stopped growing at the age of ten.
>
> Achebe (2000, pp. 59–61)

> It began with an "idea of order".
>
> Pearce (1953, p. 3)

By the time Columbus set sail in 1492, Europeans had a very clear idea of the constitution of their "civilisation". The genius of the Greek and Roman philosopher kings was their direct inheritance. Christianity anointed them "the chosen people" with divine rights to holy war and conquest over all infidel-other-enemies. The Great Chain of Being emplaced them within the planetary hierarchy between God and the "natural" world. After two hundred years of Renaissance human-ism they rose forth, phoenix rising, from the "Dark Ages" into a period of limitless human self-actualisation in and through the Arts and Sciences, to be reborn in 1490 in the form of Davinci's ***Vitruvian Man***: the embodiment of human perfection, perfectly proportioned and rendered through mathematics, science, aesthetics, at the centre of the universe. White and cis-gendered male and European (although they did not yet call themselves Europeans). "Whereas modernity gestated in the free, creative medieval European cities, it came to birth in Europe's confrontation with the Other" (Dussel, 1995, p. 12). Maintaining white Anglo-European civilisation as the planetary epicentre would fundamentally always require the violence of conquest, both physical and metaphysical. It would, thus, always be constitutive of the modernity that defined and was defined by it. Within this worldview, the self-determined, human existence of any-other-body was not a possibility.

> It appears to me that the people are ingenious and would be good servants, and I am of opinion that they would readily become Christians, as they appear to have no religion ... I could conquer the whole of them with fifty men and govern them as I pleased.
>
> Log entry, Christopher Columbus in Las Casas (1989, n.p.)

Anglo-European expansion and conquest in the late fifteenth century merely provided an opportunity for the maturation of this already existing Eurocentric worldview: one that began with the denial of the humanity of others and their construction as the anti-thesis of the White "civilised" European, to the point of being banished into ***non-being*** (Fanon, 1967). Characterised as "one of the great ideological deformations of our time" (Amin, 2010 in Ndlovu-Gatsheni, 2017, p. 17), Eurocentrism is anchored by the cornerstones of white supremacy, Evolutionism/Developmentalism, and Dualism (Dussel, 1995). These would, in turn, combine to give rise to a self-authorising knowledge architecture that created the means of reproducing a "universal" world order based on inherently racist dispositions, proclivities, and mythologies. The "New World" was thus less a discovery than a covering-up (ibid.): the centre required a periphery; the civilised required a savage; the future, a past.

Colonialism was thus not only a process of Anglo-European expansion on a physical level, but also a "mode of knowing and representation" (Andreotti et al., 2011, p. 323). Both projects were intertwined. The dispossession of knowledges, and its associated disavowal of humanity, functioned to legitimise the dispossessions of lands (Nyamnjoh, 2012). The loss of lands and the ways of life they sustained, in turn, further reinforced the "proof" of the superiority of European "civilisation". What became known as scientific racism involved the mapping of racial differences onto existing conceptions of planetary order through the natural science methods of classification (Rattansi, 2007). Categories were created based on phenotypical differences and hierarchised through the lens of white European supremacy. "Theories" of human development were extrapolated and projected onto this hierarchy accordingly, and the lines between "human" and "not-human", "civilised" and "savage", "being" and "non-being" were drawn. Scientific racism and its further incarnation in the form of Social Darwinism thus constituted the originary "social science" of Eurocentrism.

This pseudo/science subsequently provided the basis on which to rationalise and legalise the theft of lands (see Williams, 1990). The construction of "the Savage" fed Hobbes' treatises on the "state of nature" and legitimate governance. Locke's theories of property were based on the distinction that people who had not subjected to development the lands in which they lived had no claim to them, and they were therefore free to be "appropriated". Such ideas served as the basis for the legal principle, *terra nullius* (nobody's land), which redefined the lands of indigenous peoples as "empty", as a result of the determination that the people "occupying" them were undeveloped. This evolving body of "law" informed the rise of the Westphalian and international nation-state systems and their associated definitions of sovereignty, self-determination, and "peoples". And it was this framework of dominion which drove the European colonial powers to divide the African continent among themselves for settlement at the Berlin Conference of 1884, the avariciousness of which was so flagrant, that this is commonly referred to as the "Scramble for Africa".

Inventing Africa

How did the epistemicide of Eurocentrism function to *usurp* the knowledges and histories of Europe's "others"? What is the relationship between the extermination of knowledges and of peoples or cultures? With what consequences? Mudimbe's (1989) book, *The Invention of Africa,* provides an excellent genealogy that charts how Eurocentric mythologies were "factualised" through Western social sciences and humanities scholarship in order to legitimise Anglo-European conquest. This history of knowledge also illustrates the ways layers of narrative constructions formed what are now considered the "canons" of Western knowledge: Their genesis arising initially from the tales of Anglo-European explorers and travellers, followed by missionaries, soldiers and colonial administrators, artists and writers, philosophers and idealists, eventually to anthropologists and social scientists.

The interconnected and mutually reinforcing spheres of thought and practice in the disciplines of Art and (white) African/Africanist Studies, according to Mudimbe, formed the basis on which the social scientific cartography of categorical hierarchisation proceeded. Here, trade in African art and artifacts created a vehicle for Europeans to "theorise" "the African" and African cultural production in both "disciplines" through the theory of Primitivism. Artists' renderings generated visual representations of their interpretations of difference, to which White Western Africanists then attributed theories of cultural and physical variations. For example, in response to the need to account for how "the Native" could produce such valuable art, these scholars "theorised" that critical conscious apprehension was not a necessary condition of creativity: "the Native" could be "visceral" without being "intellectual". A second theory was that the art must simply have been done by others, which Mudimbe notes, was extended to many other facets of African existence, such as agriculture, astronomy, and so on. In this way, Anglo-Europeans fashioned a cartography of a racialised Eurocentric lifeworld order by theorising Africans so as to fit within the parameters of the non-human. This generated a structure of what Said (1978, p. 15) has referred to as "flexible positional superiority". That is, no matter what quality "the Native" can be attributed, positive or negative, it can be "explained" in a way that always assigns superiority to the coloniser.

Thus, the persistence of white supremacy hundreds of years following the "Dark Ages" is not (or should not be) surprising. For example, Hegel could state as a simple, almost common sense, fact that the "opacity" of Africa and the lack of "consciousness" possessed by "the blacks" demonstrated that Africans have

> not yet even arrived at the intuition of any objectivity, as for example, of God or the law, in which humanity relates to the world and intuits its essence ... He [the black person] is a human being in the rough ... This ... explains the fact that it is extraordinarily easy to make them fanatics. The Reign of the Spirit is among them so poor and the Spirit in itself so intense ... that a representation that is inculcated in them suffices to impel them not to respect anything and to destroy everything ... Africa ... does not properly have a history. For this reason, we abandon Africa, we will mention it no more. It is not part of the historical world; it does not present movement or historical development ... What we understand properly of Africa is something isolated and lacking in history, submerged completely in the natural spirit, and mentionable only as the threshold of universal history.
>
> Hegel (1830), in Dussell (1995, p. 22)

Dussel reminds us that such founding principles of Hegel's extensive work on human development would be passed on to Marx and from there to economics and sociology, and all the disciplines and subdisciplines yet to come.

Mudimbe observes that much of what constituted social science at this time involved the simple transcription and codification of artistic representations of difference into and through the lexicon of Social Darwinism. Here, theological, biological, and anthropological destinies were mapped onto conceptual themes of evolution, conquest, and difference, to be plotted within the racially hierarchised social order (1989, p. 30). Its novelty, he argues,

> resides in the fact that the discourse on 'savages' is, for the first time, a discourse in which an explicit political power presumes the authority of a scientific knowledge and vice-versa ... [A]nd the development of anthropology, from an archive of travellers' tales as a clearly visible power-knowledge political system

one which anthropologists envisioned they would serve (ibid., p. 29).

Thus, regardless of the particularities of the theory, "all repress otherness in the name of sameness, reduce the different to the already known, and thus fundamentally escape the task of making sense of other worlds" (ibid., p. 85). Despite variations in the extent, style, or form of modern/colonialist Eurocentric scholarship, Mudimbe argues that the

> methodological rules remained essentially the same: ...evolutionary, or functionalist, and still imply that Africans must evolve from their frozen state to the dynamism of Western civilization. The policies of applied anthropology had taken the view of colonialism and focused on African structures in order to integrate them into the new historical process.
>
> (ibid., p. 89)

In tandem with the "empty land" legal principle of *terra nullius* that legalised dispossession, Eurocentric strategies of social scientific erasure and usurpation created "empty" spaces for imagination, discourse, and possibility. Such conceptual space was thus available to be filled with an unbounded array of myths and fantasies – of sea monsters, and savages, and salvation. No longer would these be just the dreams of explorers, missionaries, travellers, but the "universal" "truths" of scientists. They became the staples of hegemonic social and human sciences: "deviance", "dependency", "disadvantage" – the very conditions of the global structures of inequality they have co-created and sustained. Mudimbe argues that it is this "epistemic determinism" that constitutes the "unity" of social sciences. Its conceptual and empirical force, and the institutionalised structures of Western academic practices that have grown up around it, that are what have given epistemicide such a long and healthy life in contemporary universities, in now-independent African states and around the world.

Epistemic racism, knowledge dependency, and the persisting coloniality of South African universities

> Berlin of 1884 was effected through the sword and the bullet. But the night of the sword and the bullet was followed by the morning of the chalk and

> the blackboard. The physical violence of the battlefield was followed by the psychological violence of the classroom.
>
> Ngũgĩ (1986, p. 9), in Ndlovu-Gatsheni (2018a, p. 25)

Whether historically white schools or black, the objectives of colonial education in South Africa were the same: maintaining the colonial order through training White elites to rule, and Black people to be ruled (or later, to rule themselves as assimilated independent states) (Heleta, 2016). Exploring the genealogy of this colonialist formation illuminates the ways epistemicide operates as a profound form of institutionalised racism in the contexts of education, particularly in the university. "Epistemic racism", the disregard of peoples' "epistemic capacity" (Maldonado-Torres, 2004, p. 34), and "cognitive injustice" (Santos, 2007), the refusal to recognise different ways of knowing and the parity among different knowledges, combine to form university cultures characterised by knowledge deficit and dependency (Lebakeng, Phalane & Dalindjebo, 2006; Fataar & Subreenduth, 2015; Nyamnjoh, 2012). These dynamics are further reinforced by international academic regimes, which have contributed to the persistence of epistemicide and coloniality long after the end of apartheid rule.

Drawing on Mignolo's (2009) concept of "null pedagogy", Fataar and Subreenduth (2015) observe that it operates on

> the idea that African teachers and students possess limited cognitive capacity, and little to no critical intellectual processing skills and capacity ... [Teachers] are viewed in deficit terms as bearers of pathology, as unsophisticated readers, as professionals who can only manage simple transfer pedagogies, while African children are viewed as uncritical knowledge consumers ... [and African] cultural ontological make-up renders them preponderant for rote-learning, formalistic pedagogies and tightly scripted curricula.
>
> (pp. 113–114)

The result is the use of curricula that emphasise basic literacy and numeracy skills and vocational or domestic training that serve "the colonial extractive project by underplaying the critical questioning that a more intellectual upbringing would have encouraged" (Nyamnjoh, 2012, p. 135). This type of curriculum also functions to devalue and supplant indigenous African histories, cultural practices, forms of creativity, and agency (ibid.). This further undermines the subjectivities, experiences, and bodies of African students and contributes to their sense of "internalised inadequacy" (Nyamnjoh, 2012, p. 138). As such curricula that do not reflect learners' realities "continue to be a source of alienation" (Lebakeng, Phalane & Dalindjebo, 2006, p. 73). This in turn cultivates extreme xenophilia, reflected in, for example, African exchange students downplaying their home institutions and professors while they are in the North "as they shop up for recognition by their European counterparts" (Nyamnjoh, 2012, p. 138).

Nyamnjoh (2012) argues that the legacies of conquest and coloniality have created an educational culture that "has tended to emphasize mimicry over creativity, and the idea that little worth learning about, even by Africans, can come from Africa" (p. 129). He points out that this leads to the production of scholarship that is ultimately "derivative", "imitative and uncritical" (ibid., Lebakeng, Phalane & Dalindjebo, 2006). Research is characterised by a lack of creativity and originality in relation to the methods of inquiry and analysis because it is alienated from the issues of central importance to indigenous society and the lived experiences of the majority of the population (ibid., p. 73). The situation becomes worse when African scholars are dependent on "an exhausted intellectual tradition and social science that is no longer useful in the analysis of the social world in general and African experience in particular" (ibid., p. 74). "Even the most explicitly 'Afrocentric' descriptions" argues Mudimbe, reproduce a Eurocentric frame (1989, p. 10). For Lebakeng, Phalane, and Dalindjebo (2006) this is indicative of the ongoing "mental captivity" of coloniality.

However, entrenched inequalities in the generation of educational content, opportunities, and attainment across different ethnic groups continue to reward those favoured by the colonial system, ensuring the systematic underdevelopment and underqualification of the majority Black population (Nyamnjoh, 2012; Heleta, 2016). This, however, is underpinned and made further problematic by the

> long-standing asymmetrical division of intellectual labour [that] sustains epistemic hegemony. In this context African scholars have largely functioned as "hunter-gatherers" of raw data as well as "native informants". Europe and North America have remained sites to process raw data into concepts and theories. These concepts and theories are then consumed in Africa. Africa remains a large laboratory for testing of concepts and theories.
>
> Ndlovu-Gatsheni (2018a, pp. 20–21)

Hountondji's "indices of scientific dependence" clearly map the breadth and depth of this structure of knowledge dependency (1990, pp. 10–13 in Ndlovu-Gatsheni, 2018a, p. 34):

- dependence on Northern technology, libraries, centres, and European languages, and importation of theory from the North to enlighten the data gathered in the South;
- research topics determined by Northern interests; aversion to basic research in favour of the colonial ideology of the instrumentality of knowledge and disciplined to fit Western modes of science even when focusing on indigenous knowledges
- specialisms confined to those that require African scholars in roles as native informants; brain drain from constant "institutional nomadism" of African scholars towards Northern universities; lack of communication among African scholars in favour of "vertical" North–South exchanges;
- reproduction of mediocrity which makes it justifiable to look for competent scholars in the North.

The epistemic hegemony of the Global North is internationally sustained through one-way, non-reciprocal institutional relationships. For example, because leading journals and publishers are based and controlled by academics there, Prah (1998) observes that "African academics who succeed in penetrating such gate-keeping mechanisms have often done so by making serious sacrifices in terms of the perspectives, methodologies and contextual relevance of their publications and scholarship" (Prah, 1998, pp. 27–31, in Nyamnjoh, 2012, p. 145). Citations are a one-way affair as African scholars must cite European scholars and scholarship, whereas Western academics are free to ignore theirs. "Cooperation" argues, Nyamnjoh,

> takes the form of North American and European universities calling the tune for the African pipers they have paid. Collaborative research has often worked in the interest of European and North American partners who, armed with assumed theoretical sophistication and economic resources.
>
> Nyamnjoh (2012, p. 145)

This often reduces the African partners' contributions to lesser and tokenistic roles and outcomes.

Apartheid accelerated and deepened the entrenchment of colonial Eurocentric education to maintain the dominion of the White minority population (Heleta, 2016). Historically black universities contributed to apartheid objectives and policies through the colonialist training of Black teachers and administrators. White, English-medium universities had a contradictory relationship with the apartheid state. Heleta (2016) notes that while universities constructed themselves in opposition to apartheid, they were funded by the government and were "islands of white privilege that benefited apartheid's policies" (ibid., p. 3). While not all Black academics and staff have supported Africanisation, the institutions themselves have played a significant role in thwarting positive change initiated by academics. Two high-profile examples illustrate different dynamics in relation to failures to diversify staff. In 1968, University of Capetown (UCT) was forced by the apartheid government to rescind the offer of a post to Archi Mafeje and publicly announce that no appointments would be made to non-White academics without extenuating circumstances. Nearly twenty years later, Mahmood Mamdani resigned his post at UCT as a result of conflicts resulting from his attempts to Africanise the curriculum (see Nyamnjoh, 2016; Smit, 2018).

In addition to unsupportive cultures for staff, Heleta also draws attention to the disregard by Whites and "middle-class Black, coloured and Indian South Africans" – alongside university administrators, managers, academics, and well-off students – of the everyday realities of poverty, racism, and exploitation of Black students and workers (ibid., p. 6). The lack of "transformation" of universities following the end of apartheid rule is significant. This served to expand the reach of #RMF to issues that ranged across students, staff, and service/support employees. Sitt reported last year that when someone asked Mamdani, who returned to UCT as Honorary Professor of the Centre for African Studies, 'why he had decided to return, his response was simply: "Because Rhodes fell"'.

#RhodesMustFall – Troubling knowledges at the intersections of knowledge, power, and resistance

> It is time to recognize that the norm of human presence in South Africa is "black". That recognition is central to understanding where real agency for shaping the future of South Africa is overwhelmingly located, and where "blackness" becomes so normal it ceases to exist.
>
> Former UCT Vice-Chancellor, Njabulo Ndebele (2016), in Prah (2017, p. 3)

Aside from the universities of Qarawiyyin in Morocco (AD 859) and Al-Azhar in Egypt (AD 972), having the oldest white settlement among African countries and known for its "European character", one of the two oldest "modern" universities on the continent is located in South Africa (Ndlovu-Gatsheni, 2017). Established in 1829, the South African College became the University of Cape Town in 1918. As a result of the early and inherent predisposition for racist stratification among those who would become the Dutch/Boer/Afrikaner ruling regime, it admitted Whites only. Black Africans did not have access to third-level education until the establishment of the South African Native College of Fort Hare in 1916, designed to provide an inferiorised "Bantu" education (i.e. indicating "industrial" rather than "intellectual") (ibid.). While the post-World War Two (WWII) era of decolonisation and independence had arrived for many, South Africa was entering yet another era of colonial rule under the apartheid regime. The country has thus come comparatively late to the projects of desegregation and decolonisation. The #RhodesMustFall (#RMF) movement, itself arising from longstanding histories of anti-colonialist, nationalist, and anti-apartheid movements, revitalised the language and demands of decolonisation in universities in South Africa and around the world. This section shifts to the story of the power of knowledge-political mobilisations in anti-colonial resistance and decolonial interventions, and the interconnectedness of social and epistemic struggles.

Prah observes that, "From the 1880s, the period of the high-noon of imperialist rivalries for colonial territories in Africa … the scramble for Africa, Africans started articulating their rejection of unbridled Westernisms" (2017, p. 17). Until the 1920s, the Eurocentrism of white Africanist social studies precluded the centring of Africanness (Mudimbe, 1989). Mudimbe argues that the emergence of the student-led 1930s Paris-based Negritude movement constituted a "mutation" in both the possibility and the "pertinence of an African discourse on otherness", which inaugured "a new foundation for organizing a plurality of historical memories" (1989, p. 92). The journal *l'Etudiant Noir* vitalised literary mediums for exploring difference as Black African peoples (Mudimbe, 1989; Prah, 2017; see also Sharpley-Whiting, 2002). This in turn, gave rise to greater African involvement in traditional cultural practices and the production of literature written in African languages – a celebration of "the right to name the world for ourselves" (Ngũgĩ, 1993, p. 3). This sea change, in turn, predicted the independence, black consciousness, and Pan-African movements (Mudimbe, 1989; Prah, 2017; see also Blain, 2018), a list to which Ndlovu-Gatsheni adds intellectual ideological developments such as Garveyism, African Humanism, African Socialism, and African Renaissance.

Following WWII, Prah observes that post-war socio-demographics rendered Eurocentric social sciences "inappropriate in the analysis of the contemporary Afro-Asian and Latin American worlds" (2017, p. 17). This period was further marked by

> The definitive entry of descendants of the enslaved, displaced, colonised, and racialised peoples into the existing academies across the world; proclaiming loudly that they are human beings, their lives matter, and that they were born into valid and legitimate knowledge systems; enabled the resurgence of long-standing struggles for epistemic freedom.
>
> Ndlovu-Gatsheni (2018a, p. 17)

The concurrent worldwide civic and student movements in the 1960s around identity politics, civil rights, self-determination, war, anti-colonialism, and freedom of speech brought about significant changes in the epistemological structures of universities (e.g. establishment of "African studies" departments), as well as the internationalisation of Afrocentric philosophies and scholarship. The take-up of empirical sociological methods in African scholarship facilitated the "consideration of the real history of African peoples; in scale ... from the village to national social group" providing opportunity to highlight rather than ignore the role of colonialism (Mudimbe, 1989, p. 23). Marxist analysis opened up topics and levels of analysis relating to the world economic market and capitalist economies, alongside the discussion of liberation movements, class politics, and imperialisms, and created opportunities to connect with Latin American critiques in relation to dependency theory (Mudimbe, 1989; see, for example, Rodney, 1972).

The mobilisation and the impetus of the African independence and decolonization processes in the 1960s deepened the interconnections between intellectual and political projects. The call for the Africanisation of universities occupied a central, albeit, contentious space of debate and change within this wider field of change. The postcolonial university was conceived as "a gift of nationalism" or a "partner" of the African nationalist revolution, that would actively work to cultivate Black consciousness, eliminate and promote pan-African unity (Ndlovu-Gatsheni, 2018b) through "... the transfer of intellectual leadership and administrative authority to Africans" (Mudimbe, 1989, p. 182). In African universities, more African subjects were introduced into curricula, and new oral tradition-based methods were being used in historiography to counter the misinterpretations of colonial sciences. Scholars were actively challenging the constitutions of disciplines and university departments in Nairobi, Ibadan, Dar es Salaam, and Dakar. CODESRIA (the Council for the Development of Social Science Research in Africa) was established in 1973 and brought an avowed, radical left, and uniquely "non-disciplinary" disposition to the issues of social and economic decolonisation (Ndlovu-Gatsheni, 2017). In the Global North many

African Studies Centres were set up not only for intellectual work but also to support Northern governments and NGO-led 'development' assistance programs for African countries (Olukoshi, 2006).

Yet the Africanisation project was also deeply entangled with post-independence nationalist politics and upheavals around leadership and governance. Ndlovu-Gatsheni (2017, 2018b) observes that its transformative decolonising potential was overtaken by the priorities of economic development, nation-building, and the establishment of governmental authority, whereby concerns regarding the demands of international standards and fears of isolation eclipsed issues relating to revolution, consciousness, and academic freedom. Thus, despite this "golden age" he argues that Africanisation and decolonisiation were only achieved at superficial levels, serving more as an induction into the European university regime than a substantial transformation of it. He also outlines an array of factors that, over the next several decades, diminished the role of academics in society and undermined real change in universities: the rise of authoritarian governments and dictatorships, the Cold War, economic crises, and the ushering in of oppressive and marginalising neoliberal regimes for newly independent nations (e.g. structural adjustment programmes), and the neocolonial rule of the World Bank, International Monetary Fund, and other such intergovernmental organisations. Favouring "internationalization over indigenization" brought about the devaluation of university education as a necessary and public good, and its corporatisation and neoliberalisation. This lead to managerialism, precariousness, and emigration of African academics, reduction of access to higher education and inadequate qualifications for students; and the further entrenchment of eurocentrism and epistemicide by elite academics. Despite the promotion of UCT as a "first" or "world-class", "premier university of African scholarship" (Lebakeng, Phalane & Dalindjebo, 2006), little has changed within the "neo-apartheid" system persisting since 1994. #RMF arose in the wake of unfulfilled promises of post-apartheid democracy (Heleta, 2016; Nyamnjoh, 2016; Prah, 2017).

The commencement of #RMF is typically attributed to the event on 9 March 2015 when Chumani Maxwele threw human waste on the statue of Cecil Rhodes (often referred to as the "architect of apartheid"), calling for the statue and other homages to colonial rule to be removed. Students attending the historically black universities had been protesting in the years prior (Jansen, 2017), and several Student Representative Councils across universities also had issued calls (Irvine, 2016). The statute already bore the image of "Remember Marikana", grafittied by the Tokolos Stencils Art Collective to mark the 2012 massacre of striking National Union of Mineworkers members by police. Marikana had become a symbol of post-apartheid failures, but also recalls the history of apartheid violence epitomised by other such events as the 1960 Sharpeville massacre of people protesting policies of surveillance and control of movement, Soweto in 1976 where police killed high school children and others protesting the imposition of Afrikaans in schools; and the Boipatong massacre in 1992 involving opposition politics regarding the Democratic Convention (Thomas, 2018). The profound racism experienced by Black students at white universities that were publicised in the documentary, LUISTER, inspired protests at Stellenbosch University and Elsenburg Agricultural College, followed by #OpenStellies, #WitsSoWhite, #RhodesSoWhite, and galvanised movements in European universities. The subsequent #FeesMustFall at Wits University was taken up across both historically white and black campuses (Trowler, 2018).

In his in-depth study of #RMF, Ahmed (2019) critically explores a triad of praxes underpinning the movement: Bikoism, black Feminist, and Pan-African movements and epistemologies. I briefly touch on them here as an example of a contemporary configuration of the interconnected knowledge-political dynamics and transformations of mobilisation:

> ***Bikoism***'s emphasis on the embodied politics of black Consciousness, where "blackness" is fluid and open while keeping live the tensions surrounding white allyship. This provided a foundation for the dialectic enunciations of "Black pain" and "Black liberation" as central standpoints forming the basis for new forms of Black-led decolonial activism. Central focuses involved the de-mythologisation and disruption of whiteness and white supremacy, and challenging the "Rainbow Nation" discourses of the South African state.
>
> The central role of ***Black Feminism*** and the frame of intersectionality in #RMF was an innovation on previous movements. It required centring and confronting issues of the patriarchy, genderism, homophobia and sexism that continue to undermine the movement participation and empowerment of women and LGBTQ+ people. This complexified discourses around collective engagement and extended the decolonial work of the movement beyond just a focus on Eurocentrism.
>
> ***Pan-Africanism*** enriched the "for-all" dynamic underpinning #RMF, whereby the internationalist outlook also served to centre and trouble the complex machinations of colonialism and borders, identities and belongings, xenophobia and Afrophobia with the movement, as well as the country and the continent. It also created interconnections and complementarities across the diverse contexts and scales of transformation, e.g. the environment (changing names of buildings) with the curriculum; indigenisation with the global project of de-centring Western knowledges.

The challenges made by students speak to not only the failed promises of a post-apartheid democracy, but the fundamental outcomes of a political settlement that ended the regime, but left the structures of inequalities that benefit Whites largely intact (Heleta, 2016). They tap into the extreme social, institutional, and material inequalities that have been carried forward in the legacies of coloniality and apartheid, and accelerated by neoliberalism beyond as well as within the universities. Yet the students also shifted and advanced the discourse from a focus on post-democratic transformation to one of decolonisation (Jansen, 2017).

The cultivation of this knowledge work responded to as well as played out, in and through the tensions of collective mobilisation. The mobilisation of #RMF gave rise to the term, Fallism, which Ahmed (2019) identifies as a "new grammar" that encapsulates the nature of the far-reaching change implicated in #RMF: anything other than the restoration of dignity and humanity decimated by ongoing colonialist legacies "must fall".

Epistemic freedom and the struggle for planetary survival

> Epistemic freedom is fundamentally about the right to think, theorise, interpret the world, develop own methodologies and write from where one is located and unencumbered by Eurocentrism. ... Epistemic justice is about the liberation of reason itself from coloniality.
>
> Ndlovu-Gatsheni (2018a, p. 17)

The brief knowledge-political cartographies I have mapped out in this chapter illuminate the compelling interrelationships between systemic and epistemic struggles, and the way global and knowledge justices and injustices are entangled. Through this lens, we see the cartography of Eurocentrism and epistemicide: The denial and disavowal of the humanity of African peoples, and with this, their knowledges and the ways of life in and through which knowing arises; The coloniality of being through the instantiation of racist, self-authorising pseudoscience as the basis of all knowledge and education yet to come; The erasure of African histories and overwriting of African existences, and with this, the imposition of a global systemic knowledge deficit, dependency and underdevelopment in their place; The legitimation of a world geopolitical system called forth by the universalisation of White, Western, European supremacist human and planetary hierarchies through discursive and material dispossessions. The cultivation of these knowledge violations are intertwined with the structural violences of racial subjugation, poverty, and exploitation.

Juxtaposed and intersecting are the cartographies of African/South African anti-colonial and independence movements. These chart the projects of reclaiming humanity and personhood – and the compelling interrelationships between epistemic and political emancipations. They highlight the workings of a decolonising architecture of Africanisation, central to which is the nurturing of embodied, localised, indigenous knowledges. Africanisation embodies Ngugi's notion of "moving the centre", that is, de-centring Eurocentrism by re-instantiating other epistemic and cosmological centres. These acts of creating a "pluriverse" (Mignolo, 2009) of many centres in place of the universalisation of one, transforms the global power relations of knowledge in the process. Thus, the work of "indigenising" knowledge systems multiplies rather than closes down the cultivation of epistemic resources in concert with the ways of living and being they arise from.

Looking northward from the South, from and with the African scholarship and accounts of #RMF illuminates the ways all decolonial projects are pluriversal and necessarily particular to the circumstances and histories in which they arise. Their constitution, aims, strategies (and knowledges!) will differ according to their relationships to, encounters with and inheritances of White, Western, Eurocentric coloniality. The defining dynamic of such knowledge-political projects in the North is that they are directed towards dismantling the(ir own) "centre" – decolonising the colonial centre of Eurocentrism, from within it, by looking outward, through and towards its diversification. A key driving force in #RMF has been the "unfinished business" of transforming the legacies of colonialism, imperialism, neoliberalism, and apartheid.

In the Irish case, – and while the general public would most likely disagree – the "unfinished business" still revolves around its complex imbrications in coloniality. Ireland is caught between its inheritances of being both colonised and colonisers; of being located within both indigenous and Eurocentric cosmologies. These are, of course, naturally overlapping and mutually constitutive. However, Irish people and the Irish state must be accountable to both positionalities, and to their consequences societally as well as globally. As an enthusiastic, card-carrying member of Europe, we must acknowledge and accept responsibility for our complicity in the projects and outcomes of White supremacist, Western colonial Eurocentrism, and in the geopolitics of knowledge injustices they have created and continue to exact.

In the case of university education and the tropes of "global excellence" that are so avidly promoted, this means actively and critically reflecting on and responding to our participation in the reproduction of epistemicide, every day, as administrators and practitioners of "higher" education. From course reading lists, to hiring, to the international industries of rankings and dissemination, we must step up to the project of pluriversalisation. And because the work of shifting the universal centre of Eurocentricism ultimately involves both pluralising as well as "indigenising" knowledges, knowers, and ways of knowing, we may also, in the process, rediscover and shift our own "centre", arising, collectively, from who we have been, who we are becoming, and how we may live in the future, in a world currently in great crisis.

Note

1 See Ndlovu-Gatsheni (2018b), Santos, (2007), and Warrior (1994) respectively.

References

Achebe, C. (2000). *Home and exile*. Edinburgh: Canongate Ltd. Press.

Adichie, C.N. (2009). *The danger of a single story*. [Online] TED.com. Retrieved from https://www.ted.com/talks/chimamanda_adichie_the_danger_of_a_single_story

Ahmed, A.K. (2019). *The rise of fallism: #RhodesMustFall and the movement to decolonize the university*. PhD thesis, Colombia University. Retrieved from https://academiccommons.columbia.edu/doi/10.7916/d8-n7n3-e372

Amin, S. (2010). *Eurocentrism* (2nd ed). New York: Monthly Review Press.

Andreotti, V., Ahenakew, C., & Cooper, G. (2011). Epistemological pluralism: Ethical and pedagogical challenges in higher education. *AlterNative*, 7(1), 40–50.

Blain, K.N. (2018). *Set the world on fire: Black nationalist women and the global struggle.* Philadelphia, PA: University of Pennsylvania Press.

Darder, A. (2016). Forward: Ruthlessness and the forging of liberatory epistemologies. In J.M. Paraskeva (Ed.), *Curriculum epistemicide: Towards an itinerant curriculum theory.* New York/London: Routledge.

Dussel, E. (1995). *The Invention of the Americas: The eclipse and the 'other' and the myth of modernity.* New York: Continuum.

Fanon, F. (1967). *Black skin, white masks.* New York: Grove Press.

Fataar, A., & Subreenduth, S. (2015). The search for ecologies of knowledge in the encounter with African epistemicide in South African education. *South African Journal of Higher Education*, 29(2), 106–121.

Feldman, A. (2018). Re/entangling Irish and Nigerian diasporas: Colonial amnesias, decolonial aesthetics and archive-assemblage praxis. *Cultural Dynamics*, 30(3), 173–198.

Grosfoguel, R. (2013). The structure of knowledge in westernized universities: Epistemic racism/sexism and the four genocides/epistemicides of the long 16th century. *Human Architecture: Journal of the Sociology of Self-Knowledge*, 11(1), 73–90.

Hegel, Die vernunft in der geschichte, Second Draft (1830). In Hoffmeister, J. & Meiner, F. (Eds.), *Samtliche Werke.* (Hamburg, 1955), 231–234; English, 188–190.

Heleta, S. (2016). Decolonisation of higher education: Dismantling epistemic violence and eurocentrism in South Africa. *Transformation in Higher Education*, 1(1), 1–8.

Hountondji, P.J. (1990). Scientific dependence in Africa Today. *Research in Africa Literatures*, 21(3), 5–15.

Icaza, R., & Vasquez, R. (2013). Social struggles as epistemic struggles. *Development and Change*, 44(3), 683–704.

Irvine, T. (2016). *"Rhodes must fall": South Africa's ongoing university student protests against contemporary globalization's neoliberal violence.* PhD thesis, University of California, Santa Barbara. Retrieved from https://escholarship.org/uc/item/8r00w5rr

Jansen, J. (2017). *As by fire: The end of the South African university.* Pretoria, South Africa: Tafelberg.

Las Casas, B. (1989). *The log of Christopher Columbus' first voyage to America.* Cosgrave: Linnet Books.

Lebakeng, J.T., Phalane, M.M., & Dalindjebo, N. (2006). Epistemicide, institutional cultures and the imperative for the Africanisation of universities in South Africa. *Alternation*, 13(1), 70–87.

Maldonado-Torres, N. (2004). The topology of being and the geopolitics of knowledge. *City*, 891, 29–56.

Mignolo, W. (2009). Epistemic disobedience, independent thought and decolonial freedom. *Theory, Culture & Society*, 26(7–8), 159–181.

Mignolo, W. (2011). *The darker side of western modernity: Global futures, decolonial options.* Durham: Duke University Press.

Mudimbe, V.Y. (1989). *The invention of Africa.* Bloomington, IN: Indiana University Press.

Ndebele, N. (2016, September 25). Fire destroys – but it can also forge tools to build the future. *Sunday Times (South Africa).* Opinion, 21.

Ndlovu-Gatsheni, S.J. (2017). The emergence and trajectories of struggles for an 'African university': The case of unfinished business of African epistemic decolonisation. *Kronos*, 43, 51–77.

Ndlovu-Gatsheni, S.J. (2018a). The dynamics of epistemological decolonisation in the 21st century: Towards epistemic freedom. *Strategic Review for Southern Africa*, 40(1), 16–45.

Ndlovu-Gatsheni, S.J. (2018b). *Epistemic freedom in Africa: Deprovincialization and decolonization*. Oxon/New York: Routledge.

Ngũgĩ, T. (1986). *Decolonising the mind: The politics of language in African literature*. London: J. Currey.

Ngũgĩ, T. (1993). *Moving the centre: The struggle for cultural freedoms*. London: J. Currey.

Nyamnjoh, F.B. (2012). 'Potted plants in greenhouses': A critical reflection on the resilience of colonial education in Africa. *Journal of Asian and African Studies*, 47(2), 129–154.

Nyamnjoh, F.B. (2016). *#RhodesMustFall: Nibbling at resilient colonialism in South Africa*. Mankon, Bamenda: Langaa Research & Publishing.

Olukoshi, A. (2006, November). African Scholars and African Studies. *Development in Practice*, 16(6), 533–544.

Pearce, R.H. (1953). *Savagism and civilization: A study of the Indian and the American mind*. Berkley, CA: University of California Press.

Prah, K. (1998). African scholars and Africanist scholarship. *CODESRIA Bulletin*, 3–4, 25–31.

Prah, K.K. (2017, October 20). Has Rhodes fallen?: Decolonizing the humanities in Africa and constructing intellectual sovereignty. The Academy of Science of South Africa (ASSAF) Inaugural Humanities Lecture. HSRC, Pretoria. Retrieved at: https://www.researchgate.net/publication/315684012

Rattansi, A. (2007). *Racism: A very short introduction*. Oxford/New York: University of Oxford Press.

Rodney, W. (1972). *How Europe underdeveloped Africa*. London: Bogle-L'Ouverture Publications.

Said, E. (1978). *Orientalism*. New York: Pantheon Books.

de Santos, B.S. (Ed.). (2007). *Cognitive justice in a global world: Prudent knowledges for a decent life*. Lanham: Lexington Books.

Sharpley-Whiting, T.D. (2002). *Negritude women*. Indiana: University of Minnesota Press.

Smit, S. (2018, June 5). 20 years after the 'Mamdani affair', the old adversary rejoins UCT. *Mail & Guardian*. Retrieved at: https://mg.co.za/article/2018-06-05-20-years-after-the-mamdani-affair-the-old-adversary-rejoins-uct

Thomas, K. (2018). "Remember Marikana": Violence and visual activism in post-apartheid South Africa. *ASAP/Journal*, 3(2), 401–422.

Trowler, V. (2018). Review on Jansen, J. As by fire: The end of the South African University. Pretoria, South Africa: Tafelberg. (2017) *Journal of Student Affairs in Africa*, 6(2), 131–133.

Warrior, R.A. (1994). *Tribal secrets: Vine Deloria, John Joseph Mathews and the recovery of American Indian intellectual traditions*. Indiana: University of Minnesota Press.

Williams Jr., R. (1990). *The American Indian in western legal thought: The discourses of conquest*. Oxford: Oxford University Press.

9 Making sense of race in global justice education

Insights from a racial stratification project in Ireland

Ebun Joseph

Introduction

Knock, knock, knock.
Bimpe the team leader and Siobhan looked up from across the room where they were having a conversation as Eoin walked in.
"Good morning. I am Eoin from IT, I was asked to set up a temporary laptop for the new staff member. Which table will she be using?" *Eoin asked, directing his question to Siobhan.*
"Oh, I am sorry," said Siobhan looking a little uncomfortable. "I am the new staff member and Ms Bimpe is the Manager."
Bimpe didn't react or show her irritation, as she was used to new hires and visitors to the office assuming she was at best a junior staff or the centre's service person.

... *Let's think of another scenario.*

White female business executive (WFBE) *attending a two-day conference walks over to the Black woman standing by the conference meeting room and asks,* "Do I hand you my coat?"
Black female: I'm sorry, I don't work here.
WFBE: Oh, I am so sorry. I apologise for my mistake.

The real question to ask in order to get to the crux of such incidences and why they are problematic is: what is it about this Black person that automatically makes visitors assume they must be waiting staff and not a conference attendee? These kinds of situations are a common occurrence where, for example, visitors to offices and first responders have been known to speak over the head of the Black person at an incident site to address their query to the White body in the room. While this might seem like an ordinary incident and an understandable mistake, we need to question the automatic assumption that they must be junior staff. Is this because of their age, gender, class, race, or something else?

Such experiences are insightful when race is centred in examining our social world. When we try to understand interculturalism and global justice, including how the West trades with Africa and its people and the value it places on African goods, such an enquiry cannot fully take place without an examination of race.

We cannot intervene or truly understand what people need without first understanding the underlying paradigms that marks Africa and Africans out as different or for negative treatment. It will be akin to the notion that if I don't see you then you do not/must not exist. This is like the young person hiding behind a small pole assuming because their eye view is obstructed and they cannot see the other, that the other cannot also see them. That is the colour-blind approach to racial difference which results in silencing (visibly) different groups while they are impacted by the racial order. Despite the growing significance of race in Europe today and despite Ireland's commitment to aid, trade, and development, the dearth of theoretical understanding which centralises race within these fields is egregious. The preparation of educators should commence with an in-depth understanding of race and how society and actors respond to difference for more impactful change.

This chapter thus argues for a Critical Race Theory (CRT) perspective in global justice education that includes a comprehensive understanding of racial stratification, its operation, and effects. When global education and global justice educators do not centre or acknowledge race, they skim the surface without impacting transformative learning. Based on the understanding of extensive empirical evidence from a racial stratification study in Ireland (Joseph, 2018), this chapter discusses the importance of centring race and the implication of the 'default' starting position of the Global South in the world order. The key features of racial stratification discussed within this chapter include its homogenising attributes, the interaction between class and race; how assigned racial groupings influence outcomes; and the hegemonic imaging and representation which reify racism and racial stereotypes. The chapter concludes with a discussion of the implications of racial stratification on the socio-economic outcomes of the African continent and its people, and the race consciousness required to carry out a non-racist, non-Eurocentric examination and engagement with the Global South.

Roots and definitions of race

Race is a problematic, divisive, and heavily contested concept that was constructed for the purpose of maintaining a racial hierarchy. It exists as a signifier of group and individual social status with very real social consequences (Zuberi & Bonilla-Silva, 2008). Race was conceptualised out of and for racial and racist reasons, making it difficult for it to yield good or positive results. The Europeans employed race to emphasise nobility and superiority of some groups, while at the same time depicting the inferiority of the other (Omi & Winant, 1994; Cornell & Hartmann, 1998). Race has been applied as a category imposed by others who use it as a foundation for oppression and discrimination, including the promotion of slavery in America and apartheid in South Africa. One of the most contentious uses of the concept of race is that it often assumes the ordering of racial groups, whereby Africans are inserted at the bottom and Europeans at the top (Zuberi & Bashi, 1997). The way Africans are positioned today has its origin in the hierarchal representation of raced people. Traditionally, race is a comparatively simple idea that is applied to certain outward signs of "social visibility" such as physiognomy (Myrdal, 2000, p. 96). Literature suggests that race also derives from racial systems, or ways of classifying people, usually by judging how closely their phenotype fits with the somatic norm imagery of what the different races 'look' like (Zuberi & Bashi, 1997, p. 669). This ability to categorise the other implies a power dynamic where 'Whites categorise Negros' (Myrdal, 2000, p. 96). Fanon (2000, p. 257) illuminates this point and insists that in the discourse of race, Black people in the global hierarchy become the racial 'Other'.

Undeniably, race is a social fact that shapes the concept of identity and collective representation organising social experience (Winant, 2004). Race is widely employed to socially define and categorise individuals based on their physical characteristics that are not predetermined by biological facts (Cornell & Hartmann, 1998, p. 24). The concept of race has transformed and become even more pejorative in its use to separate people into groups, such as Europeans and others (Spickard, 1992). The taxonomy of race operates in a way whereby the dominant groups exercise the power to stipulate the status and place of the less powerful, thus maintaining their own power, status, and authority (Cornell & Hartmann, 1998). Such classifications usually involve a power relation with racial designations that imply some kind of inferiority. The positioning of White Europeans at the top of the pinnacle, where they were seen as naturally superior to all other races in virtually every aspect, was vital for the imperialist expansion in all parts of the world, including the inception and practice of slavery. "The African thus became the foil against which the English defined who they wished to be" (James, 2008, p. 33). Therefore, how race is employed for the inferiorisation and superiorisation of groups makes it continuously problematic and contentious.

Race in Ireland

Conversations about race in the public sphere in Ireland very often become about Black Africans, asylum seekers, or migrants generally. Yet we are all part of race; the human race. The result is an ambivalence about race and how it either benefits or disadvantages people. Race as we can see is not value free. There is a default identity ascribed to people based on their visible traits which act as racial markers. Despite personal achievement/s, groups are homogenised and ascribed an identity based on what they look like, sound like, or where they are from. Group members are stuck with these positionings until they have either proved themselves to be different from the expected ascribed identity or they are known individually. The onus to differentiate themselves is on the migrant, particularly the visible ones.

Ireland like most countries in the Global North has been found to be a racial (Goldberg, 2002) and a racist state (Lentin & McVeigh, 2006), and also a heavily racially stratified state with a white over black dichotomy (Joseph, 2018). What this means is that Whites are stratified at the top and Blacks at the bottom. From the beginning, the society and education system is socialised by the racial order in the country which teaches and reinforces the deficit model of not only having

Blacks at the bottom but also expecting them to be there as a subservient group of aid/welfare recipients. Even with increasing diversity in society, the labour market in Ireland is still a white space of white privilege that invisibilises difference. This is further complicated by Ireland's relationship with aid where historically, we have made collections for Black babies and Ireland took upon itself the privilege and right to name those Black babies. This disempowering hegemonic process informs the background in which students learn interculturalism and global justice. In one of my black studies lectures, the students began expressing different opinions about the African continent and its people from the one they had been taught through the Irish education system, where Africa is typically portrayed as a continent of poor governance, poverty, famine, and slavery. However, re-educating students in a class that countered the deficit story by teaching about the precolonial government, communities of African countries, its music, contribution to the development in the sciences, food, oil, and pioneering in the arts, placed Africa at the centre of the students' own learning.

In Ireland, race awareness is not emphasised in mainstream education. Race is not generally discussed in society unless in response to problems involving people of black African descent in negative acts, thus making race the face of problems. Although we know society is unequal and hierarchal, from the lack of interventions specifically targeting the issues of people of African descent in Ireland, we can safely say the Irish society is colour-blind. While race is not given much eminence in Ireland, a country with racial categories like white, black or black Irish, Asian or Asian Irish as depicted in the 2016 Census means racial groups are either created, being created, or pre-existing. This is problematic because of who categorises people, the power dynamics involved, the meanings associated with the categories in terms of where, how, and with whom individuals are categorised. All these forms of human categorisation have socio-economic implications, for example, if a country is categorised as EU or non-EU; Third World, developing, or developed; or the new trend of Global North and South – which is a euphemism for poor underdeveloped country. The arrangement of these categories is either flat: that is to say, racial equality, or top-down: signifying a hierarchical ranking. These racial categories are not value free; they influence status, privileges, positive or negative judgements attached to each category, and the challenges this presents to the categorised group and its members. In the Global North generally, racial hierarchies exist where some are at the top and some are at the bottom. More specifically, Whites at the top, Blacks at the bottom. This is a problematic starting point for any group.

Understanding the racial order

Let us start with a simple question asked by Song (2004), what does it matter who is at the bottom or at the top? The only group/s that argues for the insignificance of the positioning of groups is the group at the top. This is because they are advantaged, positively esteemed, and seen as the world leaders in technology, infrastructure, education, and wealth. What this means in practical terms is that in the world order, the European is stratified at the top and Africans at the bottom. In terms of the social sphere, the European is held up as the standard of acceptable beauty, skin colour, hair texture, and femininity, as seen recently in sports where femininity is defined by a Western ideal of what that femininity should look like/be like. We see the court ruling that Caster Semenya has been judged to be too manly to participate in female races. Despite the level of natural resources in the African continent, Africans are not categorised as world leaders or at the top in any sphere of the global economy. Rather, the continent is viewed through a deficit lens. From the period of the Scramble for Africa (Chamberlain, 1981; Koponen, 1993), leaders from the continent were not invited to or involved in the decision-making about how Africa was divided, named, and subsequently plundered, with its resources, both natural and human distributed. For example, its artefacts in foreign museums that European countries are refusing to return while they indulge in mass repatriation of Africans either as failed asylum seekers or illegal migrants. The irony in this arrangement is that the supposedly unprofitable continent of Africa was important enough for the acclaimed world powers to fight over its possessions. Many people do not question how an elite and educated group of leaders scrambled over something without value. Critical race theorists (CRTs) who offer a counter story to this image of Africa argue that if the true value of Africa was acknowledged, if the West paid Africa the true value for both the human and natural resources it has taken and continues to take from the continent, Africa would not need aid (T. Zuberi, public lecture, 15 October, 2015). Rather, the Western world would in fact be indebted to Africa for generations. It has however suited the West to deny the excellence, wealth, and resources of Africa and its people while erasing the epistemological wealth of Africa. It is undeniable that the West is knowledgeable about its own culpability in the imperialist project, which it also tries to deny, rewrite, and even erase.

The result is that the African continent is racially stratified at the bottom of the racial order leaving its products and its people similarly stratified. This affects how the rest of the world views and deals with the African continent and African people. This Eurocentric ordering is one of the main reasons Mills (1997, p. 1) in the racial contract argues that white supremacy is “the unnamed political system that has made the modern world what it is today.”

The nature of racial stratification

Racial stratification is a homogenising system of structured inequality, where an assigned default starting position determines access to scarce and desired resources based on racial group membership (Joseph, forthcoming). Although the biological existence of race has no scientific merit, race is implicated in the way Blacks and Whites are separated to the bottom and top of the economic ladder. It directly and indirectly affects the lives of all people because all groups do not have the same starting point in racially stratified societies. Groups stratified higher up the racial ladder will have easier access to their labour market objectives than those lower down (Joseph, 2018). The levels of difficulty and distance in attaining the same economic goals as those at the top, progressively gets more difficult the further down the ladder a group is positioned. In essence, groups at the very bottom of the ladder have to work harder to achieve the same results as those at the top. This is not because such opportunities/jobs/status demands more, but because those at the bottom have to start from a lower position on the strata, they end up starting with a deficit and in a disadvantaged and incapacitated position. They have to contend with secondary issues which those stratified above them do not have to face. This is the key problem with racial stratification. The challenge is not really where a group is positioned (although it heavily influences both socio-economic and psychological outcomes), but where each group has to start from relative to others on the same ladder. Du Bois' (1903) argument that: "The problem of the twentieth century is the problem of the color line" holds just as true today as it did then. This line refers to the often invisible but sometimes physical divide between races. It is inherently hierarchical in nature and origin, ensuring that Whites receive better treatment, services, and opportunities, while Black people receive little to nothing. Although instituted and established by slavery, the colour line Du Bois referred to in the 1900s survived the Emancipation. It has taken on new forms today particularly with the increase in far-right ideologies, the politics of hate in fortress Europe particularly around election times, and the increasing anti-immigrant sentiments from the 45th President of the United States who has banned immigrants from certain Muslim countries, likened immigrants to snakes, called migrants from Mexico rapists and drug dealers, and disparaging protections on immigrants from African countries and places like Haiti as 'shithole' countries (see Dawsey, 2018).

Racial stratification is not a personal trouble, neither is it an accidental outcome. It is endemic to the structure of labour markets but largely unacknowledged by those in power as the colour-coded hierarchy of the labour market order is not called into question or publicly challenged (Joseph, 2018). Unfortunately, groups stratified at the top of the racial order do not readily admit to the advantages it provides, neither do they recognise the distance their automatic positioning at/close to the pinnacle of the racial ladder imposes on groups positioned below. Racial stratification is like an invisible national identity card that is carried everywhere because it is attached to individuals, groups, countries, and continents. It affects the economic outcomes of groups in a manner over which they have no personal control. By this I mean that assigned racial strata are unchangeable, though group members can change their positon on the economic ladder through personal action. Although race also interacts with other expressions of difference, such as gender and class to influence the socio-economic outcomes of actors and their inter/intra-group positioning, the impact of racial stratification is more common and has become the de facto way society is organised. Notwithstanding Ireland's or even Europe's claim of commitment to integration and equality, we are still doing race as the founding fathers of race intended. That is, instituting actions, policies, lenses, and perspectives that function in ways that guarantee the stratification of Europe, its people, and by-products at the top to maintain the present racial order.

Why class is a problem for raced people

Groups that possess phenotypic whiteness typically see the world from the perspective of class because their race is not a problem, neither does it disadvantage them. Rather, they are beneficiaries of its largess (Joseph, 2019). Many of the champions of race on the other hand typically see the world and how it is structured through race-conscious lenses. As important as class is to Marxists, the racial stratification study I carried out showed people of black African (PBAD) descent in Ireland do not directly name class as a key determinant of their outcome (Joseph, 2015). Class however plays a part in the ascribed status and positioning of migrants on the racial strata on their arrival in Ireland. The first indication of social class as an important factor in where groups are positioned on the racial strata occurred when participants in my study were able to separate Spanish, Polish, and Nigerian migrants onto different layers on a hypothetical arrangement of society (Joseph, 2018). They mainly attributed this arrangement to the gross domestic product (GDP) or perceived wealth of countries represented in the exercise. This is not directly linked to an individual's accumulation of surplus wealth, but to the perceived historical wealth of each race and nationality. In other words, rather than the individuals being classed, the historical social class of the group is by default attributed to the whole group, country, or race in what I describe as '*classed race*.' Each race is classed and then ascribed to group members on arrival as their default racial status and starting position, irrespective of individual achievement or attainment factors such as education or personal wealth. This is possible because society conflates race with nationality and skin colour.

Groups whose race is classed as higher are stratified higher in the labour market, benefiting from similarity with in-group members, and subsequently attaining greater labour market mobility vis-à-vis those whose race is classed as lower. In a similar manner, the class ascribed to the African continent is used to evaluate people of African descent. Many indigenous White Europeans have scant knowledge about the African continent and African people, and their views are typically characterised by stereotypes and negative perceptions. This stems from the definitions and teachings about Africa in Europe as 'Third World', Global South, 'developing' or 'underdeveloped'; speaking about 'slaves' rather than enslaved people. The way in which race is classed and ascribed to groups is not simply due to historical influences but also reflects current views held about group members. The negative publicity and stereotyping of not just migrants coming to take Irish jobs, but specifically of Black Africans as 'free loaders', 'spongers', 'lazy', 'slaves', and other historical imaging has infused society with much negativity about PBAD right from (and before) their arrival on Irish shores.

'Classed race' is problematic because it is predicated on the homogenisation of group members, where they are all expected to be the same, act the same, and have the same outcome. This can be a challenge particularly when group members deviate from their expected group norms. This way of homogenising people allows group members to be held accountable for their race and nationality of descent. Despite the fact that many people do not openly perform racist acts, and the response to race might be expected to be different, the historical racial positioning and prejudgement of different groups is still pervasive though covertly perpetrated. It still functions as the way in which society automatically assigns citizens and newcomers their racial position. This is evident from the parallels we can draw in Ireland from the Census, where PBAD are seen as good for 'care work' and racialised into home/human care roles such as healthcare assistants, home support workers, nursing, and social care workers. This is somehow too close to the racist era and imaging of black exploitation during their enslavement, where they were presented as people who were not suited for intellectual roles, but only good for, and happy to serve as the Help, cleaning homes and caring for other people's families.

Concerning the layering of actors within the broad categories of the white-over-black, European-over-non-European ascendancy, *classed race* separates groups that are similar onto different rungs of the strata. If we take the case of the three migrant groups from my study (Joseph, 2018), the *classed race* of each nationality is employed within the black–white dichotomy to stratify the three White European groups on to different strata, such that the group seen as the 'poorest' are stratified lower. In such cases, actual or perceived wealth (social class), operates as a darkener, as those perceived as poorer country nationals are stratified lower. The *classed race* and the socio-historical status ascribed to different groups does not only affect where its members stand on the racial order, it also influences the share of the State's resources and social status available to them, how their currency is valued and the price the North is willing to pay for their services and [by]products. If like me, you have ever wondered how the world is able to keep its black population stratified at the bottom of both the economic and racial ladder considering that race is not biological, it is because the black race, continent, countries, cultures, knowledge, and, by extension, their economic produce are all classed lower than the white race, cultures, knowledge, continents, and people. Whiteness provides Whites with advantage over their black counterparts. Interestingly, even in African countries, White Europeans are treated more favourably than Africans. Whites are esteemed more favourably than Blacks. Education from the Global North is regarded more highly, White European workers are treated as 'expatriates' rather than as 'migrants', and they are paid higher than their African counterparts and given better employment package.

How racial stratification guarantees racial inequality

> *You, your experiences, and outcomes are always going to be coloured by your skin colour.*

Another way to explain racial stratification is through its likeness to playing with adults in my childhood where children were given a head start because of their age. The older and bigger the child, the further away from the finishing line they started. This was to give the younger people who were also smaller, an opportunity to be in the game. It was a case of 'equity' rather than 'equality': giving people what they needed rather than giving everyone the same thing.

Scholarship on racial inequality is typically discussed in terms of access to resources (Kelly, McGuinness, O'Connell, Pandiella, & Haugh, 2016), and the way group members are positioned on the racial strata (Verdugo, 2008). While this is true, positioning on these strata invariably means all groups do not start from the same position. These positionings differ depending on race, skin colour, and nationality of descent. These differing starting positions serve the purpose of homogenising populaces by rewarding possessors of similar attributes (i.e. Whites with European nationality) and giving them a head start. This advantages them over those who exhibit difference, in terms of skin colour, nationality, or race. This process occurs in education, the labour market, in trade relations, in recognition, and even in social status (McGinnity, Grotti, Kenny, & Russell, 2017; Organisation for Economic Co-operation and Development, 2018). The default starting position is the key mechanism through which the racial stratification of actors is established. In other words, outcome is not based on where groups end on the strata but where they start. On arrival, immigrants are assigned a racial group based on their racial category, which in turn determines where they fit within the politico-economic system in their new country. This in turn determines their access to wealth and social status which are socially constructed as suitable for different levels on the strata (Joseph, 2018). For example, arrival as an asylum seeker in Ireland means access to only €38.80 weekly (an increase of €17.20 from March 2019); denial of access to paid employment and third-level education (this has changed since May 2019 after intense campaign for reform to the asylum system); restricted movement and limited rights. Arrival as an EU migrant on the other hand, means freedom of movement, immediate access to the labour market, healthcare services, and even access to the child benefit system for those who availed of it anywhere in Europe. Those stratified at the top are entitled to more, while those at the bottom, less.

It would be simplistic to assume that racial stratification is value free. It is not simply where a person is placed, rather it determines what social status they are ascribed, what they can and cannot get in terms of jobs and resources, where they can and cannot go, how they are treated and how people respond to them. In other words, it is not a physical position but a socially constructed one; it is not about a place on a stratum but about day-to-day experiences and outcomes. The combination of whiteness and European citizenship imputes, for example, trust of educational qualifications, and abilities and right to work in Ireland. This gives White European migrants a head start in their economic pursuits. The in[up]ward mobility of the Black African on the other hand is severely handicapped by race. In this case, visa requirements, descent rather than citizenship, racial markers such as skin colour, all serve as racialised gatekeepers restricting access to higher societal rungs, by protecting and imputing rights to those deemed to have access, in this case White migrants and White Irish natives. The groups located at the bottom of the racial ladder are thus more likely to be at the bottom of the labour market strata, namely Black Africans. The historical positioning results in groups being homogenised and group bias held about them. Race and nationality of descent are conflated, and different nationalities are viewed as homogenous. While we often hear of people visiting France, Spain, or Germany, we hear reference to Africa as if it is one big country. This process allows the ascription of stereotypes to whole populations. Unfortunately, the stereotypical image of Africa and its people in the public domain mainly portrays negativity about the group, further worsening their racial positioning at the bottom of the ladder.

Setting the stage for a non-Eurocentric/decolonial engagement with racial difference

What we need today are researchers, policy makers, and educators whose main focus is not on the difference exhibited by groups, but on their response to the differences they encounter. This section argues for a CRT perspective in global justice education that includes a comprehensive understanding of racial stratification, its operations, and effects. Racial emancipation can only occur when the overarching vector of racial inequality is eliminated (Mills, 1997; Zuberi & Bonilla-Silva, 2008). That is the elimination of white supremacy from the way society organises its people on a daily basis. It would involve removing Whites and whiteness from the centre and promoting a non-racist, non-Eurocentric view of race. To demolish these structures, we need to eliminate racialised judgement from being the main method of dealing with difference as such judgements can be biased, skewed, and predetermined based on sameness with the majority population.

Storytelling as a tool for talking about and centring race

All disciplines in the Social Sciences tell stories. Sociology, anthropology, economics, geography, all tell stories about people, the economy, and even what lies under the earth. Generated data, statistics, and narratives help us tell a story. When we consider global justice education, what kind of stories do we tell? Whose views are told and whose voice is validated? While CRT scholars advocate for the use of storytelling as both a research method and analytical tool, stories of the African continent and its people have historically been told by Whites who give perspectives that are oftentimes loaded with a black deficit. That is because stories told have mainly been the privilege of those historically influential in knowledge generation. Yet, marginalised groups are clearly able to explain their experiences if given the opportunity (Joseph, 2019). They often articulate their stories in terms different from academic discourse, but they give us an understanding of what life is really like for those marginalised and stratified at the bottom of the racial ladder. We know that biased views are handed down the generations through the stories people tell. When Brown and Black scholars write about race and racism, it is not to replace whites' perspectives but to complement and provide the broad spectrum of possibilities in our understanding and theorising about race. That is why Black and Brown people have been encouraged to tell stories (Zuberi & Bonilla-Silva, 2008), and others listen when they do (Delgado, 1989).

Storytelling has been argued to be a political act which can defend or contest social arrangements through how we portray the past, ourselves, and our fellows (Roy 1999, p. 9). It is a powerful means for creating meaning as well as for challenging myths (Delgado, 1989). Storytelling in CRT aims to expose race-neutral discourse, "to reveal how white privilege operates within an ideological framework to reinforce and support unequal societal relations between Whites and People of Colour" (Hunn, Guy, & Manglitz, 2006, p. 244). There are two main types of stories espoused by CRT scholars. Stock stories which are "stock explanations that construct reality in ways favourable to in-groups" (Delgado, 1989, p. 2438) and counterstories which are outgroup stories that seek to unseat the status quo. While "stories are attractive to all groups and they create their own bonds, represent cohesion, shared understandings, and meanings" (ibid., p. 2412), the storyteller's group influences the type of stories told. When it comes to race/racism, "Whites and Blacks tend to hear and tell very different stories" (Bell, 2003, p. 4).

Whites in the Western World are stratified at the top of the racial and economic ladder, thus they are the in-group, a term made popular by Tajfel (1970). They often tell stock stories from how they see the world, oblivious of how whiteness advantages them. Interestingly, in-group stories typically privilege the dominant group and demonise the marginalised by speaking from a standpoint that normalises the experiences, views, and needs of the dominant group (Delgado, 1989). These stories distort and silence the experiences of the dominated (Hunn, Guy, & Manglitz 2006). As Ladson-Billings and Tate (1995, p. 47) write, "... discussions of race and racism continue to be muted and marginalised." This is true today when we consider the imaging of Africa in the media and in fundraising organisations that only tell the story of poverty, sickness, and lack. In schools, a similar situation prevails where children are sold a story of an impoverished African continent without balancing it with stories about its wealth in natural and human resources. When it comes to the affairs of Africans, in-group members have been known to tell themselves comforting in-group stories. These kinds of stories according to Delgado (1989, pp. 2413–4) "make current social arrangements seem fair and natural, such that those in power are able to sleep well at night and their conduct does not seem to them like oppression". These kinds of stories include how the EU frames the displaced Syrian people as illegals, thus, making it easy for them to be left in the Mediterranean seas to their peril.

While Whites tell stock stories, Blacks/outgroups – those at the bottom, their allies, and race-conscious people tell counterstories which are stories that seek to destabilise racial stratification. These two kinds of stories do not have the same perspective, frame, or purpose. While stock stories are the dominant perspective that espouses black deficiency, counterstories are the worldview from the marginalised. When Blacks are made to be the problem and only centred when Whites want to '*fix*' them, we recreate the colonial images of black and white spaces which reify Whites and whiteness in the centre and Blacks on the margins. What I provide and encourage in this chapter is for new non-racist/anti-racist lenses and structures to look at race through understanding how the notion of racial stratification positions groups. A deracialised and decolonial stance does not proliferate a black deficit approach to race and its impact. This calls for self-policing. This is where change in society will become evident. What story does your organisation tell, and do you question that story? What story are you telling, what story do you want to tell? When you encounter difference, what are the top five stories you share? Are these stock stories or counterstories?

Race consciousness in teacher education

Have you ever wondered why two people hear the same report or witness the same thing and respond to different elements in it? From my lived experience as a scholar of black African descent in Europe, being at the centre of the phenomenon that I studied and my minority status has made a difference to the way I conduct research and the questions I ask. In this section, I share some of the basic grounding which influences how I study race and labour market differentials. From a CRT perspective, race consciousness is required to fully understand how race operates and influences outcomes. What this means in practical terms is discussed as four overarching frames with which a race theorist has to be conversant, in order to carry out a non-racist/anti-racist engagement with race or raced people. Without it, research, researchers, and the produced knowledge will be a variant of distilled stock stories that at best provide a descriptive representation of the experiences of Blacks without disrupting the ambivalence and inaction of race sceptics. This is possible because stock stories that the dominant groups tell, enable them 'explain' racial inequality without taking responsibility, and they do this by focusing on black deficit. This is because Whites often view issues of race as a problem for and of Blacks. Their understanding and engagement with race is often laden with how to solve the race problem for Blacks.

What I refer to here is viewing race as a problem of society, with the human race in the middle, meaning Blacks and Whites are centred when viewing the spectrum of how different populations are treated. This allows us to see ourselves as beneficiaries relative to others who are disadvantaged. This is required to prepare for dealing with the knowledge one encounters when working with people and groups whose outcomes is influenced by their racial categorisation. Whites have however been known to adjust their story till they find justification for the inequality in society. This is usually located in the Black body where we blame the marginalised for their marginality. The usual culprit is the language of the host community, inassimibility of Blacks, geographical distance, and cultural and ethnic differences. All of these points to the Black person as the reason for their marginality, a stance which again seeks to *fix* the Black person. The Black person is not broken but our racial, political, and economic systems are. Here I present from my own cultural learning, four race-consciousness frames required for a deracialised, non-Eurocentric engagement with racial difference.

The changing meaning of race

First is an understanding that race is not fixed. Because race is socially constructed, its meaning changes with time and across space. Race however continues to play a significant part in all spheres of life. In order to be prepared when working with groups that are raced the way we have it today, an understanding of the present paradigm of race in the country being considered and how race shapes the lives of your subjects is mandatory. While checking a deficit approach, it will also help students become aware of the unequal conditioning of people due to race, their racial categorisation, and the assigned strata. These key considerations will influence how race is nuanced in different countries, across space and time. For example, in terms of time, race in the early 2000s in Ireland meant the integration of migrants with a drive for recognition. This was coupled with claims of bogus asylum stories and Black women clogging up hospital beds which culminated in the 2004 citizenship referendum (Lentin, 2007). In the late 2000s, race transformed with the beginning signs of the return to overt anti-immigrant sentiments. This was fuelled by the recession and stories of immigrants taking Irish people's jobs (Kelly et al., 2016). The mid-2010s saw the rise of the far right, with race becoming a tool for politicians to ascend to power. In terms of place, race in Nigeria for example is different from how people experience race in South Africa, the USA, or Ireland. While there are and continue to be similarities, race is nuanced differently when it moves across time and space. The key race consciousness required is to know how race is represented in the time and space you seek to transform or work. What does it mean for you, raced and non-raced people?

Hierarchical stratification and domination

Second is the notion of hierarchical racial stratification and its connection with domination. This is because racial inequality is not simply a matter of not having the same as others with similar abilities. Rather, it is a hierarchal positioning which is linked to the dominance of one group over the other as we can see in the hegemonic relationship between the African continent, its people, and the world. In order to prepare students for a non-Eurocentric standpoint, an understanding of racial stratification and the racial order that exists in the country of the study or the group being studied is vital. This is because racial stratification as I discussed earlier is a site of otherness for PBAD and the African continent, and economic dominance for Whites. A global justice educator will need to understand how the group/s they work with are constrained by external sources such as these. If and how they manage or use it as sites of action, production, and/or resistance. Also, considering human/minority agency, everyone responds in particular ways to their racial positioning which could be static or fluid. What about how they change their place, these will alter how we engage with others whose difference we encounter in our work and travels. Lastly, educators must appreciate that the way groups are categorised as Global North or South also forces them to assimilate or fit in with a racial understanding of themselves as dictated by the North.

Management of racial difference

A third race consciousness for a non-Eurocentric engagement would involve understanding how the racial difference of the country, continent, society, or organisation being studied is viewed and managed. It is important to say here that the African continent or its people are not the problem, neither is their difference. Rather it is how we (society) respond to their difference. An inclusive concept of citizenship recognises (rather than excludes) difference (Kymlicka, 2001). All over the world, groups and marginalised people want their difference normalised and not to be the basis of their evaluation. Thus grounding a non-racist or non-Eurocentric student will include getting a clear understanding of how the racial difference of the group is being managed in the world order. Are they disparaged, despised, or esteemed? Are they recognised or seen as objects of aid thus only beneficiaries to be helped? The worldview of your group is important in order to challenge and ensure it does not unduly influence the educators' understanding and way of working with the group. In my black studies class, I asked my students what they had learnt about Africa and Africans in their various classrooms across the whole of their education. More than 90% of it was negative. The natural tendency is to believe and not challenge what we learn particularly through the formal education system. Considering everyone is not treated the same way (Joseph, 2019), there is a need to be conscious of how racial difference and sameness are treated in the Global North or South. This is not simply informational, it influences how groups are treated globally.

Difference has been managed on a skin colour basis. Although whiteness is not often reckoned as a resource, just like financial capital, it continues to advantage Whites against their non-White peers in the world of work. This is evident in the ways education from the North is esteemed higher than that from the Global South. Knowledge and education in black bodies is often undervalued as is evident in the higher unemployment rate experienced by PBAD despite their high level of education (see CSO, 2016), call-back ratio of greater than two in many European countries (McGinnity, Nelson, Lunn, & Quinn, 2009), underemployment, and "50% higher chance of being over-qualified when employed" (OECD, 2018, p. 84). In Ireland, the expectation is that White Europeans would be hard-working, punctual, trustworthy, and competent, while Blacks report experiencing disregard, disrespect, ascription of incompetency, mistrust, expectation to have poor quality education and communication (Joseph, 2019). These attributes are automatically ascribed, oftentimes before the actors even perform. It influences outcomes by disadvantaging Black workers against their White counterparts through a taste-based discrimination – where the employer has racial or ethnic preferences (Becker, 1957), because of similarities in credentials, race, ethnicity, and skin colour. Although Whites rarely openly acknowledge that possession of white skin colour advantages and oftentimes protect them in society, they enjoy the benefits of a 'solidaristic labour community' (Standing, 2011, p. 12) amongst other White populations in the Global North.

Create inclusive spaces through acceptance

Let me start this section with a direct question. Do you want to be tolerated? I have never seen anyone really ask to be tolerated. People all over the world who have experienced differential treatment because they exhibit some form of difference typically ask for their difference to be accepted. Toleration is a concept that is only espoused by those whose race/group is at the top of the racial ladder and groups socialised into regurgitating the dominant discourse because that's what is in the public domain. If given the choice between being tolerated or accepted, which would we go for, and which would we advocate for in society? When a group and their difference is not accepted, it is indicative of a superior stance against that difference/group because we only tolerate that which we abhor (Jones, 2010). When as educators, we allow ourselves take a critical examination of our knowledge and attitudes to the group/s we work with, we can begin to unearth and unlearn some of our hidden practices and pitfalls as global justice practitioners. A biased stance can alienate the very group/s we seek to help, thereby creating a gulf in the classroom of superiors and inferiors. Global justice educators must become conscious of how their use of words/presentations/descriptions impact on members of the groups we speak about during lectures.

Why race should be centred in intercultural and global justice education

Whichever way we look at it, the Global North structures access to resources, power sharing, trade, and movement around countries and continents. Being EU/non-EU, Third/First World, developing/developed world, Global North/South has implications on the social status, privileges, positive/negative regard attached to each category. Considering the various ways race impacts on labour market outcomes, it is imperative that race is central to the education of those who will be working with groups from the South. The element we centre in a study ultimately influences the results, explanations, and recommendations. If we centre gender, or class, the outcome and recommendations will be different. When race is centred in our understanding and analysis, a societal deficit is implicated, when individualistic attributions are centred, a migrant/black deficit will be implicated.

Centralising race combined with a racial stratification framework is beneficial to education because it can reach and uncover hitherto silenced experiences. The black–white binary which is a paradigm that suggests that Blacks "constitute the prototypical minority group" (Delgado & Stefancic, 2012, p. 75) is undeniably contentious and even divisive in nature. However, based on the lived experience of Black workers and on statistical evidence, the impact of race needs to be made plain (Joseph, 2018). Anything less will fuel the ambivalence of Whites about the impact of race on labour market outcomes which often silences victims and demonstrates a lack of commitment to addressing the consequences of racial inequality. Unless we centre race and name it in its entirety, it will continue to provide an unfair advantage for Whites, white culture, and countries while remaining unacknowledged yet powerful in destabilising any effort towards levelling the playing field. To provide interventions without taking cognisance of race is to disadvantage those most in need of interventions while perpetuating a culture of silence. Centring race in mainstream, first-world political philosophy is indeed challenging, heavily contested and resisted. It however should not and cannot be ignored.

Concluding comments

Black Africans' experience in the labour market in Ireland is undoubtedly connected to the evaluation placed on the African continent and its people. It continues to perpetuate stereotypes that date back to the colonial era and imaging of PBAD. The education system is complicit in reifying that image of Africa, its people, and by-products, whether in the form of its education, culture, clothes, language, and skin colour. It portrays the African continent with a single story, a story of deficit that originates from the slavery era covertly erasing its precolonial history, power, wealth, resources, and way/s of governance. This is not to say that Whites are all racist, neither is it to say they are not. Rather, that whiteness positions the White person at the centre through racial stratification – a process where White people become socialised into being in the centre. This makes seeing themselves as White difficult. While Whites racialise and use racialised naming for others, they are averse to being named as White with many feeling disoriented and affronted to be called White (Di Angelo, 2011). For deracialisation to occur, Whites and whiteness need to be moved from the centre and the human race needs to be centred in such a way that race is no longer synonymous with Blacks or 'other' but all, including Blacks and Whites. We are all race, we form race, and we all do race. That's the starting point.

References

Becker, G. (1957). *The economics of discrimination*. Chicago, IL: University of Chicago Press.

Bell, L.A. 2003. Telling Tales: What stories can teach us about racism. *Race, Ethnicity and Education*, 6(1), 3–28.

Chamberlain, M.E. (1981). *The scramble for Africa*. London: Routledge.

Cornell, S.E., & Hartmann, D. (1998). *Ethnicity and race: Making identities in a changing world*. Thousand Oaks, CA: Pine Forge Press.

CSO. (2016). Irish Central Statistics Office. Retrieved from http://www.cso.ie/en/

Dawsey, J. (2018, January 12). Trump derides protections for immigrants from 'shithole' countries. *The Washington Post*. Retrieved from www.washingtonpost.com

Delgado, R. (1989). Storytelling for oppositionists and others: A plea for narrative. *Michigan Law Review*, 87(8), 2411–2441.

Delgado, R., & Stefancic, J. (2012). *Critical race theory: An introduction*. New York: New York University Press.

DiAngelo, R. (2011). White fragility. *International Journal of Critical Pedagogy*. 3(3): 54–70.

Du Bois, W.E.B. (1903). *The souls of black folk* (p. 19). New York: New American Library Inc.

Fanon, F. (2000). The fact of blackness. In L. Back and J. Solomos (Eds.), *Theories of race and racism, A reader* (pp. 257–266). London: Routledge.

Goldberg, D.T. (2002; 1990). *The racial state*. Oxford: Blackwell.

Hunn, L.R.M., Guy, T. C., & Manglitz, E. (2006). Who can speak for whom? using counter-storytelling to challenge racial hegemony. Retrieved from: http://citeseerx.ist.psu.edu/viewdoc/download?doi=10.1.1.495.622&rep=rep1&type=pdf

James, A. (2008). Making sense of race and racial classification. In T. Zuberi, & E. Bonilla-Silva (Eds.), *White logic, white methods, racism and methodology* (pp. 31–44). Lanham, MD: Rowman and Littlefield.

Jones, P.N. (2010). Toleration and recognition: What should we teach?. *Educational Philosophy and Theory*, 42, 38–56.

Joseph, E. (2015). *Racial Stratification in the Irish Labour Market: A comparative study of differential labour market outcomes through the counter-stories of Nigerian, Polish and Spanish migrants in Ireland.* Unpublished doctoral thesis, School of Social Justice, University College Dublin.

Joseph, E. (2018). Whiteness and racism: Examining the racial order in Ireland. [Electronic version] *Irish Journal of Sociology*, 26(1), 46–70.

Joseph, E. (2019). Discrimination against credentials in Black bodies: counterstories of the characteristic labour market experiences of migrants in Ireland. *British Journal of Guidance & Counselling*, 47(4), 524-542. doi:10.1080/03069885.2019.1620916

Kelly, E., McGuinness. S., O'Connell, P., Pandiella. A.G., & Haugh, D. (2016). How did Immigrants fare in the Irish Labour Market over the Great Recession?, OECD Working Papers, No. 1284. Retrieved from: http://dx.doi.org/10.1787/5jm0v4f4r8kh-en

Koponen, J. (1993). The partition of Africa: A scramble for a mirage?. [Electronic version] *Nordic Journal of African Studies*, 2(1), 117–135.

Kymlicka, W. (2001). *Contemporary political philosophy: An introduction* (2nd ed.). Oxford: Oxford University Press.

Ladson-Billings, G., & Tate, W.F. 1995. Toward a critical race theory of education. *Teachers College Record*, 97(1), 47–68.

Lentin, R., & McVeigh, R. (2006). *After optimism? Ireland, racism and globalisation.* Dublin, Ireland: Metro Eireann Publications.

Lentin, R. (2007). Ireland: Racial state and crisis racism. *Ethnic and Racial Studies*, 30(4), 610–627.

McGinnity, F., Nelson, J., Lunn, P., & Quinn, E. (2009). *Discrimination in recruitment; Evidence from a field experiment.* Dublin, Ireland: The Equality Authority and The Economic and Social Research Institute. Retrieved from https://www.esri.ie/pubs/BKMNEXT137.pdf

McGinnity, F., Grotti. R., Kenny. O., & Russell, H. (2017). *Who experiences discrimination in Ireland? Evidence from the QNHS Equality Modules.* The Economic and Social Research Institute and the Irish Human Rights and Equality Commission. Retrieved from https://doi.org/10.26504/bkmnext342

Mills, C.W. (1997). *The racial contract.* Ithaca, NY: Cornell University Press.

Myrdal, G. (1996). *An American dilemma.* New York: Harper and Brothers.

Myrdal, G. (2000). Racial beliefs in America. In L. Back, & J. Solomos (Eds.), *Theories of race and racism, A reader* (pp. 87–104). London: Routledge.

Organisation for Economic Co-operation and Development, OECD. (2018). *Education at a Glance, OECD Indicators.* Paris: OECD. Retrieved from https://read.oecd-ilibrary.org/education/education-at-a-glance-2018_eag-2018-en#page1

Omi, M., & Winant, H. (1994). *Racial formation in the United States: From the 1960s to the 1990s* (2nd ed). New York: Routledge.

Roy, B. (1999). *Bitters in the Honey: Tales of hope and disappointment across divides of race and time*. Fayetteville, AK: University of Arkansas Press.

Song, M. (2004). Introduction: Who's at the bottom? Examining claims about racial hierarchy. *Ethnic and Racial Studies*, 27(6), 859–877.

Spickard, P.R. (1992). The Illogic of American Racial Categories. In M.P.P. Root (Ed.), *Racially mixed people in America*. Newbury Park, CA: Sage.

Standing, G. (2011). *The precariat – The new dangerous class*. London: Bloomsbury.

Tajfel, H. (1970). Experiments in intergroup discrimination. *Scientific American*, 223(5), 96–103.

Verdugo, R. (2008). Racial stratification, social consciousness, and the education of Mexican Americans in Fabens, Texas: A socio-historical case study. *Spaces for Difference: An Interdisciplinary Journal*, 1(2), 69–95.

Winant, H. (2004). *The new politics of race: Globalism, difference, justice*. Minneapolis, MN: University of Minnesota Press.

Zuberi, T., & Bashi, V. (1997). A theory of immigration and racial stratification. *Journal of Black Studies*, 27(5), 668–682.

Zuberi, T., & Bonilla-Silva, E, (Eds.). (2008). *White logic, white methods: Racism and methodology*. Landham, MD: Rowman and Littlefield.

10 Transformative learning

The future of critical education

Barbara O'Toole, Ebun Joseph, and David Nyaluke

Introduction

Readers wondering why there is reference to 'race' in a book targeting educators must realise that global justice education is not a simple, neat, and comfortable area. Rather, as the authors in this book have shown, the reality is laced with questions of power, domination, and racial stereotyping. Many chapters in this volume show how the outcomes for people from the Global South, particularly of African descent, mirror the value we place on products in trade and are echoed in the kinds of representations found in school books and are also reflected in messages conveyed by the media. These examples show that the present is not devoid of imperialist histories and impositions, but that unequal power relationships between North and South have become established and ingrained and that they persist to this day. The most urgent and recurring strand running through this book relates to how messages about Africa and African people in the Global North are predominantly situated in deficit thinking with roots in colonial processes and the privileging of Northern epistemologies. Another key conceptual idea in the book situates race at the heart of the colonial matrix of power; therefore, discussions about race are central to calls for change in the discourse.

Trade justice has occupied a central position in many of the chapters, with an examination of the persistence of economic colonialism in the contemporary global order, along with a spotlight on trade justice initiatives which retain 'value added' in African countries. The kind of injustice and power imbalance found at the heart of economic relationships between North and South has featured as an ongoing theme throughout the book; it emerges in the examination of 'sending' programmes in Chapter 4; in the privileging of Eurocentric knowledges in curricula and academic texts discussed in Chapters 6; and in the plea for White educators to recognise, unlearn, and de-centre from their privilege, which comes across in many of the contributions. We have also seen in Chapter 8 how the sources and practices of diverse knowledges were largely eliminated through the colonial mission, a process of epistemicide. Meanwhile, epistemic hegemony is maintained through the extraction of scholarship and intellectual labour in the form of 'raw data' for the benefit of the North, which is subsequently imported into African countries as 'concepts and theories'. These were some of the issues raised by the authors. In this final section, we attempt to draw together some of the main ideas and themes that have emerged in the chapters, along with offering ideas on future directions and signposting further praxis suggestions for education.

Global justice education

As explained in Chapter 1, we have framed our overall approach in this volume as *global justice education*. Although attention has been focused throughout the chapters on teaching and learning about the Global South, specifically Africa, we have also been careful to place the black/white relationship in the centre. This is because race has not only been fundamental to the investigations in many of the preceding contributions, it has also influenced the nature of the interactions between/amongst groups. Thus we call on global justice educators to be cognisant of the dynamics of North/South relations and to also recognise the power of racial ordering and stratification in everyday life, in economic relationships, and in the centring and privileging of certain knowledges.

In this final chapter our reflection continues to take place through acknowledgement of the "longstanding structures of colonial domination" (Kerr & Andreotti, 2017, p. 6) and its associated white privileging. Contemporary manifestations of such structural domination, i.e. racism and racialisation, must be seen against the backdrop of coloniality and in the "multiple material, political, social and cultural processes of colonialism" (Gebrial, 2018, p. 29).

Effective global justice education must therefore incorporate historical and geopolitical dimensions of study along with an examination of contemporary societal power issues, and it must counter and challenge manifestations of racism and injustice, both locally and globally. Furthermore, Northern thinking and teaching about Africa typically begins with enslavement in the 1600s: the arrival of White Europeans tends to be the starting point for teaching and learning about African countries. This not only continues to place Europeans at the centre of the discourse but it also obliterates the entire history of the African continent before that time. The great civilisations which spread across Africa, from the Asante Empire in modern-day Ghana, to ancient Zimbabwe, from Mali to the Zulu Kingdom in the South of Africa, all of these become obscured by the 'single story' which begins with enslavement and typically ends with poverty, famine, and disease, alongside Northern benevolence, aid, and charity. This Eurocentric narrative hides historical injustices and ongoing exploitative socio-economic relations in which Africa's resources are siphoned off for the benefit of Northern countries and people. This injustice, and the attendant epistemic violence whereby certain knowledges are centred while others are marginalised or removed, is one of the core issues this volume has sought to expose and counteract. It is indeed time to enrich our education system and our educators with other perspectives. It is time to tell other stories.

Intersectionalities

Chapter 1 highlighted how 'soft' forms of development education/global learning eschew more challenging aspects of global concerns; for example, poverty in African countries is presented in isolation from its systemic causes; charitable aid from the Global North is presented as the solution to African 'underdevelopment', while causal responsibility on the part of the Global North in perpetuating the colonial matrix of power with its attendant power imbalances is neatly elided. Global education without a critical perspective is simply 'declawed' (Bryan, 2011). As we turn to 'intercultural education', which is the main platform and policy perspective used to address the challenges of modern European multicultural societies, we contend that 'intercultural education' without political, historical, and geopolitical insights is also 'declawed'. Indeed, one might argue, along with Coulby (2006), that education can never claim to be truly 'intercultural' if it neglects broader political contexts. It is within those arenas that Northern ideologies, through the imperialist project, have led to the consolidation of white hegemony into "a dominant frame of reference for civilisation, moral development and rationality" (Leonardo, 2004, p. 146). This is the terrain examined in Chapter 9 where race was centred in the discussion, the point being that when global justice educators do not centre or acknowledge race, they simply skim the surface without facilitating transformative learning.

Intercultural education that disregards the complexity of the 'local' context (i.e. the impact of geopolitics and history, along with the centrality of race) typically ends up as celebratory and superficial (Dalal, 2008). According to Fiedler (2007, p. 7), the term 'intercultural space' in itself carries a "benign vision of evenly balanced cultural encounters"; it assumes a neutral and ahistorical context, whereas the reality is far more multi-layered and uncomfortable, with questions of power, domination, and race at its core. Such (re)framing of intercultural education incorporates deep political work and includes theoretical frameworks such as Critical Race Theory in which these issues can be brought to conscious awareness and interrogated. Martin, Pirbhai-Illich, and Pete (2017, p. 238) describe this kind of process as 'critical interculturality'. In Ireland, this is needed now more than ever.

Racial stratification in Ireland

Increased migration into Ireland over the last two decades has led to a concomitant rise in racist ideology, including 'Afrophobia', which Michael (2015, p. 5) describes as the "hostility, antipathy, contempt and aversion expressed directly and through institutional and legal means, towards people with a background in sub-Saharan Africa or who belong to the African diaspora." The impact of such sentiments is evidenced in the racial stratification of the Irish labour market, which is "rife with incidents of discrimination in both recruitment processes and workplace practices" (Joseph, 2018, p. 47). Joseph's research demonstrates that immigrants, particularly those of black African descent, fare worse in the workforce than members of the 'host' community and also than their White European counterparts. The findings point to the incongruence in which Ireland is the "world's fourth most welcoming country" (ibid., p. 52), and yet has a "colour-coded migrant penalty" by which Europeans are placed "at the top and Black Africans at the bottom of the labour supply chain" (ibid., p. 63).

This kind of racial stratification has been a long-standing phenomenon in Ireland, and is both a feature and an extension of a generalised hostility towards 'Other', including and particularly towards Irish Travellers (Ní Shuinéar, 2002; Garner, 2004; Joseph, 2018). The historic and consequently deeply ingrained perception of Africa as a continent to be 'assisted' by the charity and generosity of the North has left the African diaspora in Ireland particularly vulnerable to being on the receiving end of racist ideologies, including racial stratification. It is important at this point to trace the evolution of Ireland's 'White' identity in the nineteenth and twentieth centuries because this provides an insight into the formation of a very particular and context-specific black/white dichotomy in Ireland, one which continues to have an impact in the present day.

Understanding White identity in Ireland

The study of the construction of 'White' and 'Black' in Ireland is a relatively new field of investigation, emerging in the last two decades, most notably with writers such as Ignatiev (1995), Fanning (2002), Goldstone (2002), McVeigh and Lentin (2002), Garner (2004), Kitching (2014), Bryan (2013), and Joseph (2018), all of whom have examined the particular circumstances around Ireland's relationship with 'whiteness'. According to McVeigh and Lentin (2002), although Irish people experienced colonisation, forced emigration, famine, and attempted genocide, all of which "provided the basis for historical and contemporary forms of anti-Irish racism" (ibid., p. 8), Ireland was also "empowered by its whiteness, its Europeanness and by the advancement of Irish blocs in other countries such as the USA" (ibid., p. 8). This left Ireland 'between two worlds' in the sense that it has been "both perpetrator and survivor of racism, both thoroughly racist and determinedly anti-racist" (ibid., p. 8). Alice Feldman in Chapter 8 of this volume refers to 'colonial amnesia', saying that the long-standing history of the participation of Irish people in British colonialism and in religious colonisation, particularly in Africa, is largely unknown. Bryan (2013) frames this in terms of a simultaneous 'remembering' and 'forgetting' ("historical amnesia", ibid., p. 21): highlighting the "function that *remembering* instances of historical trauma and suffering and of *forgetting* or ignoring Ireland's role in the history of imperialism play in shaping and constituting the nation through orthodox development discourses" (p. 7, italics in original). 'Remembering' historical traumas such as the Great Famine of the 1840s serves to equate the Irish experience with contemporary famine and poverty in certain African countries. It contributes to what Bryan (2013, p. 14) describes as "an experiential empathy frame" in which Irish people perceive themselves as having a heightened awareness of poverty and suffering because of a colonised past. However, this orthodox narrative of 'imperial innocence' also shields Ireland from the more complex and uncomfortable territory surrounding its relationship with race, particularly how the Irish in the USA pursued 'whiteness' as a means of dissociating themselves from non-Europeans, specifically from African-Americans (Ignatiev, 1995; Garner, 2004; Bryan, 2013; Joseph, 2018). Garner (2004, p. 98) describes the Irish "drive for whiteness" in the USA in the latter half of the nineteenth century: "whiteness safeguarded access to the labour market, the vote and a degree of social prestige...and ensured a constant flattering comparison with occupationally and residentially segregated blacks." Similarly, Ignatiev (1995, p. 3) states that "entering the white race" was a strategy to gain "advantage in a competitive society", so that ultimately, "the Irish were located some notches away from the bottom of the labour market, above Black Africans and non-English speaking Whites" (Joseph, 2018, p. 52). These uncomfortable historical realities are obscured by the more favourable narrative of 'imperial innocence' in which Ireland holds an unblemished record in the subjugation of non-Europeans, and specifically, of black Africans.

This orthodox account of 'innocence' also shields Irish people from the uncomfortable acknowledgement of the "racialisation of Africans through the missionary movement" (Bryan, 2013, p. 16), which created "paternalistic and profoundly racist images and discourses" (ibid.) that have shaped Irish people's perceptions of Black Africans living in Ireland. Even though Ireland was one of the first conquests of European expansionism, the Irish diaspora were, according to Kitching (2014, p. 36), also "complicit in empire-building" and were "important to the working through of other colonial (e.g. anti-African, anti-Semitic) racist ideologies in/to Irish cultural life". This led to a kind of 'missionary nationalism', whereby national identity in Ireland was constructed in terms of "spiritual superiority" drawing upon "colonial ideologies of racial superiority" (Fanning, 2002, p. 16). Similarly, Bryan (2013, p. 17) states that "Irish missionaries simultaneously participated in, and actively sustained, a stereotypical and racist discourse which portrayed Africa as a 'dark', dangerous, 'benighted' continent with exotic people and landscapes". This carries forward into contemporary consciousness; with "an ongoing legacy of racism and paternalism, rooted in the collective Irish imagination ... (which) impacts upon black people in Irish society" (Fanning, 2002, p. 16). Meanwhile these "paternalistic and profoundly racist images and discourses" (Bryan, 2013, p. 17) have left a "powerful legacy in terms of shaping contemporary Irish understandings of development and in terms of influencing how Irish people perceive and interact with black people living in or outside of Ireland" (ibid., p. 17).

Irish complicity in the structural oppression of African-Americans in the USA, along with the racialisation of Africans through the missionary movement, has left a historical imprint that continues to impact on perceptions and relationships in contemporary society. This could be framed in terms of 'colonial continuities', which Heron (2007, p. 34) suggests arise from the "deeply racialised, interrelated constructs of thought that have circulated from the era of empire" through to the present day. These colonial continuities in Ireland operate in a dual manner; first they contribute to ongoing racialisation and racist ideologies, specifically towards Black Africans. And second, they bestow a sense of entitlement on the White person to contribute towards the 'betterment' of the Other (Heron, 2007). The prevalence of the 'helping imperative' in Ireland can be partially understood through a lens of 'colonial continuities' with its racialised overtones. This contributes to a climate in which superficial and celebratory modes of 'interculturalism' can prevail, where societal power issues are occluded and where softer forms of development education predominate, with an emphasis on development-as-charity. Irish society's 'mirror' of its own actions and intentions is one of global humanitarianism, innocence, and shared suffering, a narrative that leads to the elision of past and present complicity in racialised ideologies and structural injustices. As Bryan (2013, p. 22) explains:

> Irish people's role in fuelling historical and contemporary forms of racism – both at home and abroad – and their role as agents of colonialism are obfuscated by orthodox narratives about 'our' global humanitarianism 'impulse to help', and 'our' socially constructed enhanced capacity for experiential empathy. In other words, these orthodox storylines do not prompt us to reflect on how we are 'causally responsible' or self-implicated in the structures that produce global suffering and inequality.

Some of that causal responsibility has been examined in this volume, with a particular focus on economic relationships. Chapter 2, for example, examined the impact of trade imbalances on local African communities, when the added value of commodity production is stripped away to the already prosperous Global North, an ongoing situation that in itself points to Northern complicity in unjust structural relationships within the political economic system.

Troubling 'Intercultural' education

Chapter 1 made a case for *global justice education*, which grapples with historical and political realities in age-appropriate ways and which counters the prevalence of development-as-charity approaches that perpetuate colonial thinking. This section focuses on 'intercultural' education as it is currently theorised and practised in Europe, arguing for a more robust conceptualisation, followed by implementation which penetrates the surface of societal power relations and moves beyond celebratory and utilitarian modes of practice (Coulby, 2006; Bryan, 2010; O'Toole, 2015; Martin et al., 2017). It then underscores the intersectionality of intercultural education and global learning, contending that such critical pedagogy, which we have presented here as *global justice education*, holds potential to challenge and disrupt dominant educational discourse in relation to North and South, as well as to counter racial stratification and racist ideologies in the local sphere.

Interculturalism is widely understood to have emerged from European debates about assimilationism and multiculturalism. The 2008 Council of Europe White

Paper on Intercultural Dialogue claimed that "old approaches to the management of cultural diversity", namely assimilationism and multiculturalism, "are no longer adequate" (Council of Europe, 2008, p. 9), and that intercultural dialogue is now the preferred approach to replace "prior approaches to cultural diversity" (ibid., p. 18), with 'intercultural dialogue' defined as follows:

> A process that comprises an open and respectful exchange of views between individuals and groups with different ethnic, cultural, religious and linguistic backgrounds and heritage, on the basis of mutual understanding and respect.
>
> Council of Europe (2008, p. 17)

The white Paper goes on to state that 'interculturalism' incorporates the best of both assimilationism and multiculturalism:

> It takes from assimilationism the focus on the individual; it takes from multiculturalism the recognition of cultural diversity. And it adds the new element, critical to integration and social cohesion, of dialogue on the basis of equal dignity and shared values.
>
> Council of Europe (2008, p. 19)

Huge expectations have thus been placed at the door of interculturalism, a relatively new policy approach in Europe, included in which is a requirement for interaction and engagement between people ("open and respectful exchange of views"), along with an anticipation of parity of esteem between cultural groups ("equal dignity and shared values"). It is essential to interrogate the anticipations contained in the 'inter' space of interculturalism, with its implied emphasis on interaction and dialogue. First, there is the assumption that 'culture' is a neutral and benign space, "free of imperialist histories and examples of imposition" (Leonardo, 2004, p. 149), which can facilitate interaction and dialogue grounded in parity of esteem. Such a naive and ahistorical interpretation of cultural exchange serves to obscure "the fundamentals of postcolonial theory and its critical assessment of traditional European concepts of culture" (Fiedler, 2007, p. 7). It neatly bypasses the colonial matrix of power through which Europe constructed itself as the 'enunciator' and effectively set the terms for the classification and subjugation of non-Europeans, a process which has continued through the centuries (Mignolo & Walsh, 2018), the legacy of which is examined in detail in Chapter 8 by Alice Feldman. A European conceptualisation of 'interculturalism' in this historical context is deeply ironic: it obfuscates the legacy of the last four centuries through which unequal power relationships between North and South became established and ingrained and persist to this day.

The result of having such a new and relatively under-theorised policy approach, one which elides historical processes of coloniality, the ongoing unequal economic and epistemic relationship between North and South, and the prevalence of white privilege, has enabled interculturalism, as it is commonly interpreted, to side-step fundamental issues of power and marginalisation. It has facilitated the pervasiveness of intercultural rhetoric alongside "a paucity of robust measures to tackle inequality" (O'Toole, 2015, p. 96), with a predominance of 'soft' or 'celebratory' intercultural education in schools. Such approaches can then mask unchallenged and unchanged paternalistic perspectives, because, as Dalal (2008, p. 12) points out, "power relations are forgotten in the miasma of celebration".

Furthermore, intercultural education can sometimes translate into 'diversity awareness' programmes which are utilitarian rather than ideologically driven, and are designed either to prepare students to 'compete' in a world economy or to grasp superficial cultural differences for the purpose of studying or working overseas, rather than supporting them to engage with and interrogate societal power dynamics. Martin et al. (2017, p. 237) argue that the field of intercultural education in the USA is driven by globalisation "and the need for greater intercultural sensitivity and competence in for example, commerce and education", while in the UK this has been determined by "the field of foreign language acquisition" and preparing students for their "study abroad semesters". This kind of 'interculturalism', driven by the economics of globalisation, tends to be acritical and utilitarian and to bypass questions of societal power. As Bryan (2013, p. 9) states, despite an ostensible commitment to 'inclusion' on the part of contemporary organisations in Ireland, the preoccupation is "with producing workers with the cultural fluency needed to participate in the global economy than they are with enabling students to critically engage with issues of global injustice and unequal interdependence". Manifestations of white privilege and social injustice in Irish society, such as racial stratification in the workplace (Joseph, 2018) and the prevalence of racist incidents, remain unchallenged, with people identified as 'Black' the most targeted group in reports of racial abuse in Ireland in 2017 (Michael, 2018).

Intercultural education that fails to take a critical perspective can reinforce and perpetuate the superior views of White students towards those from the Global South, including towards Africans and people of African descent who are living in Ireland. Moreover, intercultural education without a global justice dimension can unintentionally subjugate minorities through symbolic violence, because it remains either in the safe domain of celebration or in the empty territory of rhetoric, and it ultimately risks failing to challenge dominant discourses and colonial continuities which perpetuate violence and discrimination in local and global spheres. This is the challenge for contemporary educators, and this is the terrain that global justice education, as we have described it in these chapters, needs to occupy.

Directions, challenges, and recommendations

Some authors in this book have pointed to concrete and tangible ways of approaching global justice education in schools and universities. Our job here is not to rehearse this material, but rather to examine some overarching themes and trends that have emerged throughout the chapters in order to move forward with and further support this work. The following sections contain ideas on creating a firmer landscape for such critical approaches in and to education.

Intercultural education in a White Irish teaching workforce

It is impossible to discuss global justice education in Ireland without returning to the overall demographic of the teaching profession in this country, which has already been referenced or discussed by a number of chapter authors. Research from Keane and Heinz (2015) has pointed to the particular demographics from which teachers in Ireland are typically drawn, as in, "homogenous with regard to nationality, ethnicity and first language, with the great majority from White Irish (settled) and English-speaking backgrounds" (Keane & Heinz, 2015, p. 3). Their research points to the 'diversity gap' in teaching in Ireland (Heinz & Keane, 2018) in that it is a predominantly white profession with an ethnically diverse student body. According to the 2016 Census, 82.5% of the Irish population were recorded as 'White Irish', whereas in 2014, 98–99% of the entrants to the teaching profession were 'White Irish' (Keane & Heinz, 2015; CSO, 2016). Many writers in these chapters have discussed the challenges inherent in encouraging learners to critically engage with global issues and to move beyond a 'single story' of Northern (white) supremacy and Southern (black) underdevelopment. This challenge is exacerbated in the mainly white context of teacher education and teaching, in which predominant perspectives may be rarely if ever countered.

The Migrant Teacher Project

The Migrant Teacher Project (MTP)[1] has set out to challenge and change this pattern of homogeneity within the teaching profession. Established in Ireland in 2017 and initially funded by the Department of Justice and Equality through the Office for the Promotion of Migrant Integration, it is located in one of the Dublin teacher education colleges, Marino Institute of Education (MIE). The Project aims to increase the participation of Immigrant Internationally Educated Teachers (IIETs) in the Irish primary and secondary education sectors through providing information, advice, and continuous professional development (CPD) to teachers from migrant backgrounds who have qualified outside of Ireland. This will, it is hoped, enable them to continue their profession in Irish schools. The MTP specifically aims to address Action 27 of the Migration Integration Strategy (Department of Justice & Equality, 2017), which states that, "proactive efforts will be made to attract migrants into teaching positions, including raising awareness of the Irish language aptitude test and adaptation period for primary teaching". Between November 2017 and July 2019 more than 700 teachers who gained their qualification in another country expressed interest in the Project, and in July 2019, 34 teachers from 17 different countries graduated from a Bridging Programme entitled 'Being a Teacher in Ireland', which aimed to support them in building their knowledge of the Irish education sector and ultimately to teach in schools (Donnelly, 2019). The Project comes at a time of secondary school teacher shortages in Ireland and has received broad support from across the education sector. This convergence of interests between the Irish State and the MTP means that this is a timely intervention which may help to disrupt, even in a small way, the make-up of the teaching profession, and begin to close the diversity gap between students and teachers in this country.

Critical race theory

In Chapter 9, race was centred in discussions about global learning. Although development education/intercultural education, or what we have presented in this book as *global justice education*, is concerned with people and groups who are raced in their lived experience, educators in Ireland (the majority of whom are White, as we have seen above) may not be provided with grounding in the subject of race and its operation. All the authors of black African descent in this book have particularly drawn from CRT and scholarship on decoloniality in framing their contributions, and we see this as a major signpost of the relevance of CRT as a tool that provides necessary insights and that speaks to the significant areas of marginality these authors have presented.

CRT is both a theoretical and methodological framework that centralises race and focuses its effects on social, economic, and political systems, and how they influence the relationship and outcomes between majority and minority groups (Joseph, 2019). Rather than viewing outcomes in isolation, CRT defines a kind of racial consciousness as a necessary element in fostering and understanding the contested position of those in power vis-à-vis racialised and subjugated minorities. Its strengths therefore, include its direct approach on the effects of race and racism and that it doesn't obscure societal power dynamics and the study of whiteness as the site of dominance and subjugation. CRT emphasises the importance of investigating human experience within the broader context of world society. Most importantly, CRT resists colour-blind, race-neutral, ahistorical, and apolitical perspectives (Delgado & Stefancic, 2012). While mindful of the limitations of CRT, for example that it tends to homogenise white people into positions of power and privilege, and that consequently it may not draw groups together to fight against racism, we nevertheless recommend the inclusion of this framework as a core element of teacher education, particularly because of its strong pursuit of the goal of social transformation and the eradication of racism. CPD programmes with intercultural education as their focus would particularly lend themselves to the inclusion of CRT as part of their curricula, and we return to such possibilities later in the chapter.

Yellow Flag programme

A further recommendation we would make, arising out of the contributions in these chapters, is for a nationwide implementation of the Yellow Flag programme in schools and in higher education institutes (HEIs) across Ireland (Titley, 2009; Power, 2012). The 'Yellow Flag' initiative was developed and pioneered in 2008 by the Irish Traveller Movement (ITM) as an innovative intercultural education programme, involving eight steps a school takes in promoting diversity and inclusion, culminating in the awarding of a 'Yellow Flag' in recognition of the school's work and commitment to diversity. These steps comprise: intercultural and anti-racism training for staff and management; engaging with the community; establishing a diversity committee; undertaking an intercultural review; monitoring, evaluation, and information dissemination; curriculum work; and establishing a Diversity Code and Anti-Racism Policy (Power, 2012, p. 5). The premise underpinning the programme is to provide schools with assistance and support to carry through with intercultural initiatives in order to move them beyond policy statements and into practice:

> Despite there being a commitment to policy level relating to these challenges, practical progress in the area of intercultural education has been very slow. Many so-called initiatives remain simply statements of intent and put unrealistic expectations on schools and teachers to deliver interculturalism without the necessary supports.
>
> Titley (2009, p. 11)

A clear strength of the initiative, apart from the foregrounding of race education for staff, is that it involves the whole school at both policy and implementation levels; it has a structured approach with a clear sequence of possible activities and leads to a visible and high-profile award for the school. We would argue for the extension of the Yellow Flag initiative, with accompanying CPD, to a wider number of schools, and we recommend that higher education be incorporated into this broader scope, building on a successful pilot programme that was carried out in Froebel College of Education in 2010–11 (Power, 2012). A national roll out of the Yellow Flag programme, with its emphasis on social justice, anti-racism, and diversity awareness, would be invaluable in moving towards an educational landscape which prioritises critically informed social justice education.

Decolonial learning spaces

Fiedler (2007, 2008) and Andreotti (2014) call for postcolonial learning spaces, which introduce a critical and radical dimension to global learning. Within these spaces, intercultural education would move beyond soft and celebratory manifestations, towards an in-depth examination of the complex and uncomfortable terrain of the '*inter*' component of cultural exchange and engagement. Andreotti (2014, p. 20) states that such learning spaces would make it impossible for us to turn our backs on difficult issues, "such as the persistence of relations of dominance, the complexities and paradoxes of crossing borders, the gap between what we say and what we do, or our own sanctioned ignorances".

Understanding the 'decolonial' in decolonial learning spaces

Decolonial theory, as explained in Chapters 1 and 8, has made and continues to make a significant contribution to the re-examination and critiquing of modernity as a tool of Western domination over other cultures and knowledge systems globally. How does this thinking translate into the creation of 'decolonial learning spaces' and what kind of work needs to be undertaken in such fora?

The first task for educators who seek to engage in this work is to undertake an analysis of (Western) modernity in the light of decolonial theory. This calls specifically for an examination of the 'logic of coloniality', by which we mean the twin concept of modernity/coloniality, as introduced and explained in Chapter 1. Andreotti (2011, p. 392) argues that the strongest message of the 'decolonial turn' is that moving beyond Eurocentrism requires a deep and comprehensive understanding of the 'darker side of modernity' along with a realisation and acknowledgement of the power relations within coloniality, which Mignolo (2018) refers to as the 'colonial matrix of power'.

The second key message is that an educator cannot remain neutral after an analysis of modernity within the decolonial framework. There is a strong emphasis in decolonial theory on how one is implicated in the modernity/coloniality logic not only as a victim, if that is the case, but also as reproducer of the hegemonic view and practice of modernity. Decolonial theorists therefore envisage that those who become aware of these dynamics will see this as a call to action in order to participate in the work of decoloniality (Mignolo, 2015). Hence the importance of 'decolonial learning spaces', which could also become sites of activism and change.

The third message from decolonial thinking is the importance of recognising, respecting, and embracing the diversity of worldviews and sources of knowledge which come from ***pluriversality*** (see Chapter 8). Decolonial theorists advocate for a "world in which many worlds coexist" (Mignolo, 2011, p. 328; Vάzquez, 2015, p. 100) and suggest that embracing such diversity will lead us to enter into open dialogue with others in learning and teaching. This dialogue across global divides can bring us into relation with the diversity of the world, which, as Vάzquez points out, is always in "excess of our own world of meaning" and is "at once humbling and empowering" (ibid., p. 95). The compilation of chapters in this book has in itself been a project of creating a ***decolonial learning space*** in which we engaged in open dialogue across a range of perspectives. Within this investigative framework we created a space in which core issues of relevance to Irish education could be interrogated, and where 'colonial amnesia' could be brought into critical consciousness, examined, and re-framed. This volume has underlined the importance of creating a community of educators and learners, a community of Black and White allies working together to promote and model critical educational approaches. Extending and consolidating such spaces is the next task.

Continuous professional development

What is striking about many of the chapter contributions in this book is that an established programme of CPD currently features in many of these educators' attempts to counter the dominant discourse in the higher education sector, and by implication, through the multiplier effect, into the education system as a whole. For example, two relevant Master's programmes in Marino Institute of Education (Master in Education Studies, *Intercultural Learning and Leadership* and Master in Education Studies, *Inquiry-Based Learning*), which are accredited by Trinity College, Dublin, have been in existence since 2012 and 2018 respectively, and have largely been taken up by primary and secondary school teachers and school leaders (principals, deputy principals, and assistant principals). The MA in *Race, Migration and Decolonial Studies* at University College Dublin (UCD) described by Alice Feldman in Chapter 9 has been in place since 2016. The first *Black Studies* module in Ireland was initiated in UCD in 2019 and was led by Ebun Joseph. The Proudly Made in Africa (PMIA) Fellowship in UCD Business School as explained by David Nyaluke in Chapter 2 is a further instance of how this type of work has entered the academy. Moreover, the piloting of the Yellow Flag programme in Froebel College in 2010–11 represents a blueprint for other HEIs to follow (Power, 2012). All of these are examples of the kinds of decolonial learning spaces that are recently or currently in existence in the formal education sector in Ireland, and specifically in HEIs (and there are many more examples of this kind of work). There is a nascent network of educators in Ireland that can be further expanded and developed, where colleagues can support each other and grow the movement for change. Initiatives from colleagues overseas, such as the 'diversity discussion circles' at the University of Amsterdam (Icaza & Vázquez, 2018), could be learnt from and established in HEIs here as "safe spaces for encounter and dialogue" (ibid., p. 117), which could also become a focal point for the processes of unlearning and self-reflexivity emphasised by many authors in this book.

International decade of people of African descent

Finally, the United Nations (UN) has declared 2015–2024 as the International Decade of People of African Descent. This book challenges the dominant discourse in relation to teaching about African countries and African people in schools and universities in Ireland and the Global North. Its core task was to counter educational philosophies and processes that maintain discriminatory practices and to preserve stereotypical, prejudicial, and deficit perceptions. Using trade justice as its starting point, and colonial structures and structuring as its backdrop, it took its investigations across a sweep of broad themes and topics, including 'sending programmes', representations of Africa in the media and textbooks, inquiry-based learning, epistemicide and knowledge justice, and racial stratification. Through these endeavours we hope this book makes a contribution towards achieving what the UN has called on Member States to do as part of the International Decade of People of African Descent, including:

> Take measures to ensure that public and private education systems do not discriminate against or exclude children of African descent, and that they are protected from direct or indirect discrimination, negative stereotyping, stigmatization

and violence from peers or teachers; to this end, training and sensitization should be provided to teachers and measures should be taken to increase the number of teachers of African descent working in educational institutions.

UN (2015, p. 16)

Note

1 Many thanks to Dr Emer Nowlan for her support with this section. Migrant Teacher Project: https://www.mie.ie/en/Research/Migrant_Teacher_Project/.

References

Andreotti, V. (2011). (Towards) decoloniality and diversality in global citizenship education. *Globalisation, Societies and Education*, 9(3–4), 381–397.

Andreotti, V. (2014). Critical literacy: Theories and practices in development education. *Policy & Practice: A Development Education Review*, 19, 12–32.

Bryan, A. (2010). Corporate multiculturalism, diversity management, and positive interculturalism in Irish schools and society. *Irish Educational Studies*, 29(3), 253–269.

Bryan, A. (2011). Another cog in the anti-politics machine? The de-clawing of development education. *Policy & Practice: A Development Education Review*, 12(Spring), 1–14.

Bryan, A. (2013). 'The impulse to help': (Post) humanitarianism in an era of the 'new' development advocacy. *International Journal of Development Education and Global Learning*, 5(2), 5–29.

Coulby, D. (2006). Intercultural education: theory and practice. *Intercultural Education*, 17(3), 245–257.

Council of Europe. (2008). *White Paper on intercultural dialogue: Living together as equals in dignity*. Strasbourg: Council of Europe.

CSO. (2016). Irish Central Statistics Office. Retrieved from http://www.cso.ie/en/

Dalal, F. (2008). Against the celebration of diversity. *British Journal of Psychotherapy*, 24(1), 4–19.

Delgado, R., & Stefancic, J. (2012). *Critical race theory: An introduction*. New York: New York University Press.

Department of Justice and Equality. (2017). *migrant integration strategy 2017–2020: A blueprint for the future*. Ireland: DoJE.

Donnelly, K. (2019, January 30). Opening school doors to migrant teachers. *Irish Independent Newspaper*.

Fanning, B. (2002). *Racism and social change in the Republic of Ireland*. Manchester: Manchester University Press.

Fiedler, M. (2007). Postcolonial learning spaces for global citizenship. *Critical literacy: Theories and Practices*, 1(2), 50–58.

Fiedler, M. (2008). Teaching and learning about the world in the classroom: Development education in culturally diverse settings. *Policy & Practice: A Development Education Review*, 7(Autumn), 5–17. http://www.developmenteducationreview.com/issue7-focus1

Garner, S. (2004). *Racism in the Irish experience*. London/Dublin: Pluto Press.

Gebrial, D. (2018). Rhodes must fall: Oxford and movements for change. In G.K. Bhambra, D. Gebrial, & K. Nisancioglu (Eds.), *Decolonising the curriculum*. London: Pluto Press.

Goldstone, K. (2002). Christianity, conversion and the tricky business of names: Images of Jews and Blacks in nationalist Irish Catholic discourse. In R. Lentin, & R. McVeigh (Eds.), ***Racism and anti-racism in Ireland*** (pp. 167–176). Belfast, Ireland: Beyond the Pale Publications.

Heinz, M., & Keane, E. (2018). Socio-demographic composition of primary initial teacher education entrants in Ireland. ***Irish Educational Studies***, 37(4), 523–543.

Heron, B. (2007). ***Desire for development: Whiteness, gender and the helping imperative***. Ontario, Canada: Wilfrid Laurier University Press.

Icaza, R., & Vázquez, R. (2018). Diversity or decolonisation? Researching diversity at the University of Amsterdam. In G.K. Bhambra, D. Gebrial, & K. Nisancioglu (Eds.), ***Decolonising the university***. London: Pluto Press.

Ignatiev, N. (1995). ***How the Irish became white***. New York & London: Routledge.

Joseph, E. (2018). Whiteness and racism: Examining the racial order in Ireland. ***Irish Journal of Sociology***, 26(1), 46–70.

Joseph, E. (2019). ***The Centrality of Race and Whiteness in the Irish Labour Market***. http://enarireland.org/the-centrality-of-race-and-whiteness-in-the-irish-labour-market/

Keane, E., & Heinz, M. (2015). Diversity in initial teacher education in Ireland: the socio-demographic backgrounds of entrants in 2013 and 2014. ***Irish Educational Studies***, 34(3), 281–301.

Kerr, J., & Andreotti, V. (2017). Crossing borders in initial teacher education: Mapping dispositions to diversity and inequity. ***Race, Ethnicity and Education***, 22(5), 647–665.

Kitching, K. (2014). ***The politics of compulsive education: Racism and learner-citizenship***. Oxon, NY: Routledge.

Lentin, R., & McVeigh, R. (2002). ***Racism and anti-racism in Ireland***. Belfast, Ireland: Beyond the Pale Publications.

Leonardo, Z. (2004). The colour of supremacy: beyond the discourse of 'white privilege'. ***Educational Philosophy and Theory***, 36(2), 137–152.

Martin, F., Pirbhai-Illich, F., & Pete, S. (2017). Beyond culturally responsive pedagogy: Decolonising teacher education. In F. Pirbhai-Illich, S. Pete, and F. Martin (Eds.), ***Culturally responsive pedagogy: working towards decolonisation, indigeneity and interculturalism*** (pp. 235–256). London: Palgrave Macmillan.

McVeigh, R., & Lentin, R. (2002). Situated racisms: A theoretical introduction. In R. Lentin & R. McVeigh (Eds.), ***Racism and anti-racism in Ireland***. Belfast, Ireland: Beyond the Pale Publications.

Michael, L. (2015). ***Afrophobia in Ireland: Racism against people of African descent***. Dublin: ENAR.

Michael, L. (2018). Reports of Racism in Ireland. July–December 2017. 17th+18th Quarterly Reports of iReport.ie European Network Against Racism. Retrieved from http://enarireland.org/wp-content/uploads/2018/08/iReport_1718_Final.pdf

Mignolo, W. (2011). ***The darker side of Western modernity: Global futures, decolonial options***. Durham: Duke University Press.

Mignolo, W. (2015). Global coloniality and the world disorder: Decoloniality after decolonization and dewesternization after Cold War, Paper presented at ***13th Rhodes Forum, World Public Forum "Dialogue of Civilizations" Rhodes***, Greece. Retrieved from http://wpfdc.org/images/2016_blog/W.Mignolo_Decoloniality_after_Decolonization_Dewesternization_after_the_Cold_War.pdf

Mignolo, W. (2018). The decolonial option. In W. Mignolo & C. Walsh (Eds.), ***On decoloniality: Concepts, analytics, praxis***. Durham/London: Duke University Press.

Mignolo, W., & Walsh, C. (2018). ***On decoloniality***. Durham: Duke University Press.

Ní Shuinéar, S. (2002). Othering the Irish (Travellers). In R. Lentin, & R. McVeigh (Eds.), *Racism and Anti-Racism in Ireland*. Belfast: Beyond the Pale Publications

O'Toole, B. (2015). 1831 to 2014: An opportunity to get it right this time? Some thoughts on the current debate on patronage and religious education in Irish primary schools. *Irish Educational Studies*, 34(1), 89–102.

Power, C. (2012). *ITM Froebel report on diversity in Irish higher education*. Dublin, Ireland: Irish Traveller Movement.

Titley, A. (2009). *The Irish traveller movement Yellow Flag programme: A handbook for schools*. Dublin, Ireland: Irish Traveller Movement.

United Nations. (2015). International decade for people of African descent 2015–2024: Recognition, justice, development. https://www.un.org/en/events/africandescent-decade/pdf/African%20Descent%20Booklet_WEB_English.pdf

Vázquez, R. (2015). Decolonial practice of learning. In J. Friedman, V. Haverkate, B. Oomen, E. Park, & M. Sklad Team (Eds.), *Going Glocal in higher education: The theory, teaching and measurement of global citizenship* (pp. 92–100). Middleburg, VA: Drvvkery, University College Roosevelt.

Index

Notes: Page numbers in **bold** denotes tables and page numbers followed by 'n' denotes note numbers